AF477764

CITIZENSHIP EAST AND WEST

A PUBLICATION OF THE GRADUATE INSTITUTE
OF INTERNATIONAL STUDIES,
GENEVA

Also published in this series:

The United States and the Politicization of the World Bank
Bartram S. Brown

Trade Negotiations in the OECD
David J. Blair

World Financial Markets after 1992
Hans Genberg and Alexander K. Swoboda

Succession Between International Organisations
Patrick R. Myers

Ten Years of Turbulence: The Chinese Cultural Revolution
Barbara Barnouin and Yu Changgen

*The Islamic Movement in Egypt: Perceptions of International
Relations 1967–81*
Walid M. Abdelnasser

*Namibia and Southern Africa: Regional Dynamics of Decolonization
1945–90*
Ronald Dreyer

The International Organization of Hunger
Peter Uvin

CITIZENSHIP EAST AND WEST

Edited by
André Liebich and Daniel Warner
with Jasna Dragovic

KEGAN PAUL INTERNATIONAL
London and New York

First published in 1995 by
Kegan Paul International Limited
UK: PO Box 256, London WC1B 3SW, England
USA: 562 West 113th Street, New York, NY 10025, USA

Distributed by
John Wiley & Sons Limited
Southern Cross Trading Estate
1 Oldlands Way, Bognor Regis
West Sussex, PO22 9SA, England

Columbia University Press
562 West 113th Street
New York, NY 10025, USA

Set in 10/12pt Palatino
by Intype, London
Printed in Great Britain by TJ Press, Padstow, Cornwall

ISBN 0 7103 0491 9

British Library Cataloguing in Publication Data
Citizenship, East and West
I. Liebich, Andre
326.6

ISBN 0–7103–0491–9

US Library of Congress Cataloging in Publication Data
Citizenship, East and West / edited by André Liebich and Daniel Warner with
Jasna Dragovic.
222pp. 22 cm. – (Publications de l'Institut universitaire de hautes études
internationales, Genève)
Includes bibliographical references and index.
ISBN 0–7103–0491–9
1. Citizenship – Europe, Eastern. I. Liebich, André, 1948- . II. Warner, Daniel.
III. Dragovic, Jasna. IV. Series.
KJC5114.C58 1995
342.4′083 – dc20
[344.0283]

94–14172
CIP

CONTENTS

CONTENTS

Hungary

After Czecho-Slovakia

Perspectives

ACKNOWLEDGEMENTS

We gratefully acknowledge the financial support of the East European Programme of the Fonds national suisse de la recherche scientifique and the hospitality of the Graduate Institute of International Studies. We also thank Brenda Newman Watson for editorial help in the early stages of this manuscript, Professor Roland Ruffieux for his comments on the final manuscript, and Jasna Dragovic for her invaluable help throughout.

André Liebich   Daniel Warner

CONTRIBUTORS

David Campbell Assistant Professor of political science at the Johns Hopkins University, where he teaches international political theory and U.S. foreign policy. He is the author of *Writing Security: United States Foreign Policy and the Politics of Identity;* and *Politics Without Principle: Sovereignty, Ethics and the Gulf War* as well as co-editor of *The Political Subject of Violence.*

Jasna Dragovic Teaching Assistant at the Graduate Institute of International Studies and lecturer at The Colgate University Geneva Programme. A graduate of Princeton University and the Institut d'études politiques, Paris, she is preparing a thesis at the Graduate Institute of International Studies on Serbian intellectuals in the 1980s.

Tamas Földesi Professor and head of the department of philosophy at the Law School of the Eötvös Lorand University. Member of the Committee for the elaboration of human rights provisions in the Hungarian Constitution. Author of *Problems of Free Will* (English translation), *Proof in Philosophy* (German translation), *Truth about Truth* (Slovak translation) and more recently (in Hungarian) *Human Rights; The Dilemma of Justice;* and *Justice and Law.*

Guy S. Goodwin-Gill Professor of law at Carleton University, Ottawa, and editor-in-chief of the *International Journal of Refugee Law.* He has published widely on legal and policy issues relating to refugees and immigration.

Olga Gyarfasova Research Fellow at the Centre for Social

Analysis, Comenius University, Bratislava. Formerly, fellow of the Institute for Human Sciences, Vienna and of the Institute of Sociology, Slovak Academy of Sciences. Research projects on social communication and social problems of Slovak society during the transition period.

Pierre Hassner   Research Director, Centre d'Etudes et de Recherches Internationales and professor, Institut d'Etudes Politiques, Paris. A specialist on international relations and political philosophy, his publications include *Vents d'est Vers l'Europe des Etats de droit?* (with Pierre Grémion) and *Totalitarismes* (with G. Hermet and J. Rupnik) as well as recent articles in *Esprit*.

Krzysztof Jasiewicz   Director of electoral studies, Institute of Political Sciences, Polish Academy of Sciences and visiting professor of sociology, Washington and Lee University, Lexington, Virginia. Co-author of the series of political attitude surveys entitled *The Poles of '80, '81, '84, '88, '90*. Recent publications include contributions to the *Journal of Democracy; Bound to Change: Consolidating Democracy in Eastern Europe* (edited by P. Volten); and *The European Journal of Political Research: 1991 Political Data Yearbook*.

André Liebich Professor of the history of international relations at the Graduate Institute of International Studies, Geneva. A specialist in political theory and Central and East European studies, his publications include *Between Ideology and Utopia: the Politics and Philosophy of August Cieszkowski; L'Avenir du socialisme en Europe? Le Libéralisme classique,* and *L'Europe centrale et ses minorités: vers une solution européenne?* (with André Reszler).

Kenneth Minogue   Professor of political science at the London School of Economics and Political Science. Member of the Thatcher Foundation and a Director of the Centre for Policy Studies. Author of *The Liberal Mind; Nationalism; The Concept of a University; Alien Powers: The Pure Theory of Ideology;* and presenter of the television series, *The New Enlightenment*.

Gabor Nagy   Assistant Professor, Department of Sociology of Law, Eötvös Lorand University, Budapest, specializing in the political and sociological context of the legislative process. Formerly, postgraduate scholar, Hungarian Academy of Sciences, fellow, US Congress, Washington, D.C., visiting fellow, University of Groningen, Netherlands. Elected to Budapest City Council in 1990 and chairman of its Committee on Human Rights, Minorities and Religious Affairs.

Piotr Ogrodzinski Assistant Professor, Institute of Political Sciences, Polish Academy of Sciences, Warsaw, and coordinator of the East European Research Group, Stefan Batory Foundation. Specializing in the concept of civil society, comparative studies of transformation in East-Central Europe, and English political theory, he is the author of *Five Papers on Civil Society* (in Polish) as well as of recent articles in philosophical and social science journals.

Peter Paczolay Associate Professor at the Eötvös Lorand University, Budapest, chief counsellor at the Constitutional Court, head of the Political Science Department, Jozsef Attila University, Szeged. Former fellow of the Woodrow Wilson Center, Washington, D.C.

Martin Palous Lecturer in philosophy at Charles University, Prague, currently working on post-totalitarian political culture. Former spokesman for 'Charter '77' and later member of the Czechoslovak Parliament. Deputy Minister of Foreign Affairs from 1990 to 1992. Author of numerous samizdat' and other articles.

Daniel Warner Research Fellow and assistant director of the International Training Course in International Security and Arms Control at the Graduate Institute of International Studies, Geneva. Author of *An Ethic of Responsibility in International Relations* and recent articles dealing with political theory, refugees and human rights.

Edmund Wnuk-Lipinski Professor of sociology as well as founder and director of the Institute of Political Studies, Polish Academy of Sciences. Editor-in-chief of the quarterly *Sisyphus: Sociological Studies*. Solidarity advisor at the Polish Round Table and leader of a group of sociological advisors to the parliamentary Solidarity faction. Numerous publications on social structure, inequality, social policy and the political transformation of post-communist countries.

INTRODUCTION

The outcome of the political transition in Eastern Europe depends not only on the politics pursued but on the understanding of politics in the countries involved. A key aspect of such understanding is the notion of 'citizenship', an ancient term of striking contemporary relevance not only in Eastern Europe but in the West as well. What then are the dynamics of citizenship in Europe's new democracies and how do emerging solutions to the question of citizenship there respond to the concerns that the issue of citizenship has raised and continues to raise elsewhere?

These questions prompted the project which has led to this volume. Conceived in 1991, it focussed on Poland, Hungary and, what was then Czecho-Slovakia, as countries already grappling with the issue of post-communist citizenship. Independent thinkers in these countries had previously concentrated on human rights without reference to the historic distinction between *droits de l'homme* and *droits du citoyen*. They had legitimized the concept of civil society but at the cost of neglecting the state and the problem of citizenship. Finally, they had not yet known a new Europe where human mobility on the one hand and political disintegration on the other, would make the problem of political membership, defined as citizenship an acutely pressing issue.

There were thus already good reasons to undertake an inquiry into the issue of citizenship and, in the last few years, these reasons have become compelling as the issue of citizenship has shown itself to be far more intractable than originally imagined. Although the three, now four, countries singled out here have recently promulgated or are in the process of formulating new citizenship laws, the meaning of citizenship for their new politics remains uncertain. It is an open question whether a distinct, well-grounded and coherent notion of citizenship must emerge as the outcome of a broad democratic transition or whether such a notion is the pre-requisite to a successful democratization. There is no doubt, however, that reflection on citizenship remains at the heart of political thought and processes in those countries which embarked earliest and most vigorously on the post-communist road.

While the issue of citizenship stands near the top of the political agenda in the first post-communist states, in other countries it has exploded with unequalled intensity. The demise of the Soviet and the Yugoslav federations (in addition to the dissolution of Czecho-Slovakia discussed here) has transformed eight states into twenty-seven. The process of disintegration is probably not complete, as events unfold in the Caucasus, former Yugoslavia and even in the Russian Federation. Among the innumerable consequences of this unprecedented transform-ation, comparable to the wave of post World War II decolonializ-ation, has been growing attention to the definition and practice of citizenship as litmus tests of democratic commitment.

To be sure, the question of citizenship is not posed in identical terms everywhere throughout the post-communist world. Those states which enjoy continuity must define themselves in relation to pre-existing formal citizenship norms and state attitudes. Even such states, however, find their position radically changed as they are called upon to include or exclude former citizens now outside their borders and as they reflect on their own transformed identities. New states must establish the meaning of their own citizenship to themselves and to the outside world. Given the tension between state and nation so characteristic of the area, the definition of citizenship, political or ethnic, inclus-ive or exclusive, looms ever larger as the key to the assessment of emerging political régimes.

The questions formulated at the outset of this project in the context of Poland, Hungary and Czecho-Slovakia are also those which are posed in other countries. They are questions of per-sonal *identity*: 'Civis romanus sum,' said the Romans but what does it mean to describe oneself as 'civis hungaricus' or, for that matter, 'civis livonensis' or 'civis helveticus'? They are questions of formal *obligation*: what are the legal and moral claims that an individual and a state can make upon each other on citizenship grounds? They are also questions of social *attitude*: How do individuals see themselves qua citizens? What characteristics do they impute to their fellow citizens? What ties are established among individuals by virtue of a common citizenship?

The contributors to this volume were invited to address these questions from a variety of national and disciplinary perspectives. Poles, Hungarians, a Czech, a Slovak, nationals of several British Commonwealth countries, of the United States and of France contributed as did political theorists, jurists and sociologists. Inasmuch as the volume presents a current 'snapshot' view of the citizenship question, participating historians refrained from formally investigating the geneology of conceptions of citizenship in their countries of reference or from engaging in extended diachronic comparisons. Several contributors chose to examine citizenship primarily in theoretical terms, within the liberal tradition and as an urgent problem of personal identity. Others analysed elements of political culture and public opinion which bear upon current definitions and redefinitions of citizenship in their countries. Still others inquired into the emerging legal provisions which will structure and formalize concepts of citizenships in the states of the area.

The questions raised and the arguments presented in this volume are therefore numerous, vast and multifaceted. Kenneth Minogue, defining citizenship as one of the roles we play in the modern world, posits an alternative between a citizenship of participation and one of compliance and warns of the danger of overloading this role. Daniel Warner's distinction between the objective, state element of citizenship with its vertical contract and the subjective, nation element with its horizontal contrast poses the problem of exclusion from citizenship or negative identity. André Liebich pleads for the recognition of multiple citizenship as a solution to the dilemmas of multiple identity. Krzysztof Jasiewicz, contrasting exclusive and inclusive notions of citizenship, brings out the relevance of this contrast to Poland's present-day cleavages. Gabor Nagy sketches the background to the new Hungarian law on citizenship and examines the terms of that law. Martin Palous looks at the Czech doctrine of citizenship, particularly in the light of the problem of continuity, and he analyzes the constitutional circumstances of the division of Czecho-Slovakia. Olga Gyarfasova, on the basis of recent opinion research, charts the uncertainties and alternatives that confront Slovak citizens in their new state identity.

Not surprisingly, these contributions provoke vigorous rejoinders that spill over beyond the question of citizenship, however broadly conceived. Current Eastern European political issues figure prominently. Among these is the debate over the spectre or prospect of the 'Third Way', over lustration or de-communization, over political apathy as a portent of democratic unviability, over the significance of the division of Czecho-Slovakia. Citizenship comparisons abound, with examples drawn from the classical past and from these countries' own history, as well as from American and Western European experience, particularly that of France and Switzerland. Conceptual and geographic dichotomies are refined and challenged so as to illuminate the ethos of each of the countries examined. In his magisterial summary, Pierre Hassner applies a dialectic of universality and particularity to distinguish between what has been established and what remains to be ascertained with respect to the issue of citizenship.

The title of this volume is 'Citizenship, East *and West'*. The contributors recognized very early in the course of their exchanges that it was simply not feasible within a single volume to systematically analyze the variants of citizenship which lie outside the Eastern European area examined here. They did not forego comparison but rather they tended, at least initially, to approach the issue of citizenship as if it were dynamic in the East and static in the West. They implicitly assumed, if only for heuristic purposes, that changes and aspirations in Eastern Europe could be measured against a presumed stability of conceptions of citizenship elsewhere.

As reflection continued and as events unfolded, the fallacy of such assumptions of stability became clear and the fallacy is explicitly recognized as such in this volume. Lately, German citizenship law founded upon the sacrosanct principle of German origin (*ius sanguinis*) has come under challenge and will, no doubt, soon be revised. An amended French citizenship law has already opened a breach in the entrenched republican principle of citizenship for all those born in France (*ius soli*). These contradictory changes are matched by others elsewhere and at different levels: The move towards a common European Union citizenship flounders even as the provisions of the Maastricht Treaty are being put into place. Switzerland refuses to join a larger political entity because it will not dilute its concept of citizenship but, at the same time, it broadens its citizenship laws to facilitate acquisition and dual citizenship.

The question of citizenship lies open both in the West and in the East. It is hoped that this volume will contribute to the debate on citizenship by illuminating directly several important cases in a crucial area and by putting into focus the question of citizenship elsewhere. The future of citizenship is inseparable from the future of politics, for citizens of all countries.

André Liebich
October 1993

PROBLEMS

TWO CONCEPTS OF CITIZENSHIP

Kenneth Minogue

'All the world's a stage', remarks Jacques in Shakespeare's *As You Like It*, and all the men and women 'merely players'. The idea that human beings are essentially composed of the roles they play is perhaps the best way of distinguishing the modern world from traditional societies. Traditional societies take their bearings from the facts of nature, such as gender, or seniority, by which the needs of order assign to each person a set of rights and duties. These in their turn largely determine each person's voyage through life. The convenience of this scheme is that it provides a decision procedure which, in principle at least, solves problems of conflict. On the other hand, it is largely static and inflexible. The modern world emerges as roles multiply, and opportunities become available to individuals not on the basis of supposedly natural indicators, like gender and seniority, but on the basis of abilities, which are infinitely variable according to circumstance. In the modern world, individuals create their lives largely out of their talents and energies. And one of the roles they must come to terms with is that of citizen.

It is a role in which great hopes have been invested. The French revolutionaries thought that the role of *citoyen* and *citoyenne* could supersede the unfortunate divisions of the *ancien régime*. Many countries have tried to improve the quality of their democracy by setting up courses in how to be a citizen – often to the detriment of education. To be a citizen is thought more honorific than being a mere subject. These hopes are the context of our concern with citizenship.

Citizenship and Political Philosophy

In philosophical terms, one must start with Hegel because the distinction he made between the state and civil society is both the theory from which the Communist historical blind alley began, and the point of reference which allows us to understand just what it was that went wrong. Hegel's follower Marx identified the individuality of civil society with bourgeois selfishness; individuality was thus construed as a moral fault. Communism consequently became the project of destroying civil society (which is an arena of inequality) in order to incorporate all human activities within the social world of the community. Now individuality is, precisely, the capacity to play roles, and therefore Communism must be recognized as a rejection of the entire notion of playing a role. Indeed, rejection of individualism, understood as the capacity to engage in self-chosen roles, is entailed by *any* project of building a perfect society. No perfect society can work so long as individuals may choose roles for themselves, because different roles have different consequences. Plato necessarily made justice the orchestrating virtue of his *Republic* because to have more than one virtue would open up the possibility of uncertainty, even conflict, as to which virtue ought to prevail. Utopian writers in pursuit of perfection are certainly right in this belief: the human being who plays a variety of roles – religious, social familial etc. – will find that these roles make conflicting demands upon him.

Most writers who take their bearings from the republics of classical antiquity tend to make a grand performance of citizenship, but Hegel does not, and for excellent reasons. As he comes to consider civil society in *The Philosophy of Right*, he lists the roles whose character he has adumbrated as he builds up his account of the state. In abstract right, there is the *person*, distinguished from the natural world. In morality, the *subject*, the person distinguished from others, where this term emphasizes subjectivity rather than the fact of subjection to a civil authority. In the family there is the *family member* and in civil society the *burgher* or *bourgeois*. In talking of needs, Hegel recognizes 'the composite idea which we call man.'[1] Now the state in Hegel

---

[1] Hegel, *Philosophy of Right*, remark to paragraph 190. 'Man' may also be used honorifically, as it is, for example, in *The Magic Flute*. Sarastro says that Tamino is better than a prince – he is a . . . Man! This is a classical sense of man as a *telos* of development. It has provoked much admiration in the modern world, but is dangerous in that it turns into a criterion which many actual human beings may fail – with fatal results.

is the form of association which includes but transcends all other aspects of human association. It is therefore not limited to political participation, but largely expressed in what human beings do in the many roles of everyday life. Membership in the state for Hegel does not involve a wholly new role and a new relationship with one's fellows, as it does perhaps for Rousseau. Rather, citizenship, as membership in the state, is what underlies all the more active things people are constantly doing. And only derivatively is it, for most people, having an active concern in the governance of the state.

Patriotism, Hegel tells us 'is simply a product of the institutions subsisting in the state, since rationality is *actually* present in the state, while action in conformity with these institutions gives rationality its practical proof'. He goes on to remark that:

> Patriotism is often understood to mean only a readiness for exceptional sacrifices and actions. Essentially, however, it is the sentiment which, in the relationships of our daily life and under ordinary conditions, habitually recognizes that the community is one's substantive groundwork and end.[2]

Citizenship as a Spectrum

These remarks justify us in suggesting that ways of understanding citizenship may be arranged along a spectrum, such that if we go too far in either direction, citizenship disappears altogether. At one end of the spectrum is despotism, in which the individual is completely subject to the will of a master. Custom and culture no doubt mitigate many of the worst consequences of this condition, but there is no real recognition of citizenship at all, and this remains the condition of much of the so-called Third World. Further along the spectrum we come upon the theory of European monarchic absolutism, most brilliantly stated by Hobbes in *Leviathan*, published in 1651. Here the individual is largely a subject, and he gains from the state the peace and order which allows him to pursue *his* projects. Citizenship consists in enjoying the benefits of being subject to the laws of an equal association. A little further along the spectrum we encounter Rousseau, for whom in *The Social Contract* of 1762,

[2] *Ibidem*, paragraph 268, and Remark.

citizenship was access to a universal level of being; nevertheless, this citizen is quite distinctly a subject as well. And finally, at the other end of the spectrum, we encounter the Marxian project, which may stand for all visions of a perfect society, in which the individual is entirely absorbed in the activity of the community, without energy, activity or identity left outside to allow any kind of separate existence. At this end of the spectrum human beings are associated together so closely that the 'watery' and therefore somewhat cool relationship appropriate to fellow citizens within the state is excluded altogether.[3] For the essence of states is that the public realm in which they most evidently subsist must be partnered by both a social and a private sphere of life. Politics is commonly about how these spheres fit together.

We may thus use the tradition of political philosophy to generate two models of the state which in turn reveal two corresponding models of citizenship itself: one, loosely associated with Hobbes, emphasizes that the state is an association of individuals equal in their subjection to law. The other, loosely associated with Rousseau, identifies the state with a community of equals actively involved in legislating and deciding public business for themselves. Both models allow some scope for both obedience and participation, but each emphasizes the one rather than the other.

In setting up our inquiry this way, we may claim to be in the central stream of the tradition of political philosophy. Philosophers have always been concerned with specifying just what kind of association a state is, and each concept has as its counterpart a conception of the role of the citizen. Aristotle, for example, distinguished citizens of a *polis* from slaves, wives and children in a household.[4] Locke was concerned to distinguish patriarchal from civil power.[5] In our own century, Michael Oakeshott found the postulates of civil association distinct from those of what he called 'enterprise associations'.[6] And we have seen that Hegel performs an exercise of just this kind. The point of these inquiries is to make sense of a fluid and confusing political reality, and also to disentangle confusions. Aristotle, for example,

---

[3]Oakeshott, M., *On Human Conduct*, Oxford 1975, p. 110.
[4]Aristotle, *Politics*, Book 1, c. 7
[5]Locke, J., *Two Treatises of Government*.
[6]Oakeshott, M., *op. cit* (note 3), especially the second essay 'On the Civil Condition'.

thought that Plato gave too much to communal life and not enough to the diversity which politics presupposes; later idealist philosophers have thought that modern individualism overemphasizes the daily pursuit of the satisfaction of desires and fails to recognize communal involvement.

Our question is: What concept of citizenship fits most appropriately into the conditions of the modern state? To some extent we are interested in a practical problem – namely, what is the appropriate way in which those previously living in a version of a full and perfect community (and necessarily, of course, a grotesque parody of this aspiration) move to a condition of statehood? And in considering this question, we might keep in mind certain elementary facts of the civil lives of those living in liberal democracies. Most citizens, for example, limit their participation in politics to the act of voting. In Britain, about 75% of people bother to vote in national elections, and in American presidential elections, it is less than 50% these days. In Australia it is much higher, because failure to vote carries a small penalty. But we may say that those who take a serious interest in politics – *le pays politique* as the French call it – must be of the order of 10%, with large variations depending on what you call a 'serious interest'. National politics (like the monarchy) has about it these days an element of soap opera, and is enjoyed as a dramatic spectacle. But none of this constitutes serious participation in politics.

Citizenship as Participation

These realities explain why it is that the ideal of participation is so lively an issue among many intellectuals in the West today. Critics of Western society interpret low voter turnout as a symptom of 'alienation'. Many people, it is said, despair of being able (as the common phrase has it) 'to control the conditions of their lives'. As a witty left-wing politician put it: 'If democracy changed anything, they'd have abolished it long ago'. These are critics who look back with nostalgia to the classical past, and believe with Rousseau that participation is an essential condition of self-determination, and therefore of freedom itself. Their criticism of Western society often takes the form of attacking 'hierarchy', by which they mean the functionally convenient practice of making major decisions at the top of an organization. As egalitarians, they would like all decisions to be taken after full consultation and discussion with everyone marginally involved. This was the programme of university turbulence in the 1960s, and these days one version of it is presented as the political version of Japanese industrial success. It is hard to detach the ideal of participation from the belief that there are imaginable conditions (rationality, for example, or a properly working system, or social justice, or enough time to thrash out all the issues in an ideal speech situation) in which participation would arrive at a unanimously agreed conclusion. In that case, neither authority nor coercion would be needed in a modern state, and we should have arrived at a perfect community.

This, of course, is one version of socialism, but it generally comes before us as the *telos* of democracy. The basic objection to it must be that citizenship as participation in the governing of *all* institutions would leave no space for a civil society in which individuals may contract with each other on whatever terms they choose. It is, like much of socialism, a profoundly reactionary idea because it excludes social mechanisms which would allow genius and eccentricity to flourish. Western societies have not one but two ways in which individuals may manage their relations to each other. These have been analysed in a famous work by Albert Hirschman.[7] Individuals may influence institutions sometimes by participation, or 'voice' (as Hirschman calls it), but they may sometimes respond by withdrawing and moving on to something else, which he calls 'exiting'. Obviously most economic services in a competitive modern economy are subject to exit. The state, by contrast, is not something which, short of exile and immigration, can be easily abandoned in favour of a preferred option. It can only be influenced through participation in the processes of politics. Now those who believe in participation as the basic democratic activity, and in democracy as the ideal form of social cooperation, are generally hostile to capitalist enterprise and its opportunities for 'exit'. Their project, at its extreme, is to turn all decisions into collective decisions, and the result would seem to be that the role of citizen has swallowed that of the consumer and producer, not to mention what Hegel called the *burgher* or *bourgeois*, and to some extent even the role of moral agent. In

[7]Hirschman, A., *Exit, Voice and Loyalty: Responses to Decline in Firms, Organisations and States*, Cambridge, MA 1970.

this conception, it is *as citizens* that we produce, consume, associate with each other and even respond aesthetically to the world.

An influential version of this vision is found in T. H. Marshall's famous account of the development of modern Western societies, *Citizenship and Social Class*.[8] Marshall detected what he thought was a trend in modern history in which the oppressed populace of medieval Europe first acquired civil rights (the very basics of justice) in the course of the 17th century, next acquired political rights in the suffrage battles of the 19th century, and then entered into a promised land of economic and social rights in the 20th century. (He is, of course, generalizing British experience.) Citizenship turns into a guarantee of the satisfaction of needs, and the individual as citizen is locked into administration by the state from the cradle to the grave.

Marshall's theory clearly postulates a mechanism whose point is to make the state the servant of individual needs. It is a theory which carries the attractive suggestion that the peoples of the modern state advance in citizenship by actively subjecting the state to their demands. But the rhetoric of this view is misleading. No doubt *in making* demands upon the government, the individual is politically active. But in demanding the material benefits which are the essence of the economic and social rights described by Marshall, the individual as citizen of a participatory state is economically passive. This is certainly not what Rousseau was thinking of. He would almost certainly have regarded much of what passes for active participation in politics today – street demonstrations, for example – as essentially passive. But participatory theorists have linked the idea of participation to the satisfaction of needs and packaged the combination as a revival of classical republican virtue.

It is clear that opinions about citizenship raise very much wider questions, and in particular questions about what is a proper human life. There is a considerable difference between the classical conception of an active, self-sacrificing patriotism, and the modern conception of a life of satisfied individual needs. That the campaign for this latter conception of citizenship can be presented in the language of classical republicanism tells us something about the imprecision of political language. It can allow our understanding of the political role of citizenship to

[8]Marshall, T. H., *Citizenship and Social Class*, Cambridge 1950.

drift so that it turns into the business of managing the details of production and consumption.

Rousseau, as the most notable exponent in modern times of the idea of citizenship as participation, was thinking about something quite different. His focus was on the city republics of the ancient world, in which needs were satisfied within the household, and the realm of politics was a sphere of human freedom. Life was lived under laws, and the citizen was active not in attempting to secure benefits for himself – quite the contrary! – but in being able to participate in the making of laws and taking of decisions in which he would further participate as a subject. Rousseau assumes a world of virtuous citizens, patriotic to the core and therefore subordinating their material needs to the good of the city. There is no conception of virtue irrigating contemporary participatory theory, except the virtue of being content with an equal share of the goods of the community. It has nothing heroic about it.

It should be clear from this that in looking too hard merely at the concept and role of citizenship, we might well miss a vital consideration: it matters a great deal what it is that government takes as its responsibility. Rousseau assumes – perhaps not firmly enough, or consistently enough, but he does assume – that material needs will be satisfied in a private and domestic realm which is no direct concern of the state. The business of government is thus justice (not social justice) and foreign policy. This gives a grandeur to the citizen deciding the laws under which he will live, a grandeur lacking to the citizen-consumer of a modern welfare state whose participation would largely consist in demanding insurance, medical services, pensions and other direct material benefits.

Citizenship as Compliance

The essential question, therefore, is what the government is charged to do. And that brings us directly to our second conception of citizenship, which we may call the ideal of compliance. Here a state is understood as an association of individuals (in the classic version these individuals will be patriarchs, the fathers of families whom they are accustomed to govern and protect) subject to the laws made by a sovereign. They have no duty other than that to comply with the laws and to obey the commands of the sovereign power. The liberty they enjoy may not be a very grand ideal – it is merely the silence of the law – but it is a solid basis for the conduct of individual life.

There are some politicians in Britain – a famous one is Tony Benn – who think that being a subject is a demeaning situation to be in, and that the British do not really enjoy freedom because they are not guaranteed a set of things they can call their 'rights'. Rights or not, they certainly enjoy, roughly speaking, the same basic set of liberties as are enjoyed in other free societies; indeed, Britain has in previous centuries been taken as the very model of liberty. But we may explain the basic situation by the analogy of language. Those who speak any particular language (the Germans, for example) are subjects of what we might call a linguistic association. They are subject to the rules of grammar which *constitute* communication and expression, in this case in the German language. These rules in no way determine what sentences they will choose to utter in concrete situations. German speakers are entirely free, so long as they abide by the rules of communication in German, to say anything they please. It is certainly true that other rules (and other vocabularies) would be possible in communication, but what matters to the speaker of a language is that he should comply with the rules, for this is the condition of reciprocal comprehension.

This analogy brings out one of the central issues in the dispute between our two conceptions of citizenship. On the participation model, a citizen is only free – indeed a citizen is only actually a citizen – by participating in and thereby determining the law. But this is a very peculiar doctrine, because the decisions of assemblies are taken by majority vote, and there is always a minority which voted against the law in question. If we take the theory seriously, then I am, as a citizen, oppressed by every law against which I voted. Rousseau understandably found this a difficult problem and he solved it by the theory of the *volonté générale*. There is, in principle, always a correct law, and in a legitimate society, the majority will infallibly alight upon what that law should be.

An even more serious problem arises in contemporary versions of the participatory model. The classical republicans whom Rousseau admired were in the paradigm case deciding upon either foreign policy, or upon a *law*.[9] Each of these is a discipline on the citizen requiring the exercise of certain virtues: this is why the citizen in Rousseau might have to be forced to be free; his virtuous decision when focussing upon the general issue might give way to self-partial weakness amid the confusions of life itself. The participating citizen in the contemporary world, however, is conceived of as concerned largely with the satisfaction of his needs. He is concerned with services and benefits. But there is no such thing as a right distribution of benefits unless one assumes a universal model human being with a determinate schedule of needs. In such a universal model, there would only be a single way of life in the community. But the essence of the modern world is that communities are composed of a great variety of ways of life and judgements about what is valuable. What this means is that the central problem of contemporary politics is that of judging the distinction between those things which should be decided politically in terms of laws, and those which should be decided individually in terms of entering and exiting from loyalties and associations.

Hobbes, in giving an account of civil association, gave fewer hostages to fortune than Rousseau. He did not have to assume a form of association in which a certain kind of majority would make the right decision, because he was entirely sceptical about the idea of right decisions. The problem to which states are a response was, in his view, the diversity of human tastes, judgements and opinions, and the propensity of human beings to come into conflict with each other because of scarcity of resources, pride of self-regard and mistrust of the intentions of others. The solution was that each of the members of the association should agree with each of the other members jointly to obey the rules and commands of a third party called the sovereign. Now, what this solution assumes is twofold.

Firstly, the actual content of the rules does not greatly matter. No doubt some rules are better than others, and there are certainly some laws which are actually harmful to those who must endure them. This fact must be recognized by various kinds of limitations on the law. One such limit in Hobbes is the law of nature which provides axioms of peace; another is that if the subjects feel threatened they will withdraw their allegiance. But

---

[9]There were, of course, exceptions to this, as in trials, or questions such as ostracism. But we are, of course, dealing with an idealized *polis* in any case.

laws are laws, everyone has to put up with them, and very little in human happiness really depends on having *this* law rather than *that*. Whatever is best administered *is*, usually, best. On the other hand, a very great deal of human happiness does depend on whether a society remains peaceful and orderly on the one hand, or falls into civil war on the other. Particular laws are not worth fighting over. It is taken for granted here that, while human beings no doubt have needs to be satisfied, their real business in life is quite different. They are creatures put on earth to be tested, and how they respond to the challenges of life will have a bearing upon their eternal destiny. As always, disputes in political philosophy ultimately reveal conflicting conceptions of the point of human life.

There is, however, a second assumption behind the Hobbesian theory, an assumption which Hobbes barely had to mention because the sovereigns of his time only violated it in one specific area, namely their interest in the religious opinions of their subjects. This is the assumption that sovereigns command such laws as are necessary to peace and good order, and that beyond such essential matters, they leave things alone. It is the duty of individuals, who in a commonwealth enjoy the benefits of peace, to make their own way in the world and to provide for their families. Since the time when Hobbes was writing, we have acquired democracy, which has to some extent curbed the propensity of sovereigns to engage in their favourite hobby, war. Governments have also learned, however, how to siphon off wealth from the economy in order to give benefits to their electors. Governments in liberal democratic countries tax and spend in benefits and other costs of government between 40% and 60% of the GNP. In these circumstances the actual details of government are likely to become a serious concern.

Indeed, governments which dispose of this proportion of the resources of the state can no longer be said merely to *rule* a society, but rather to *manage* it. They cannot help but be involved extensively in the details of both production and consumption. Indeed, the state now becomes involved not merely in legislating and regulating, but also in producing goods and influencing attitudes; the state itself is also in an important way a consumer of what is produced, in some respects a monopsonist which can determine a market by being the largest buyer. In these circumstances, an ideal of participation becomes not the revival of a classical form of citizenly virtue, but a necessary condition of efficient management. If society were to consist primarily of independent-minded individuals each pursuing their own projects, then a managed society of the kind we have evolved would not be possible. It is only possible to the extent that individuals, in part or all of their lives, are drawn into society as a single cooperative productive enterprise.

The Inflation of Citizenship

My argument should reveal, then, that the issue of citizenship lies at the centre of political controversy. It is always on the edge of being turned into a utopian ideal. The whole Marxist adventure took off when the early Marx misinterpreted the Hegelian state as a mere ideal, a form of false consciousness masking the actual greed of civil society. But the attempt to incorporate the whole of human life within the role of citizen led on to the totalitarian state. It is a remarkable fact that today some of the rhetoric of Marxism is being employed at times for a project which runs, at least superficially, in the opposite direction. Thus Michael Joyce, president of the conservative Bradley Foundation in Milwaukee, suggests that 'Americans are clearly willing and eager to take control of their daily lives again . . . Americans are ready for what might be called "a new citizenship", which will liberate and empower them'.[10] The message here is that the state has reduced its members to clients and consumers of a highly inefficient organization, and that both morality and efficiency demand a more active population taking responsibility for many of the things currently done by the state. We may expect increasing idealism about citizenship in proportion as politicians become more and more unpopular as a result of the creeping oligarchy of our time.

Citizenship is, in fact, no less dangerous than any other ideal. Treated as the central virtue of modern life, it easily destroys the fragile balance of forms and virtues on which a modern state depends. It can, for example, lead to an excessively active involvement of the population at large in the details of legislation and political decision. It has often been pointed out that modern democracies only work precisely *because* most people

[10]Joyce, M., 'Philanthropy and Citizenship', 22 *Imprimis* (1993), p. 3.

limit their political activity to the elementary act of voting. There used to be, in the 1950s, a vogue for academic articles praising apathy as a necessary virtue in modern states, and contemporary political parties regard their own activists as a mixed blessing. (The political enthusiasm of youth movements must be regarded in our century as especially pernicious.)

But even the simple act of voting has its dangers. Understood as the emblem of democracy, it has also been recognized as an irrational diversion of time and energy which, except in unlikely circumstances, will have no real effect upon the decision at all. For the only circumstance in which my vote would *determine* which candidate has been elected would be if that candidate were elected by a majority of just one. There are, no doubt, other considerations which might be advanced, but the question of why it is that people actually do bother to vote has long been one of strong interest to political scientists. And the reason is clearly that voting is an act which establishes us with a virtuous identity, as civilly responsible, in our own eyes. Such symbolic acts we feel are important. But this situation has very clear dangers. It might mean, and sometimes does, that *in voting* we are usually pretty confident that *our own* vote is not going to affect the outcome. Voting thus comes to belong in that area of our actions where we posture before the world as having this or that virtue, an act of conspicuous moral consumption, as it were. But clearly if increasing numbers of people vote along these lines, then democratic decision-making will tend to become severed from reality, and that may have serious long-term consequences.

Our conclusion must be that citizenship is one of the roles we play in the modern world. It is an important role, but one which must not be accorded an exaggerated status. No doubt having such an emblem of citizenship as the right to vote is an important element in the status of those who have previously been peripheral to politics – a point made vigorously about women and blacks by Judith Shklar.[11] But the real character of a modern state lies not in any particular role, but in a balance of roles, and the more roles there are, the more we all become virtuosos in how we finesse conflicts between them. And this

---

[11]Shklar, J. N., *American Citizenship: The Quest for Inclusion*, Cambridge, MA 1991, ch. 1.

is why both Hobbes and Hegel played down citizenship in their accounts of the modern European state.

Citizenship is essentially the implicit morality which underlies our roles as moral agents, economic actors, aesthetically sensitive individuals, voters, members of families and all the rest of the forms of life in which we are involved. What holds these things together is a form of moral probity, the performance of the duties appropriate to each. The balance between the notional state which Hegel felt it necessary to formulate, and the civil society whose importance we recognize now more than ever, rests upon the incorruptible public official. For what we call 'corruption' on politics is the invasion of Hegel's 'state' by the considerations of civil society. Logically, this is the precise opposite of the Marxist project, but we now know that the two imbalances between these two spheres culminate in the same kind of disaster: a society in which *both* private life and public life have collapsed into each other. And the only solution to this disaster, as a practical problem, is the slow and unambitious rebuilding of the barriers between spheres and activities. It is certainly not the positing of some grand ideal of citizenship to save us from our human frailty.

DISCUSSION 1

André Liebich launched the discussion by commenting that in Kenneth Minogue's promenade through the portrait gallery of philosophers, Hobbes came out looking better than Rousseau, and he invited the participants to continue the promenade. The invitation was taken up by Pierre Hassner, who evoked Benjamin Constant's view that the state existed only to protect private life, and that of Alexis de Tocqueville, whose nightmare was the welfare state. Hassner emphasized, however, that the main figure underemphasized in Minogue's philosophical gallery was John Locke. He argued that Hegel's pessimistic and reluctant recognition of the sphere of political economy and his belief in the need for war set him apart from modern concerns, whereas Locke fully realized the central place of capitalism in our lives. What then would be the Lockean citizen, asked Hassner? Kenneth Minogue responded that, in fact, Locke still believed in the law of nature, and that Hassner's attribution to Locke of the thesis that the central business of modern society is the pursuit of prosperity was incorrect; this was actually Marx's vision and his critique. Minogue reiterated his argument that individuality was the essence of modern society and took issue with Hassner's portrayal of Hegel. According to Minogue, Hegel was not pessimistic; he believed that all are free in the modern world. Nor was Hegel in favour of war; he was simply attempting to explain it.

Martin Palous engaged the discussion from another point of view. Locke was important, Palous recognized, but could one really continue speaking as if the world of Locke, Rousseau and Hegel had not been fundamentally changed by both world wars? These had pitted diametrically opposed visions, *Kultur* vs

Civilisation, and they had given rise to countless crimes committed in the name of the state, culminating in Auschwitz. Without endorsing the argument of utter dissimilarity, Kenneth Minogue agreed that World War I was indeed a historical milestone as it ushered in the modern phenomenon of totalitarianism.

Piotr Ogrodzinski remarked that another philosopher missing from the discussion was Immanuel Kant, whose idea of history as a sphere of freedom to be created was particularly relevant to Eastern Europe today. Kant's categorical imperative could be defined as a statement on how free people should live together in society. This added a valuable dimension to Locke's insights on the structure of rule and on the creation of a sphere of private property as well as to Hegel's doctrine of the state. Kenneth Minogue responded that although Kant's merit was to recognize the impossibility of combining the moral and the natural spheres, his mistake was to believe that the way in which the state is constituted determines what any particular government will do.

André Liebich concluded the discussion by asking whether much of Kenneth Minogue's argument concerning compliance and participation did not actually involve a distinction between substance and procedure. In his closing statement, Minogue reiterated his thesis that in modern society some roles absorb others; citizenship is in fact one role among many, and it is in danger of being overloaded.

A.L.

CITIZENSHIP IN ITS INTERNATIONAL DIMENSION

André Liebich

The nexus between state and citizen represents the lowest common denominator of any reflection upon citizenship.[1] Whatever the significance and the values we impute to citizenship, whatever our view of the continuity and the changes in the meaning of the concept, it has been generally agreed that citizenship concerns life *inside* the state. The premise which I propose to explore is that the future significance of citizenship will lie increasingly *outside* the state. Here, I shall attempt to look, first, at the past transformations and understanding of citizenship; second, at the present meaning of citizenship; and, third, at the implications of a future citizenship which would be exercised outside the boundaries of its own state.

The Classic Citizen

'There is no more dynamic figure in modern history than the Citizen,' writes Ralf Dahrendorf.[2] This conviction underlies our discussions here too, inasmuch as the assumption behind this volume is that very recent changes in Central and Eastern

---

[1] 'Nationality as a legal term denotes the existence of a legal tie between an individual and a State . . .' Randelzhofer, A., 'Nationality', in *Encyclopaedia of Public International Law*. Published under the auspices of the Max Planck Institute for Comparative Public Law and International Law under the direction of Rudolf Bernhardt, Amsterdam 1985, p. 417. Note that, in English, boats have nationality and individuals have citizenship but, in legal usage, nationality replaces citizenship. Indeed, the *Encyclopaedia of Public International Law* has no entry for citizenship.

[2] Dahrendorf, R., 'Citizenship and Beyond: The Social Dynamics of an Idea', 41 *Social Research* (1974) p. 673.

Europe oblige us to re-examine the notion of citizenship and, possibly, adapt it to new circumstances.

The past dynamics and metamorphoses of citizenship were mapped out most illuminatingly by T. H. Marshall over forty years ago.[3] Exploring the evolution from civil through political to social citizenship, Marshall charted the course of modern political values from the 18th to the 20th century. Correcting Marshall's whiggish assumptions, B. S. Turner brought Marshall's idea of social citizenship up to date by enlarging the scope of the concept even further.[4] Yet more recently, other critics have continued to push the thesis that citizenship, even social citizenship, is ineffective so long as it coexists with class inequality and dependence.[5]

One reads such elaborations on the concept of citizenship with a sinking feeling. It is difficult to avoid the conclusion that the specificity of citizenship is being dissolved in a blurred landscape where the concept of citizenship merges imperceptibly with values such as fairness and solidarity and perhaps many others.[6] This risk of merger and confusion is all the greater because innovations in the concept of citizenship *overlay* rather than replace earlier ideas. No theorist of social citizenship will give up political or civic citizenship (in Marshall's terms) or indeed any other earlier conceptions, all seen as prerequisites for effective citizenship. Apparently, conceptions of citizenship are cumulative.

Thus, even as discussion of citizenship strays further from its

[3]Marshall, T. H., *Citizenship and Social Class*, Cambridge 1950.

[4]In Turner's view we are on the eve of an expansion of citizenship rights to animals and, with the acceptance of environmentalism, to plants as well. Feminists and others argue that reproductive freedom is a citizenship issue since without this right women become second-class citizens. Turner, B. S., *Citizenship and Captialism*, London 1986, p. 98.

[5]Esping-Anderson, G., *The Three Worlds of Welfare Capitalism*, Princeton 1990.

[6]Harvard University's Center for European Studies runs a 'Citizenship and Social Policy' study group. The extent to which the latter part of the title dominates the former is apparent from the group's readings. To cite but a few typical examples: 'Equity in the Finance and Delivery of Health Care'. 'Resource Allocation in Health Care: The Allocation of Lifestyles to Providers', 'Social Class and the Health Service'. One would almost believe that health is the essence of citizenship and, if this were the case, one cannot be surprised that the initial draft of the Slovenian citizenship law admitted only the healthy to citizenship. See Nakarada, R., 'The Mystery of Nationalism: The Paramount Case of Yugoslavia', 20 *Millennium* (1991), p. 378. Article 13 (4) (5) of the present Lithuanian citizenship law bars 'persons who are chronic alcoholics or drug addicts; and persons who are ill with especially dangerous infectious diseases'.

Greek origins the classic notion of citizenship survives, however uncomfortably. Few theorists of citizenship can resist a yearning for the ancient, original notion of citizenship in its mythical Athenian garb as codified by that non-citizen, Aristotle. The notion of the citizen as free participant in politics, as 'one who rules in addition to being ruled', exercises a magical hold on the political imagination. Preserved throughout the ages in republican tradition, the Athenian citizen as ideal may well be today the last gasp of industrial age Hellenism. Even the most hard-bitten advocates of social citizenship, fully aware that Aristotle's citizen is an idle male slaveowner of whom they should disapprove, and themselves completely dedicated to an opposing vision of citizenship, allow themselves to be charmed or inhibited by the Aristotelian vision.[7] Citizenship is thus asked to bear a heavy burden. It is called upon to be all things to all people. Citizenship is civil rights, political participation, social welfare. It is identity and recognition. Citizenship is the common good. It is the consciousness of community. To paraphrase Leszek Kolakowski's statement about socialism, all one can really say of citizenship is that it is a good thing.

The Citizen Today: Rights

Let us therefore approach the concept of citizenship from another vantage point. What does citizenship mean to the individual citizen in a 'normal', i.e., democratic and developed state, of the sort familiar to some and aspired to by others? After all, citizenship has to do with citizens and, I would suggest, it is they who can tell us most about the meaning of their own citizenship to them.

In the first instance, it would seem, citizenship has to do with rights. Even in one's daily routine, and certainly at the first brush with the law, the citizen is aware of the procedural and substantive rights enjoyed in the 'normal' state. Whether it is the right to appeal a traffic ticket or an income tax assessment, to receive one's mail uncensored or to install a satellite dish on one's roof, the citizen is a legal subject endowed with rights. But is this, in fact, the citizen? None of the rights mentioned above are refused in the 'normal' democratic state to the resident

[7]For a recent and representative example see Heater, D., *Citizenship: The Civic Ideal in World History, Politics and Education*, London-New York 1990.

non-citizen. True, *in extremis* the citizen does enjoy certain rights denied to his or her non-citizen neighbour: for example, guarantee against expulsion from the state's territory or against refusal to allow re-entry or, usually, protection against extradition.[8] I shall return to these issues later because they are at the heart of my argument. At this point, let us simply note that the measures mentioned are hardly the stuff of which daily life consists. From the point of view of the blessedly humdrum life of the individual in his or her home environment, the rights of the citizen and non-citizen are little different. Justice is even blinder than we once thought.

The reason behind this indifferentiation of rights lies, in the first instance, in the universalization of human rights in our era. Whereas the French Revolution still extolled the rights of man *and citizen*, the Universal Declaration of Human Rights speaks only of mankind. Broadly speaking, citizenship is no longer a basis of rights or a precondition to the enjoyment of rights; it has itself become a right among others, universally bestowed: 'Everyone has a right to a nationality', says article 15 of the Universal Declaration. When one adds to this ringing affirmation of universalism a strong partiality for *individual* rights in the letter and spirit of the Declaration, citizenship may become superfluous. Who needs to live as a citizen in a given state if that state respects its commitment to universal rights for citizen and non-citizen alike?[9]

The Citizen Today: Entitlements

In the second instance, citizenship has to do with entitlements, the satisfaction of claims. The state has always been a protector

---

[8]Although most international instruments guarantee re-entry (or entry, for nationals born abroad) only to citizens, the case has been made that the Covenant on Civil and Political Rights protects permanent (non-national) residents and this principle has been expressly incorporated into the 1986 Strasbourg Declaration on the Right to Leave and Return. See Hannum, H., *The Right to Leave and Return in International Law and Practice*, Dordrecht-Boston 1987.

[9]International Human Rights Law has codified in a number of covenants the principle that 'states are obliged to secure human rights for everyone within their jurisdiction, whether citizens or not'. Eide, A., 'Citizenship and International Law: the Challenge of Ethno-Nationalism', in *Citizenship and Language Laws in the Newly Independent States of Europe*, seminar held in Copenhagen, January 9–10 1993. Published by the Danish Center for Human Rights, the Danish Helsinki Committee et al., Copenhagen 1993.

and a provider; indeed, to a large extent this is what defines the state. Protection against transgression, from outside and inside, is every citizen's expectation. It may be today that in some countries private police forces absorb a greater share of national income than does public law enforcement; mercifully, however, there is no ambiguity about the public nature of the armed forces.[10] In addition to serving as a community of defence, the state is also expected to sustain, to a greater or lesser extent, the population it is protecting. From the poor laws of early modern times which called upon the indigent to turn to their own commune for sustenance, the 'normal' state has created a huge, complex and costly array of social programmes. In an incomparably more efficient and direct way than the early poor laws, however, these programmes are contributory, sustained directly through social insurance schemes or indirectly through the fiscal system.

Where now stands the citizen in the web of entitlement? To be sure, he or she is solidly grounded within it. The point I would stress, however, is that grounding of the resident and contributing non-citizen is practically as solid as that of the citizen. Inasmuch as the protective mission of the modern state is concerned, this mission is defined – because the state itself is defined – above all, in territorial terms. The state defends those who find themselves on its territory, just as attackers can hardly distinguish the citizenship of their victims. The providing mission of the state, too, tends towards universality and indifference toward citizenship. After all, the various entitlements – unemployment insurance, old age pensions, state health care (where applicable), public education – do not derive logically from the status of citizen. They are either the concrete and specific manifestations of universal human rights or rightful compensation for the individual's labour and fiscal contribution, whether he or she be a citizen or not. True, there are still exceptions to this principle but the trend is clear and, in my view, expanding.

[10]In the United States 'Private guards outnumber federal, state and local law enforcement officers by more than 2 to 1,' *International Herald Tribune*, 12 July 1993.

Citizens and Non-Citizens

The 'normal' state is thus made up of citizens and non-citizens, living and working side by side, undistinguishable from one another in all respects of daily life as they pay their taxes, consult their doctor or send their children to school. Is there really never a difference among these individuals? As the tradition of citizenship teaches us, of course there is a difference: The citizen participates in politics and stands ready to defend the state with his (or, more rarely, her) life. These are weighty privileges and obligations which deserve respect in both paradigmatic and practical terms.[11] Nevertheless, I would argue that their significance is declining and is increasingly irrelevant to the lives of most individuals.

Participation in political life means, for most people, voting and, for a few people, standing for office. It is a truism that the nature of mass politics makes the individual vote unimportant on a national level. There is general consensus that it must be exercised – 'vote for the party of your choice, but vote' – but there is no illusion about its effectiveness. Voting belongs to the rituals of the 'normal' state, bearing about the same significance as church weddings do for marrying non-believers. In this light, the pathetically low level of electoral participation in the first post-communist elections in Eastern Europe is a sensible and understandable phenomenon. Post-communist citizens have had enough of the ritual and symbols of ineffective voting under the previous regime. A measure of their present freedom is the liberty to abstain from such ritual in its new, democratic version.

The citizen's capacity to stand for office is certainly not symbolic. On the other hand, it is not, primarily, a civic issue but a professional one. With the growing costs and demands of political life, politics is not a manifestation of one's identity as citizen but a career option much like others. The requirement that only citizens stand for public office is not a test of civic virtue but an eligibility criterion of the same significance as the age or residence requirement. Indeed, what is one to make of rules that deprive citizens of the right to stand for office because they are of unsuitable age (below thirty-five for U.S. senators; over

[11]Janowitz, M., 'Observations on the Sociology of Citizenship: Obligations and Rights,' 59 *Social Forces* (1980), pp. 1–24, argues that there is an imbalance between 'rights' and 'obligations' whereby the latter are given short shrift. I share his perception though not necessarily his regret.

seventy-five for Canadian senators) or because they do not reside in the right part of the state or perhaps not even within the state at all?

These remarks are not intended to belittle the citizen who votes or who stands for office. On the contrary, they aim at underscoring the fact that citizenship functions as originally intended when it take place in its original conditions. As political theorists, including Geneva's most famous sage, Jean-Jacques Rousseau reminded us long ago, the citizen's terms of reference cannot be large. Citizenship, in its original conception, is the prerogative of the inhabitants of small political units. The citizen's politics can only be local politics. From the point of view of the issue which concerns us here, therefore, the growing trend in 'normal' states towards extension of the suffrage in local elections to resident non-citizens is of fundamental importance. In this most sacrosanct preserve of citizenship, in the exercise of the key political right to vote, the distinction between citizen and non-citizen is being effaced.

Voting is an occasional and sporadic activity; standing for office is the concern of very few. What obligations and privileges of citizenship remain for the vast majority of citizens whose main concerns lie outside the sphere of politics?

The principal obligation associated with citizenship is that of military service. However equally a state may treat its own citizens and the non-citizens resident on its territory in other respects, it will only draft the former not the latter. One can only be expected to die for one's own state, not for another's. True, one might volunteer to die for a state to which one does not belong, for instance for ideological or mercenary reasons, but one could not be required to do so and such alien zeal might even embarrass the state. There is surely no closer nexus than that of citizenship and military duty.[12]

The apparent intractability of this fundamental obligation of citizenship conceals, it seems to me, a number of far-reaching

[12]In the current debate in the Baltic states on citizenship the liberal position is to deny citizenship not to all Russians present but only to those who came with, worked for, or are in any other way connected with the Soviet/Russian forces stationed there. The basic sources on this very rich debate are to be found in *Citizenship and Language Laws, op. cit.,* (note 9) and an overview in 'CIS, Baltic States and Georgia: Nationality Legislation (April 1992)', 4 *International Journal of Refugee Law* (1992) pp. 230–47.

changes.[13] First, the very notion of a military draft contradicts the classical ethos of citizenship. Classical citizens should spring to the defence of their state; they should not need to be drafted. Second, discrimination on the basis of gender violates the principle of equal and universal citizenship. Women must be susceptible to undergo military service on the same terms as men. The notion of a male-only draft flies in the face of all modern human rights concerns and will be contested by both sexes. Of course, a possible solution would be to draft both men and women but, for other reasons, it is more likely that the draft will be dropped for both. Among these other reasons are such practical considerations as the cost of a conscript army, the increasing complexity of weapons systems and the consequent professionalization of war. Ironically, one of the main arguments today in favour of universal military service is its role in creating good citizens. We seem to have forgotten that it is not armies who should create good citizens but good citizens who should create armies.

Extrapolating from the question of military service, one might see public sector employment as a privilege of citizenship. In contrast to earlier eras, today one expects one's soldiers, or at least their commanders, to be citizens and one also expects one's judges and diplomats and other high public servants to be citizens. The logic behind these expectations is a logic of loyalty. Those who serve the state can be trusted to serve it best if they are its members; *'on n'est jamais servi aussi bien que par soi-même.'* On reflection, however, this logic does not hold up. As in the case of political participation, the identification of the individual public servant with the state may not be very strong. Like the private citizen, the public servant too is awed by the size of the state and swayed by the tug of numerous other loyalties of a personal, familial, professional, religious or other nature. Conceding that the quality of citizen is an insufficient guarantee, states often require of their public servants that they swear an oath of office – why does the tacit oath of citizenship not suffice? – and subject them to security investigations well beyond those

[13]'In the democratic welfare state ... employment rather than military service is the key to citizenship', writes Pateman, C., 'The Patriarchal Welfare State,' in Gutman, A., (ed.), *Democracy and the Welfare State*, Princeton 1988, p. 239, and Soysal, Y. *Limits of Citizenship*, (forthcoming) explores the implications for citizenship and membership of the *Gastarbeiter* phenomenon in a way which parallels the argument advanced here.

inflicted on the simple citizen. Clearly, citizenship alone is an insufficient condition for public service employment (unlike Athens where recruitment was by lot). On the other hand, the expansion of the realm of the state's activities and the state's need for specialists, buttressed by the ethos of rights and the logic of entitlement discussed earlier, means that the public sector is effectively opened to non-citizens. In short, citizenship does not suffice for entry into the public sector and the public sector does not confine itself to citizens.[14]

Citizenship is thus not a sufficient status for many purposes associated with citizenship and, it must be added, citizenship is no longer (if it ever was) supreme in any moral sense. A corollary of the universalisation of individual rights is the acceptance of universal responsibility by individuals. 'My country right or wrong', or any other similar argument founded on the obligations of citizenship does not carry any weight when invoked against universal or international norms of conduct. Citizenship may be a good thing, but it is no excuse and no defence.[15]

Tomorrow's Citizen

It citizenship therefore an insignificant factor to the modern man or woman? It is certainly not insignificant to those who are deprived of it, to the stateless whom Hannah Arendt has called 'the most symptomatic group in modern politics'.[16] Nor is it insignificant to those whose citizenship is ill-regarded because they have the misfortune to be citizens of a country deemed

[14]In order to preserve the principle that public servants should be citizens, states have naturalized national sports stars, university professors and candidates for high public office (including Adolf Hitler). Bois, P., 'Nationalité et naturalisation', in Centlivres, P. (ed.) *Devenir suisse*, Geneva 1990, pp. 13–45.

[15] Walzer, M., *Obligations: Essays on Disobedience, War, and Citizenship*, Cambridge, MA 1970, dealing with citizenship as a moral choice rather than a legal status explores further the issue raised here.

[16]Arendt, H., *The Origins of Totalitarianism*, New York 1951, p. 276. I would not disagree with two Hungarian intellectuals who have recently written of citizenship, in a Marshall-Turner sense, as a sort of certificate of entry or eligibility which 'offers the chance of forming part of a modern civilization that transcends frontiers and continents'. Csepeli, G. and Orkeny, A., 'Conflicting Loyalties of Citizenship and National Identity in Eastern Europe', in Plichtova, J. (ed.), *Minorities in Politics*, Bratislava 1993, p. 46.

hostile or unworthy and who thus bear, personally, the stigma attached to their state.[17]

In these cases as well as, I would argue, in many others, the significance of citizenship only comes to the fore when one steps outside the borders of the state to which one belongs or in which one happens to live.[18] It is only then that the question of my statehood, my citizenship, becomes a vital issue governing my life and defining my identity.[19] It is then that the mechanisms of exclusion, of participation and of recognition – all part and parcel of earlier conceptions of citizenship – come to the fore once again, outside their earlier context.[20]

The transformation in the understanding of citizenship from something relevant to one's life within the state to something which acquires relevance when one leaves one's state is symbolically incarnated in the *passport*.

Within the state a driver's licence will do just as well, but as soon as one leaves one's own territory the passport becomes the individual's most fundamental prop. The institution of the passport, confined a century ago to the barbaric peripheries of Europe, tsarist Russia and the Ottoman Empire, has now become universal.[21] States affirm their sovereignty by requiring passports from those who would enter their own territory. They exercise their power *vis-à-vis* other states by recognizing some passports and refusing others. They exercise their power *vis-à-*

[17]What is it like these days to be an Iraqi, Lebanese, Libyan, or Yugoslav travelling through Europe and North America? In this connection one may reflect on the case of the enterprising firm which sold Canadian passport covers which could be slipped onto U.S. passports in situations where Americans felt threatened.

[18]Soysal, *op. cit.*, (note 13) argues along these lines with particular reference to *Gastarbeiter* and a post-national membership model where formal citizenship is not the principle criterion for the distribution of rights and privileges.

[19]There may well be excessive emphasis on the link between citizenship and identity in present circumstances. Citizenship is, at best, one possible expression of identity and it may even be losing its status as an unquestioned symbol of identity. 62% of French people surveyed declared that for them French national identity was symbolized by French cuisine. Safran, W., 'State, Nation, National Identity and Citizenship: France as a Test Case', 12 *International Political Science Review* (1991), p. 227.

[20]On exclusion as a defining element of citizenship see Shklar, J. N., *American Citizenship*, Cambridge, MA 1991, with special reference to the case of American slavery. On recognition, see Taylor, C., *Multiculturalism and 'The Politics of Recognition'*, Princeton 1992.

[21]A recent headline 'Cows to be Given Passports', *The European*, 10–11 December 1992, underscores not only the universality of passport requirements but perhaps also the depreciation of citizenship referred to earlier.

vis their own citizens by issuing – or perhaps refusing to issue – passports to them.

If one has any doubts about the value of a passport it will suffice to read the advertisements, even in such mass publications as the *Economist* or the *International Herald Tribune*, promising a passport or a second passport to those who have everything but not this.[22] Can one be really surprised that, in popular parlance, citizenship has come to be identified with the passport and that the symbol of citizenship outweighs the fact of citizenship itself?

One may lament this state of affairs in terms of the inherent dignity of citizenship but it is a condition which is unlikely to experience much improvement because there is little likelihood that international mobility will be stemmed, at any level, in the near future. Every day, one sees the privileged, easily recognizable at any European airport, who work in one state but reside in another. Every day too, if one cares to do so, one can see those less privileged who assail Europe's land borders, with variable success. The notion that citizens of one state may aspire to live in another is not new – emigration and immigration are age-old phenomena – but their present-day implications for the notion of citizenship have not been thought through.[23]

The classical citizenship solution to the problem of immigration is naturalization of immigrants and, possibly, automatic or semi-automatic attribution of citizenship to their descendants. Obviously, naturalization laws vary greatly from one state to another and they tell us a great deal about the self-definition of that state.[24] They may also raise questions about the ethics of assimilation, the nature of nationalism and other issues which do not concern us here. With respect to present-day immigration, however, all past solutions are founded on a false prem-

---

[22]'The national passport has changed its meaning,' writes a French theorist, 'it no longer expresses . . . allegiance to an autonomous power but rather, a conditional right of access to the "cosmopolis" of communications and modern financial transactions'. Balibar, E., 'Propositions on Citizenship', 98 *Ethics* (1988), p. 729.

[23]It might be noted that immigration/emigration are not equivalent phenonomena from the point of view of the state. Whereas the right of the state to control immigration is relatively uncontested (e.g., the recent German debate on asylum), the right to control emigration is not generally recognized.

[24]Brubaker, R., *Citizenship and Nationhood in France and Germany*, Cambridge, MA 1992, is exemplary in this regard. See also his 'Traditions of Nationhood and Politics of Citizenship,' 9 *States and Social Structures Newsletter* (1989), pp. 4–8.

ise: they assume that immigration is definitive, that the process of movement which brought the immigrant to a given country is final and will not be repeated.[25]

There is no reason today to make such an assumption of permanence. Market conditions change and those countries which looked attractive to immigrants at one point may not seem so in a few years. Communication facilities make travel uncomplicated, at least on a technical rather than a legal level, and encourage further movement among those who have already uprooted themselves once. Even more significantly, immigrants can stay in touch with their countries of origin and return to them when material or political conditions allow. In short, the permanent immigrant gives way to the more or less long-term but still temporary sojourner.[26]

Let it be noted that this phenomenon has consequences both for the state of origin and for the receiving state. At any given moment, there are large numbers of foreign citizens living, say, in Switzerland and a perhaps equally large number of Swiss living abroad. In a few years, the former may no longer be in Switzerland and many of the latter may be back in their homeland. The question of their citizenship status, and of those who succeed them, will remain.

What should a state do in the face of such mobility? It may, of course, make the acquisition of citizenship impossibly difficult so as avoid bestowing citizenship on those for whom a given country was but a transit point among others.[27] This sol-

[25]This assumption is connected with the preeminence of territoriality as the organizing principle of the modern polity. Elaborating on my earlier argument, one could say that the modern state tends to treat all on its own territory equally but assumes that all on its territory are its own. For a far-reaching reflection see Ruggie, J. G., 'Territoriality and Beyond: Problematizing Modernity in International Relations', 47 *International Organization* (1993), pp. 139–74.

[26]'Il faut accepter cette évidence que les immigrés vont rester en Europe. Alors, autant en faire de vrais citoyens', declares one of the immigrants' principal advocates, 'Un Entretien avec M. Daniel Cohn-Bendit' *Le Monde*, 27 June 1991. Contrary to the curiously reluctant reasoning expressed here ('we might as well make them citizens . . .'), my point is that we must make immigrants citizens not because they will stay, but even though they will not stay.

[27]One may argue that in acting this way the state is returning to the time-honoured notion that exclusion is an essential dimension of citizenship. No one can be a citizen if all can be citizens. See Shklar, *American Citizenship, op. cit.,* (note 20) reiterated in another context by Guillaume, P.,' Nationalité et citoyenneté', in Colas, D., Emeri, C., Zylberberg, J. (ed.), *Citoyenneté et nationalité: perspectives en France et au Québec*, Paris 1991, p. 111. On the other hand, Eide, *op. cit.,* (note 9), asks pointedly why denial of citizenship to some is necessary to secure recognition, respect and freedoms for others as well as to fulfill the requirements of morality, public order and general welfare.

ution, not unjust in itself as long as resident aliens are treated equitably, will be resisted by most parties: citizens who see in it a lack of confidence in their country's force of attraction; citizens and non-citizens who see discriminatory treatment in stringent citizenship requirements; and last but not least, non-citizens who seek citizenship as a guarantee of the right to return to the country where they are living. For this latter category, the importance of citizenship arises, once again, only outside the borders of the state in question.[28]

The alternative solution is to bestow citizenship easily and generously. All those who are born in or have lived in a given state for a determined, not excessively long, period of time may apply for its citizenship. This solution is compatible with modern notions of rights in that it tends towards equal treatment of the entire population of a state and universalizes a single status.[29] To function properly, of course, this solution must contain the safeguard of allowing an 'opting out' from citizenship.[30] After all, no one should become or remain a citizen without his or her consent. If this condition is respected, who can say that the civic virtue of the newly naturalized citizen is inferior to that of the native-born citizen?[31]

Personal mobility plus accessible naturalization has revolutionary implications for the traditional understanding of citizenship. Above all, it raises the prospect of multiple citizenship,

[28]Another problem is that of foreign-born nationals. This problem much exercises, for example, 'The Federal League of Americans around the Globe', which contrasts recently relaxed citizenship rules in other countries with, purportedly, restrictive U.S. rules for the foreign-born children of U.S. citizens. (Advertising Supplement), p. 7, *International Herald Tribune*, 29–30 August 1992.

[29]The present British solution, that of having different categories of citizens, for instance, those with a right of abode and those without, is not a happy one. As Denis MacShane has pointed out, the last previous case of an European state issuing passports for different categories of holders was that of Nazi Germany. The notorious 'J' was inserted, however, at the request of Switzerland 'Goodbye to Englishness', *New Statesman*, 7 February 1992.

[30]A further safeguard must make naturalization irrevocable. Arendt, *op. cit.*, (note 16) argues that the possibility of revocation is the first step towards a totalitarian polity.

[31]These issues are at the heart of discussions concerning the new French citizenship law. In contrast to the argument developed here it has been affirmed that the requirement of application for citizenship by any native-born (in this case, the children of first generation immigrants) is inherently discriminatory. 'Est-il logique [de] considérer que le fait d'être né de tel père ou de telle mère crée un lien plus fort avec le pays que le fait d'y être né, d'y avoir vécu et d'y avoir été scolarisé?' asks a socialist deputy in the National Assembly, *Le Monde*, 13 May 1993.

not as an oddity or an exception but as a normal and widespread phenomenon. The final argument of this paper is that we must come to terms with this prospect and, indeed, that we should foster it as a desirable outcome.

At present, dual or, *horribile dictu*, multiple citizenship has approximately the same moral status as polygamy does in relation to monogamy.[32] A number of states tolerates dual citizenship, particularly when the status occurs 'through no fault' of the individual concerned.[33] However, many of the new states arising in East and Central Europe are prohibiting dual citizenship, for conjunctural reasons connected with past (and possibly future) immigration. Even those established states which tolerate multiple citizenship do so with distaste, considering it only as an inconvenient anomaly.

It is time, I would maintain, to praise multiple citizenship. There is no good reason why the pluralism which we extoll in politics or ideology or society should stop short of the institution of citizenship. There is no good reason why individuals who possess multiple identities and who have earned multiple citizenships should not be allowed to express and exercise them. As the exclusivity of citizenship loses its hold and the prospects of a supranational citizenship falter (at Maastricht or Schengen), multiple citizenship emerges as an increasingly attractive option. In this respect, as in others, one should not shrink from declaring 'pluralism or barbarism'.

To be sure, multiple citizenship is not without its inconveniences It requires states to sign numerous bilateral conventions, for example, to avoid double military service or double taxation, and it requires individuals to be aware of such conventions. It increases the protection afforded individuals abroad by allowing them to turn to more than one diplomatic representation but it reduces their security by depriving them of any diplomatic protection when they are in one of their states of

[32]On the legal distaste for but practical increase of dual citizenship, see Hammar, T., 'State, Nation, and Dual Citizenship', in Brubaker, W. R. (ed.), *Immigration and the Politics of Citizenship in Europe and North America*, Lanham-London 1988, pp. 81–96.

[33]One of the main 'hold-outs', the United States, changed its position in 1990 when a State Department ruling admitted (retroactively) the right of U.S. citizens living abroad to retain their citizenship upon becoming citizens of another country. On the other hand, Germany is only beginning to discuss the possibility of dual citizenship. *International Herald Tribune*, 16 February 1993.

citizenship. Generally speaking, however, the inconveniences of multiple citizenship accrue to the state, whereas its advantages belong to the individual.

Conclusion

The Hungarian author György Konrad, in a particular burst of exuberance here in Geneva, once stated that passports should be like credit cards; one should have as many as one could afford.

The image may be somewhat crass and I would not argue that a passport or citizenship be a matter of sheer convenience or of purchasing power. Still, it seems to me that the passport should be more like a credit card than, say, like a birth certificate. Whereas the latter is a unique and unchangeable document, as constraining as one's genetic code, the former is a contract accepted in full recognition of the responsibilities it entails and a promise of access to certain benefits. There are material limits to the number of cards one may draw on just as there are moral and practical limits to the number of passports one may carry.[34]

Above all, what falls by the wayside here is the quality of exclusivity. States, at least unitary states, may still claim exclusive domination over territory. They do not and should not possess exclusive domination over individuals. 'Their' citizens may be not only 'their' citizens but those of another state. If this forces states to reduce their claims and to harmonize their laws and policies with those of other states, so much the better!

---

[34]In commenting on this paper, Kenneth Minogue has pointed out that with each additional citizenship an individual opens himself/herself up to an almost algebraic increase in liability to charges of treason. This is true, but attenuated by the fact that the question of treason comes to the fore primarily at times of war and democratic states do not wage war on each other, as Kant told us and as recent political science studies have laboriously confirmed.

CITIZENSHIP AND IDENTITY: A DOUBLE READING OF THE IDENTITY CRISIS

Daniel Warner

The subject of citizenship in the East and West is extremely topical. Unlike many other topical issues, however, the problem of citizenship in the East and West touches on fundamental problems involving the organization of society and the place of the individual in that society. In fact, the problems of citizenship evoked are tied to the deepest undercurrents in political and social life. While we will be touching on current problems, we will also be dealing with fundamental issues that have been brought to the surface by current events.

Integration and Disintegration

In the West, we are witnessing profound changes in traditional patterns of migration. The United States, my native country, is receiving an influx of immigrants from Latin America and Asia that is changing the demographic structure of the society from its original European basis. Recent discussions in France about the wearing of veils in schools also point to fundamental shifts in migration patterns away from traditional European sources, and, hence, fundamental shifts in the demographic structure of that society. The implications of these shifts are being manifested in various ways, such as the attacks on Korean-American owned stores in Los Angeles and the rise of the National Front in France. The long-term implications of these patterns are more difficult to comprehend; it is not easy to predict to what degree and how societies integrate new members.

More importantly, however, this Western integration of non-traditional members is part of a larger and more complex integration pattern. In addition to a changing migration, the West is also witnessing profound structural changes. In North America, we see this with the trade agreements between the United States and Canada, and eventually Mexico. But most importantly, we are witnessing higher forms of integration within the European Community. Instead of people moving from one place to another, as in the case of migration, we are seeing European borders changing from what were once rigid brick walls to supple cell walls that will permit the free movement of people, goods and services within a number of countries. Whereas in the case of migration people change countries, in the case of integration the borders themselves have changed in the sense of permitting freer access. Western European integration is changing the meaning of sovereignty, and, hence, of citizenship, and calls into question the very reason for migration and its significance. In the West, changing migration patterns and structural integration raise fundamental questions about traditional social attachments.

If within Western Europe and North America migration and integration have accentuated greater fluidity in social attachments towards larger units, the situation in the East[1] shows a marked contrast. The breakups of the Soviet Union, Yugoslavia and Czechoslovakia have resulted in smaller social units and more localized forms of attachments. The births and rebirths of various nation-states remind us that the inevitability of higher and higher forms of integration is not to be taken for granted; or, if it is, it will not be a linear progression.[2] If one intuitively argues that societal interdependence will occur with developing technology and improved transportation – what is generally referred to as complex interdependence – the situations in the former Soviet Union, Yugoslavia and Czechoslovakia point to another solution to the organization of social and political life. As Walker Connor noted already in 1972; '[a] global survey illustrates that ethnic consciousness is definitely in the ascend-

[1] The terms East and West are used as general categories with no value attachment or deeper meaning intended. Indeed, the same phenomenon that is taking place in the former Soviet Union, Czechoslovakia and Yugoslavia is also taking place in Canada. We refer to East and West, therefore, for the sake of convenience.

[2] For the notion of the inevitability of higher and higher forms of integration, see Linklater, A., *Men and Citizens in the Theory of International Relations*, London 1982.

ancy as a political force, and that state borders as presently delimited, are being increasingly challenged by this trend.'[3]

'[S]tate borders as presently delimited' are being challenged in both the East and the West. Integration and disintegration are both dramatic transformations in the traditional spatial delimitations of the basic organization of political and social life, whether into larger or smaller units.[4] Political theorists have long debated the relationship between the individual and society within a clearly defined community, and international relations specialists and international lawyers have long debated the relationship between communities defined as nation-states. Integration and disintegration call into question the society being considered by the political theorists and the nation-states being observed by the international relations specialists and international lawyers. In short, today we are confronted with the problem of defining the major actors in both political theory and international relations not only in terms of who they are, but in terms of what they are. The level-of-analysis problem raised by J. David Singer[5] and Kenneth Waltz[6] in the late 1950s and early 1960s focussed on the subjectmatter of international relations. Waltz, for example, examined the causes of war in terms of man, the state, or the structure of the international system. Our current problem, we argue, is that even if we accept the state as the major actor – which we should for the purposes of a discussion on citizenship – we are not sure what that state is.

It is in this sense that we can return to our earlier observations

[3]Connor, W., 'Nation-Building or Nation-Destroying?', 24 *World Politics* (1972), p. 327.

[4]'In Western Europe there is integration: frontiers eroding, a single currency on the way, a groping to co-operate in foreign and security policy. In the East there is disintegration: new states being born, new currencies created, border posts going up, separate armies being formed'. *The Economist*, 7 December 1991, p. 33. While *The Economist* refers to these trends as 'fusion' and 'fission,' a recent United Nations report makes a similar observation using different language: 'Two contradictory trends, toward enlarged unity and fragmentation, seem to be occurring concurrently: the tendency toward broadened regional arrangements in Europe, North America and other regions illustrates the first while the developments in the successor States of the Soviet Union, Yugoslavia, Czechoslovakia and Ethiopia, along with a host of other countries, dramatize the second.' UN Economic and Social Council, Doc. E/CN.4/1993/35, 21 January 1993, p. 36.

[5]Singer, J. D., 'The Level-of-Analysis Problem in International Relations', 14 *World Politics* (1961), pp. 77–92.

[6]Waltz, K., *Man, the State and War*, New York 1959.

about migration, integration and disintegration. Whereas migration threatens individual identity, integration and disintegration threaten the state's identity. While one may speculate as to the relationship between the different patterns of integration in the West and disintegration in the East, and the reasons for those differences,[7] I would prefer to make the general observation that patterns for both; i.e. integration and disintegration, fusion and fission, integration and fragmentation, are different responses to the same modern crisis of identity. And we understand citizenship in the largest sense to be related to the entire question of identity for both the individual and the state. A citizen's identity is tied to the state that he or she is a citizen of, in the sense that citizenship is the constitutive element of political identity.[8] But, as our examples from the West and East have suggested, states themselves are going through a form of identity crisis. In sum, then, the question of citizenship/identity in the East and West is part of the larger modern (post-modern?) crisis of identity, a crisis that is acute for both individuals and the state.[9] Thus, while Etienne Balibar talks of a 'new citizenship' in France,[10] we would argue that the problematic of 'new citizen-

[7]For some speculation on this relationship, see: Warner, D., 'Humanism and Identity', translated into Russian and appearing in the *Newsletter of the Tolstoy Society*, 5 1993, p. 6. John Lewis Gaddis discusses this in terms of integration and fragmentation. Gaddis, J. L., *The United States and the End of the Cold War*, Oxford 1992, pp. 196–216. Gaddis suggests that 'the problems we will confront in the post-Cold War world are more likely to arise from competing processes – integrationist versus fragmentationist – than from the kinds of competing ideological visions that dominated the Cold War'. (p. 201) Gaddis feels that there is a kind of dialectic tension between the two processes. John Ruggie analyzes the overall changes in territoriality as 'the emergence of the first truly postmodern political form...' Ruggie, J. G., 'Territoriality and Beyond: Problematizing Modernity in International Relations', 47 *International Organization* (1993), p. 140. Ruggie goes on to ponder 'whether the modern system of states may be yielding in some instances to postmodern forms of configuring political space', (p. 144) and refers to 'unbundled territory'. (p. 171)

[8]For an interesting discussion of identification from the individual to the national and international levels from a psychological point of view, see Bloom, W., *Personal Identity, National Identity and International Relations*, Cambridge 1993.

[9]In fact, the individual and state levels of identification can be encapsulated within Bloom's national identity dynamic. Bloom says that the national identity dynamic 'describes the potential for action which resides in a mass which shares the same national identification'. Bloom, W., *Idem*, p. 53.

[10]'Yet whatever the future redistribution of political power may be, several of the problems raised by discussions of the "new citizenship" will still have to be faced. These include racism and the status of immigration (or rather of the "communities that have issued from immigration") in France'. Balibar, E., 'Propositions on Citizenship', 98 *Ethics* (1988), p. 723.

ship' in certain traditional immigration countries is also very much related to the problem of 'new citizenship' in 'new countries'. 'New citizens' exist in both traditional and new countries, and, thus, there is a double reading of the identity crisis.[11]

Elements of Citizenship

But what is citizenship? What are the elements that constitute political identity? We are aware that Aristotle said that 'the nature of citizenship . . . is a question which is often disputed: certainly there is no general agreement on a single definition'.[12] In terms of the larger question of the relationship between citizenship and identity, Herman van Gunsteren says: 'Citizenship is an answer to the question, "Who am I?" and "What should I do?" when posed in the public sphere'.[13] Citizenship is the expression of a public identity. This public identity encompasses two elements: it includes the existence of a public authority made up of citizens who constitute the authority[14] and it includes the status following from the possession of citizenship. Citizenship is at once the recognition of an official position and the ability to use the rights and privileges following from that position. A citizen is one who is protected by the state and at the same time uses the state to advance her claims on the basis of equality with fellow citizens.

This public identity, in a more general sense, can be separated into three elements: the civil, political and social.

> The civil element is composed of the rights necessary for individual freedom – liberty of the person, freedom of speech, thought and faith, the right to own property and to conclude valid contracts, and the right to justice. The last is of a different order from the others, because it is the right to defend and assert one's rights in terms of equality with others and by due process of law. This shows

[11]With all due respect to Richard Ashley's 'Untying the Sovereign State: A Double Reading of the Anarchy Problematique', 17 *Millennium: Journal of International Studies* (1988), pp.227–62.

[12]Aristotle, *Politics*, E. Barker (ed.), Oxford 1946, p. 93, cited in Heater, D., *Citizenship: The Civic Ideal in World History, Politics and Education*, London-New York 1990, p. vii.

[13]van Gunsteren, H., 'Admission to Citizenship', 98 *Ethics* (1988), p. 731.

[14]See Shklar's discussion of Rousseau on this point: Shklar, J., *American Citizenship: The Quest for Inclusion*, Cambridge MA 1991, p. 34.

us that the institutions most directly associated with civil rights are the courts of justice. By the political element I mean the right to participate in the exercise of political power, as a member of a body invested with political authority or as an elector of the members of such a body. The corresponding institutions are parliament and councils of local government. By the social element I mean the whole range from the right to a modicum of economic welfare and security to the right to share to the full in the social heritage and to live the life of a civilised being according to the standards prevailing in the society.[15]

To rephrase Marshall, our understanding of the first two elements is that the civil element of citizenship is a position from which, on the basis of equality, people can make certain claims against each other and/or against the government. The political element is that which allows an individual to participate in the decisions of the government or to be a member of that government. Since I will link the civil and political elements together, I will discuss their relationship before examining the social element.

What is the relationship between the civil and political elements? Can one have the civil element without the political element? To some extent, I imagine the answer is yes. That is, blacks in the United States did have certain civil rights before they were given the right to vote. Foreign workers in most countries have certain rights even though they are not part of the political system. Moreover, one could argue that the internationalization of human rights has created a situation wherein individuals have certain rights regardless of their citizenship. Human rights theory is citizen-specific blind; it posits a set of fundamental rights that supersede national legislation. Human rights are carried out through the particular state mechanism, but they are universal and should not be abrogated by a specific state. From the human rights and natural law points of view, the civil element can precede the political element.

Can one have the political element without the civil element? First, the question could be dismissed by saying that

<hr>

[15]Marshall, T. H., *Citizenship and Social Class*, Cambridge 1950, pp. 10–11. For an excellent discussion of Marshall's famous study and Anthony Giddens' critique of Marshall, see Held, D., *Political Theory and the Modern State*, Cambridge 1989, pp. 189–213.

the political element is in itself a civil element. That is, we could argue that the right to vote or hold office is constitutive of the civil element and cannot be separated from it. Second, we would argue that the possession of the political element implies the civil element. Whereas one might be in a minority in a given society, the ability to participate and eventually hold office in that society should be a form of guarantee for the civil element. The political element is the forum within which the civil element is expressed. Thus, whereas one could imagine the civil element without the political element, the political element seems inextricably tied to the civil.

Instead of separating the first two elements, as I have done briefly, I think it more fruitful for our purposes to join them together in terms of the larger theme of our concerns. Both the political and civil elements are part of what could be called the 'objective' element in citizenship.[16] In terms of political theory, we would argue that the objective political and civil elements are part of the vertical contract between citizens and a government. Together, these elements form the basis of the legal structure of any state and constitute the structural basis within the state. (The question of human rights and its universality is an exception to the state-centric model we are focussing on when considering citizenship.) The civil and political elements are part of a common practice based on common rules: what Terry Nardin calls 'practical association'[17] and Michael Oakeshott a 'civil' association.[18] The objective element forms the structural basis of political practice. In discussing a universalist ethic in terms of rationality, David Miller says '[w]e can interpret the significance of social boundaries in contractual or quasi-contractual terms . . . we are to think of nations as "mutual benefit societies" in which our special obligations to fellow countrymen are derived from our common participation in a *practice* from which all may expect to benefit . . .'.[19] The objective,

[16]See Introduction to Hobsbawm, E. J., *Nations and Nationalism since 1780: Programme, Myth, Reality*, Cambridge 1991.

[17]Nardin, T., *Law, Morality and the Relations of States*, Princeton 1983; 'International Ethics and International Law', 18 *Review of International Studies* (1992), pp. 19–30.

[18]Oakeshott, M., *On Human Conduct*, Oxford 1975.

[19]Miller, D., 'The Ethical Significance of Nationality', 98 *Ethics* (1988), p. 651. (italics added)

contractual practice of the civil and political elements allows the society to function in so far as the practice is actualized.

It is important to note that for Nardin and Oakeshott this structural basis is neutral. That is, the practical association allows the society to function as it wishes to function, but the rules allowing it to function have no inherent bias or purpose; they are the basis of a *modus vivendi* and nothing more. Thus, for Nardin and Oakeshott, the civil and political elements can remain independent from the third element of political identity and citizenship, the social element.

This assumption is not evident. If the objective element *allows the society to function in so far as the practice is actualized and followed*, one of the major concerns of any discussion on citizenship is the degree to which the objective element is sufficient in and of itself, and the degree to which the objective element and practice can be and have been separated from the social element. One of our purposes is to see to what extent the objective element is necessary *and* sufficient, and to what extent and how it must be related to the subjective element. To return to the language of Oakeshott and Nardin, we want to see to what extent citizenship is merely a practical or civil association and to what extent it is an enterprise or purposeful association. Or, perhaps, we wish to see to what extent those distinctions can be made.

The social element of citizenship is the horizontal contract in society: the subjective element in citizenship, or the 'purposeful' association, in Nardin's term, or 'enterprise' association, in Oakeshott's terminology. In other terms, we could say that the civil and political elements constitute the state, and that the social element constitutes the nation. Whereas the civil and political elements can be studied in legal documents, the social element is much more difficult to discern.

> [N]ationality is essentially a subjective phenomenon, con-
> stituted by the shared beliefs of a set of people; a belief that
> each belongs together with the rest; that this association is
> neither transitory nor merely instrumental but stems from
> a long history of living together which (it is hoped and
> expected) will continue into the future; that the community
> is marked off from other communities by its members'
> distinctive characteristics; and that each member recog-

nizes a loyalty to the community expressed in a willingness to sacrifice personal gain to advance its personal gain.[20]

When discussing the civil and political elements, I paused for some reflections on the relationship between the two before grouping them together within the objective, vertical contract. Now that I have presented the objective and subjective elements of citizenship – the vertical and horizontal contracts – I will do more than pause to discuss their relationship. For I have come to the nub of the discussion, and the heart of what I believe to be the major issue involving citizenship. For it is in the relationship between the objective and subjective elements of citizenship that one can see most clearly the interdependent relationship between individual identity and state identity.

Citizenship and the Nation-State

What are the possible relationships between the horizontal and vertical contracts, the subjective and objective elements of citizenship? We will examine three. First, we could assert that the vertical and horizontal contracts are symmetrical, that there is, in Michael Walzer's phrase, a 'historic fit' between the legal system of a state and the nation or community of people who reside within that state.[21] This ideal of the nation-state is assumed within the concept of nationalism.

Nationalism is a political programme, and in historic terms a fairly recent one. It holds that groups defined as 'nations' have the right to, and therefore ought to, form territorial states of the kind that have become standard since the French Revolution. Without this programme, realised or not, 'nationalism' is a meaningless term. In practice the programme usually means exercising sovereign control over, so far as possible, a continuous stretch of territory with clearly defined borders, inhabited by a homogeneous

[20]Miller, D., *Ibidem*, p. 648.

[21]See Walzer, M., *Just and Unjust Wars*, New York 1977. My discussion of Walzer's understanding of the nation-state relationship and a summary of the major criticism of Walzer on this point appear in Warner, D., *An Ethic of Responsibility in International Relations*, Boulder 1991, Chapter 2. For an interesting discussion of the state/society relationship from a neo-Hegelian perspective, see Charvet, J., 'Hegel, Civil Society and the State', in Navari, C. (ed.), *The Condition of States*. Buckingham 1991, pp. 167–82.

population that forms its essential body of citizens. Or rather, according to Mazzini, it includes the totality of such a population: 'Every nation a state and only one state for the entire nation.'[22]

This ideal type of symmetry between the nation and the state has been placed in historical perspective. For example, Marshall maintains that the three elements, our two contracts, were united in earlier times and that each of his three elements belongs, in its formative period, to a different century: '[c]ivil rights to the eighteenth, political to the nineteenth, and social to the twentieth.'[23] Others talk of the 19th century as part of a larger modern philosophical yearning.[24] William Connolly, who has eloquently described many of the complexities of modernity,[25] speaks of the demand for the ideal of the alignment of the horizontal and vertical in terms of nostalgia or homesickness:

And the demand [for the alignment] is monumentalised through memory of previous times when this symmetry is said to have existed, times when a politics of place was intact as in the Greek *polis*, or in a few nineteenth century states or in the local politics of some sections of early nineteenth century America. It is a homesickness that construes correspondence between the scope of common troubles and a territorial place of action to form the essence of democratic politics. It is a nostalgia for a politics of place.[26]

Discussions that call into question the symmetry of the nation-state and those that highlight the importance of the nation-state as an ideal lead us to question the relationship between the state and the nation. In other words, what happens when there is no symmetry? We have referred to the nation-state as an ideal because it is an ideal. Connolly mentions limited examples, and other writers also point to the fact that the ideal has been a

[22]Hobsbawm, E., 'Nationalism', *New Statesman and Society*, 24 April 1992, p. 23.
[23]Marshall, *op. cit.* (note 15), p. 14.
[24]See Hobsbawm, *op. cit.* (note 16), pp. 30–2 and Marshall *op. cit.* (note 15), pp. 10–12.
[5]See Connolly, W., *Political Theory and Modernity*, Oxford 1989, Chapter 5 on homesickness.
[6]Connolly, W., 'Democracy and Territoriality', 20 *Millennium: Journal of International Studies* (1991), p. 464.

very rare exception in history and is not relevant to our modern experience. ('The term "nation-state", based as it is on assumption of ethnic homogeneity and political representativity is, in empirical terms, inappropriate to the modern world'.)[27] Thus, we should recognize that, in reality, the vertical and horizontal contracts are usually separated. Whether or not the elements were united in previous times, it is the separation of the different elements – often their confrontation and/or overlapping – that confronts us today.[28] Realistically, therefore, we must talk of the differentiation between the horizontal and vertical contracts and the subjective and objective elements. Nardin and Oakeshott could not have posited two different types of association if the ideal nation-state fit existed. It is the separation of the two axes, the differentiation between the elements, that renders the problem of the nature of citizenship so complex.

So, moving away from the initial relation of symmetry, we could speculate on the separation, even accepting that at one time there was symmetry. We could say that there was initially separation, followed by a historic fit, and then a subsequent separation. One could say, for example, that an ethnic community formed a nation which became a state. In this sense, there are really two contracts. From the initial state of nature, there was the initial contract to form the community, and then there was the contract by the community to form the state.[29] On the other hand, we could speculate that the state created the community in the sense that the governmental structure imposed a certain order which itself became constitutive of the meaning of society. The state may have been merely laws and

[27]Halliday, F., 'State and Society in International Relations: A Second Agenda', 16 *Millennium: Journal of International Studies* (1987), p. 220. David Campbell discusses this split in these terms: '[A]ll states are marked by an inherent tension between the various domains that need to be aligned for an "imagined political community" to come into being – such as territoriality and the many axes of identity – and the demand that such an alignment is a response to (rather than constitutive of) a prior and stable identity. In other words, states are never finished as entities; the tension between the demands of identity and the practices that constitute it can never be fully resolved, because the performative nature of identity can never be fully revealed'. Campbell, D., *Writing Security: United States Foreign Policy and the Politics of Identity*, Minneapolis 1992, p. 11.
[28]For a brief commentary on Marshall's view of the tension between civil and political rights and social citizenship, see Heater, D., *op. cit.* (note 12), pp. 100–1.
[29]'[T]he theory of a contract of government really postulates, as an a priori condition, the theory of a contract of society'. Barker, E., Introduction in Gierke, O., *Natural Law and the Theory of Society, 1500 to 1800*, London 1934, p. XII.

rules, but the practice of those laws and rules created deeper attachments and involvements.

In either case, it is within the relationship between the two contracts – whether there be a historic fit or not – that I feel that Nardin and Oakeshott have missed an important point. By emphasizing two separate forms of association and ignoring the dynamic between the two, they have rendered inaccessible the fluidity of the relationship. Our brief discussion here is not a chicken and egg discussion (which came first, the horizontal or vertical?) but a more important presentation of the possible relationships between structural practices and the attachments that go into the creation of those rules or allow them to be actualized.

The second and third possibilities of the relationship between the different elements of citizenship assume that there has always been estrangement from the ideal. One can assume that there has always been a separation between the two contracts, and speculate about reasons for the existence of the ideal of symmetry. Whether one argues for the primacy of the horizontal or vertical axis, discussions of their primacy lead to speculation about the reasons for their continued separation, the importance or priority of the contracts, and eventually the reasons for the ideal of symmetry of the axes to form the historic fit. If Connolly's comment about nostalgia for the *polis* or *homesickness* is valid, it is very similar to Steven Lukes' criticism of the communitarians: ' "We" cannot become ... pre-modern'.[30] The communitarians, I would argue, are not nostalgic for a notion of place, they are nostalgic for the notion of place having meaning, for the horizontal and vertical contracts to be symmetrical (again?).

It is left for others to speculate on the implications of demythologizing the ideal within the nation-state. To see one of the elements without necessarily trying to combine the two is to deny all of the emotions of patriotism. It is to view citizenship as a commodity like any other practical association. While we will not develop this in our present discussion, we note how

[30]Lukes, S., 'Return to a World We Have Lost', *New Statesman and Society*, 19 August 1988, p. 35. For a general introduction to the recent writings on communitarianism, see Mouffe, C., 'The Civics Lesson', *New Statesman and Society*, 7 October 1988, pp. 28–31. For a more complex and detailed analysis, see Gardbaum, S., 'Law, Politics, and the Claims of Community', 90 *Michigan Law Review* (1992), pp. 685–760.

powerful the forces are which reject this possibility. Nardin's separation functions on the level of the relations between states. We have difficulty imagining the separation of practical and purposeful association in terms of citizenship functioning within a state. To demythologize the ideal of symmetry and to posit estrangement as the norm is not to deny that the ideal of symmetry and the historic fit is still a powerful force.

The significance of citizenship, therefore, depends on a reading of the relationship between the subjective and objective elements, whether one assumes symmetry or estrangement. Whereas it is relatively simple to write laws about what is required to be a citizen, it is much more difficult to anticipate the consequences of those laws for the society at large in terms of the social element. Conversely, while it is understandable for an ethnic group to want to expand its territorial domain, the movement from ethnic group to nation to nation-state is a much larger project. Any discussion of citizenship, therefore, tells us how one conceives of the very fundamental relationship between those living within a given society and the limits of that society in terms of attachments.

Citizenship as Exclusion

The relationship between the elements also tells us something about the limits of that society in a deeper sense, however. Even if we reject the social element in citizenship and only focus on the practical association, citizenship still has its limits. It is in this sense that the previous discussion has been positive. We have tried to elaborate on various implications of what it means to be a citizen; we have not looked at what it means not to be a citizen. For, whatever we say it means to be a citizen, we cannot forget that citizenship is a statement of belonging that is naturally exclusive. To say that I am a citizen of a country is to both include myself within the framework of other citizens, whether objectively or subjectively attached, or both, *and* to say that this group that I am a part of excludes others. '[E]thnic strife is too often superficially discerned as principally predicated upon language, religion, customs, economic integrity, or some other tangible element. But what is fundamentally involved in such a conflict is that divergence of basic identity which manifests itself in the "us-them" syndrome'.[31] Membership in any group is a form of division between insiders and outsiders,[32] and one cannot ignore this negative, exclusive element in a full discussion of citizenship. As van Gunsteren notes: '(Citizenship) is a scarce resource that can remain a resource only as long as certain boundaries are maintained. The price for effective standing and equality among citizens apparently is inequality between citizens and non-citizens, between insiders and outsiders.'[33]

Membership as a general principle includes a decision-making process. That is, there are certain members, or the entire membership, if possible, who decide who will be new members and who will be excluded. What is important about this process is not the form of the process itself, but the criteria on which the decision is made. The criteria are, as as we have noted, of positive and negative sorts. The positive says that we want this person to be a member with us, either because the person is like us or because the person is like what we want a member to be. Walzer says that 'admissions policies are shaped partly by arguments about economic and political conditions in the host country, partly by arguments about the character and "destiny" of the host country, and partly by arguments about the character of countries (political communities) in general',[34] before going on to discuss admissions policies with analogies to neighborhoods, clubs and families.

Van Gunsteren distinguishes three positive requirements for citizenship:

1) The prospective citizen must be capable of dialogic performance. He must, within limits, be ready to argue with

---

[31]Connor, W., *loc. cit.* (note 3), p. 341.

[32]This phrase has come to be associated with R. B. J. Walker's work. His latest book is entitled *Inside/Outside: International Relations as Political Theory,* Cambridge 1993.

[33]van Gunsteren, *loc. cit.* (note 13), p. 731. Antony Black makes a similar point: 'Certainly there exists amongst us humans a very ancient sense of community, based upon the corporate interests of one linguistic or territorial group against another, the ultimate rationale for which has always been the entirely 'rational' one that in a world of limited resources and competitive populations, whether animal or human, it makes eminent sense to exclude outsiders'. Black, A., 'Nation and community in the international order', 19 *Review of International Studies* (1993), p. 86.

[34]Walzer, M., *Spheres of Justice: A Defence of Pluralism and Equality,* New York 1983, p. 35.

other citizens, to talk and listen to them, and to form his judgment on the basis of such dialogue . . . 2) The prospective citizen must be capable and willing to be a member of this particular historical community, its past and future, its forms of life and institutions within which its members think and act . . . What this comes down to in the Dutch admission practice is that prospective citizens are required to know the Dutch language and to respect the law of the land . . . 3) In order not to be forced to sell themselves or their autonomous judgment into dependence, the prospective citizens should have a reasonably secure access to the means of their continued existence. They must own property or have access to another source of income, for example, from a job, social security, or the welfare state.[35]

But what should be stressed is the negative factor. Having decided that we want some people to be members, we are also saying that there are others whom we do not want to be members with us. The criteria that we establish for membership also imply what we do not want; membership and non-membership cannot be separated, just as citizens and non-citizens cannot be separated. Thus, in terms of Van Gunsteren's criteria, we would assume that those incapable of 'dialogic performance', those incapable of being or unwilling to be a member of a particular historical community, and those not having a means of existence and autonomy would not be welcome.

While the first part of my argument stressed the positive elements of citizenship, I must conclude on a rather pessimistic, negative note. For the crisis of identity that we have emphasized for both the individual and the state has greatly exacerbated the importance of the negative element. Instead of talking about the constructive elements of citizenship, in terms of equality and community, we, in modern times, use the notion of citizenship as a means of negative affirmation. In speaking of the importance of myths for nations and exclusion, David Miller says that 'nations need a common view about what they are now; a view about what distinguishes membership in this nation from membership in others'.[36] But, more specifically, Hobsbawm says: 'And because we live in an era when all other human

<hr>

[35]van Gunsteren, *loc. cit.* (note 13), p. 736.
[36]Miller, *loc. cit.* (note 19), p. 656.

relations and values are in crisis, or at least somewhere on a journey towards unknown and uncertain destinations, xenophobia looks like becoming the mass ideology of the 20th-century *fin de siecle*. What holds humanity together today is the denial of what the human race has in common'.[37]

Citizenship has always had an exclusive element. In the ancient Greek city-states, supposedly the cradle of democracy, women and slaves were not citizens, only 'resident foreigners'.[38] In Rome, the status of citizenship was given only to the residents of Rome and served to distinguish them from the people living in the conquered territories.[39] In describing nation-building in England and France, William Bloom states that 'The important point . . . is that regardless of conscription methods, all across a specific territory – in this case England and France – men were engaged in a similar endeavour, an endeavour which was defined by opposition to an outside culture'.[40] Many of the general strikes at the turn of the 20th century were attempts to change electoral laws to make them more inclusive.[41] The exclusive element, we argue, has been worsened by the current individual/state identity crisis. It is as if the pressures and uncertainties of technology and integration have caused nationalist and patriotic feelings to be based solely on the nega-

[37]Hobsbawm, *op. cit.* (note 16), p. 26.

[38]Aristotle, *The Politics*, cited in Salam, N. 'The Emergence of Citizenship in Islamdom', M.LL. Thesis, Harvard Law School 1991, unpublished, p. 2. Rob Walker makes this point concerning the construction of the outsider in classical Greece: 'As Francois Hartog has argued, Herodotus works with a complex rhetoric of representation in which Greek self-identity is defined in relation to non-Greek'. Walker, R. B. J. *op. cit.* (note 32), p. 66. Indeed, as Heater notes, 'Citizenship in the Greek city-state was parochially practical but exclusive'. Heater, D., *op.cit.* (note 12), p. 16.

[39]See Salam *loc. cit.* (note 38), p. 3.

[40]Bloom, W., *op. cit.* (note 9), p. 66.

[41]Seligman, A., *The Idea of Civil Society,* New York 1992, p. 104. Indeed, Seligman goes on to make the following point: 'Bearing in mind the generally ecstatic response to the first free elections in East-Central Europe in 1989, we should recall that the principles of universal citizenship that we in the West take for granted are not of all that long standing and were not won without a struggle. To take the case of England as an example, suffrage was extremely limited and was broadened only gradually throughout the nineteenth century. The first Reform Bill of 1832 left five out of six adult males disfranchised, and the Reforms of 1867–68 increased male suffrage only to about 30 percent of the population. The further reforms of 1884–85 left a population of 31.5 million with an electorate of still only 5 million males, that is to say, it left about one-half of the male urban working class beyond the pale of citizenship. The principle of universal political citizenship was not recognized even in England until 1918'.

tive element. As Hobsbawm states: 'The characteristic nationalist movements of the late twentieth century are essentially negative, or rather divisive . . . Time and again they seem to be reactions of weakness and fear, attempts to erect barricades to keep at bay the forces of the modern world . . .'.[42]

In reaction to this negative element, one could say that all particular memberships should be abolished in order to arrive at the largest possible universal community: Linklater's idea that I mentioned earlier. For certain cosmopolitans, any form of citizenship is wrong since it inherently separates 'them' from 'us'. ('Citizens of the World' would be an obvious exception.) What I have tried to highlight are several of the problems on both the positive and negative sides of that separation in terms of the complexity of what it means to be a citizen. In other words, I have tried to show that separation between citizens and non-citizens in and of itself is not a problem, but rather that the difficulty lies in the understanding of what the separation means.[43] One cannot argue about insiders and outsiders until one can clearly define what it means to be an insider and to be an outsider.[44] If one is born in the United States, one is automatically a citizen of that country, no matter what one's parental status may be. This accident-by-birth citizenship begs the enormous complexity of establishing criteria for choosing new citizens, just as do lotteries.

This element of exclusion can be seen in both the objective and subjective elements of citizenship. Legally, one can be excluded from citizenship in a country but can develop profound social attachments through permanent residence. On the other hand, one can legally be a citizen of a state while remaining excluded from the nation or society of that country.

In general, however, we focus on exclusion from citizenship in the legal sense. Each state has the right to decide on what

[42]Hobsbawm, *op. cit.* (note 16), p. 164.

[43]See Connolly, W. E., *Identity/Difference: Democratic Negotiations of Political Paradox*, Ithaca 1991.

[44]For some of my own comments on the difficulty of selecting members, see Warner, D., Review of *Democracy and the Nation-State: Aliens, Denizens and Citizens in a World of International Migration*, 9 *Refugee Abstracts* (1990), pp. 63–65; Warner, D., Review of 'The Ethics of Refugee Policy', 2 *International Journal of Refugee Law*, (1990), pp. 521–3.

basis citizenship in that state can be acquired.[45] '[N]either the European Convention on Human Rights nor any other international human rights convention recognizes the right to a certain citizenship as a human right. Consequently, it must in principle be left to each State to determine the conditions for acquiring its citizenship'.[46] That right is an integral part of a state's self-definition. Nonetheless, whether it be the state's right to determine its citizenship criteria or some international authority's function to determine citizenship legally, the relationship between the subjective and objective elements cannot be decided by legislation. The relationship between the objective and subjective elements are worked out within the society and in forms of dialogue with those outside the borders. The relationship is an ongoing process that is expressed through various fora. Debates about citizenship put into focus the political identity of citizens and non-citizens in terms of the state's identity. It is in this sense that debates about citizenship are the prism through which the double identity crisis can be observed.

[45]Although James Hathaway has proposed an international authority to determine forms of refugee admissions. Hathaway, J., 'Reconceiving Refugee Law as Human Rights Protection', 4 *Journal of Refugee Studies* (1991), pp. 113–31. Hathaway, however, does not clarify whether the refugee admissions is merely a juridical status or whether it has deeper meaning. For my criticism of Hathaway's proposal, see Warner, D., 'Refugee Law and Human Rights: Warner and Hathaway in Debate', 5 *Journal of Refugee Studies* (1992), pp. 162–9.
[46]Report on Human Rights in the Republic of Estonia, Ad Hoc Committee on Relations with Eastern Europe, Parliamentary Assembly, Council of Europe, Strasbourg 1991, p. 14.

COMMENT ON PAPERS BY DANIEL WARNER AND ANDRÉ LIEBICH

David Campbell

World politics is increasingly marked by the irruptions of accelerated and nonterritorial contingencies upon our political horizons, irruptions in which a disparate but powerful assemblage of flows contest borders, put states into question (without rendering them irrelevant), rearticulate spaces and re-form identities.[1]

Of foremost importance amongst these flows is the mobility and internationalization of capital. Through technological changes that enabled the disaggregation and globalization of production, as well as the instantaneous transfer of money world-wide (a development most often signified by reference to the switch from Fordist to flexible accumulation strategies); through development strategies which encouraged export processing zones in the 'Third World' and investment zones in the 'First World'; and through political changes which deregulated international financial practices, established the conditions for the various Euromarkets, and made transnational ownership possible such that capital could maximize and/or exploit those opportunities, 'the geography and composition of the global economy changed so as to produce a complex duality: a spatially dispersed, yet globally integrated organization of economic activity'.[2]

---

[1]This commentary draws these points from my 'Thinking Beyond Sovereignty: Towards a Political Prosaics of World Politics', in Fawn, F./Larkins, J./Newman, R. (eds.), *Beyond International Society*, Milton Keynes, forthcoming 1994.

[2]Sassen, S., *Global City: New York, London, Tokyo*, Princeton 1991, p. 3. The amount of literature on these developments is obviously large, but an informative starting point can be found in Hirst, P./Thompson, G., 'The Problem of "Globalization": International Economic Relations, National Economic Management and the Formation of Trading Blocs', 21 *Economy and Society* (1992), pp. 357–96.

Although recent transformations have had a wide-ranging impact on economic spatializations, the flow of capital is not alone in the challenge it poses for the state. Just as capital, goods, services and information circulate in a transnational space, so too does labor in the form of migratory workers. Indeed, the two developments are linked because labour migrations tend to retrace (albeit in reverse) the circulation of capital between the developed core and the less developed periphery, thus explaining why there have been sizeable labour movements from high-growth areas (such as South East Asia) to industrialized economies (such as the United States), even when those economies are subject to poor growth and substantial unemployment.[3]

Of course, commodity flows (even if one of those 'commodities' is people) do not exhaust the factors which are contesting a geopolitical interpretation of world politics. The challenges of ecological destruction, population movements, border cultures, political dispossession, nationalist conflicts, postcolonial identities, new military orders, media and information technologies, and transgressive social practices organized around the signs of gender, class, ethnicity, religion, and race (to provide an incomplete account), all serve to destabilize modes of political organization and intellectual understanding dependent upon secure grounds, hermetic spaces, or rigid segments.

Marked by this 'centrifugation of power', a sense of dislocation and homelessness can prevail: indeed, as Wendy Brown notes, 'we are today very susceptible to getting lost'.[4] Or, as Daniel Warner has poignantly suggested in another piece, 'we are all refugees'.[5] In response to this sense of dislocation and homelessness, identity politics (i.e. understanding and practicing politics in terms of ethnicity, race, gender, sexuality, region, continent, nation, state) emerges to provide a sense of situation, a feeling of location and an air of certainty about our place in the world. In Brown's formulation, 'Identity politics emerges as a reaction, in other words, to an ensemble of distinctly postmod-

---

[3]Sassen, S. *The Mobility of Labour and Capital: A Study in International Investment and Labour Flow*, Cambridge 1988. See also Dixon, M./Jonas, S. (eds.), *The New Nomads: From Immigrant Labor to Transnational Working Class*, San Francisco 1992.

[4]Brown, W. 'Feminist Hesitations, Postmodern Exposures', 3 *differences: A Journal of Feminist Cultural Studies* (1991), p. 66.

[5]Warner, D., 'We Are All Refugees', 4 *International Journal of Refugee Law* (1992), pp. 365–72.

ern assaults upon the integrity of communities producing identity'.[6]

It is in this maelstrom that the meaning of citizenship has been put into question, and it is in response to that question that the papers of André Liebich and Daniel Warner are directed. Citizenship, and the community to which it refers (the state), have been, as both Liebich and Warner recognize, the basis for identity politics in the modern period. In consequence, the assaults on identity and the means of its production can be most readily located at the political intersection of the state and citizenship. To do so, however, requires a thoroughgoing problematization of the state as the community in which identity is produced and located. That identity has been and is constantly materially problematized by the flows and forces of globaliz- ation mentioned above. Without drawing a sharp distinction between 'the material' and 'the "ideational"', it is nonetheless fair to say that this material problematization has yet to be matched by an equivalent intellectual articulation.[7] It is equally fair to say that while each of these papers recognizes the par- ameters of this issue, and while each proceeds somewhat differ- ently from that recognition, neither goes as far in pursuing the logic of these challenges as I would argue is necessary.

André Liebich begins his argument by noting that 'the nexus between the state and citizen represents the lowest common denominator of any reflection upon citizenship', a statement which makes reasonably clear his intent not to question the meaning of 'the state' in this formulation. This is reinforced when he argues that while citizenship is concerned with life *inside* the state, his interest is in what citizenship *outside* (or perhaps in-between) states would look like, particularly given that he maintains 'the significance of citizenship only comes to the fore when one steps outside the borders of the state to which one belongs or in which one happens to live'. The concern of the argument is thus with potential new domains of citizenship, rather than whether the old domains still hold. For Liebich, this focus is essential, for otherwise the broadening of the category of citizenship (or perhaps the questioning of its lowest common denominator) means the concept loses its distinctiveness.

[6]*Ibidem*, 1991, pp. 66–7.
[7]This point is the primary concern of my 'Thinking Beyond Sovereignty', *op. cit.* (note 1).

Liebich's argument operates in terms of a contrast between the 'fact of citizenship' and 'the symbol of citizenship', where the former refers to the instrumental rights and responsibilities entailed by the legal category (i.e., formal political participation, military service, government employment, and social services), while the latter indicates the political importance granted to the sign of one's home, especially in the form of a passport. Liebich 'laments' some of the implications of citizenship's political functions, particularly as he argues that the material differences between citizens and non-citizens embodied in the 'facts of citizenship' – all the more so in our era of mobility – are daily diminishing and 'increasingly irrelevant to the life of most individuals'. As a consequence, Liebich hails the possibilities of multiple citizenship, arguing that states should be satisfied by their dominion over territory rather than control over people.

Liebich's proclivity for pluralism is to be praised as both ethical and realistic. However, his desire to loosen the exclusive relationship between the state and its people seems to me to miss the central importance (an importance that I, like Liebich, wish were not the case) of disciplinary strategies concerning the population for the existence and meaning of the state.[8] Simply put, a state cannot be a state by territory alone. To be sure, for a theorist such as Rousseau, for a people to be free they had to inhabit a contiguous territory. But the notion of a territory in which all could wander as the basis for community (a 'civi-territorial complex,' in Connolly's reading of Rousseau and Tocqueville) was unthinkable.[9] Which is not to say it should remain unthought, just that in imaging such a possibility one should not be blind to the obdurate investments that lie in its way. This is most obviously the case with respect to the fact that states and their population controls are part of the mechan-

[8]Indeed, state authorities seek to regulate the movement of some flows (such as labor) to a greater extent than they do others (such as capital). See Goodin, R. E., 'If People Were Money . . .', in Barry, B./Goodin, R. E. (eds.), *Free Movement: Ethical Issues in the Transnational Migration of People and Money*, University Park, PA 1992.

[9]"The line of correspondence [in Rousseau] is clear: to be free you must belong to a people; to be a people you must have a common identity burned into you; to be a flourishing people you must exclusively inhabit a contiguous territory; to flourish freely as a territorialized people you must stringently limit contact with the foreign. Wandering must be curtailed along a variety of dimensions'. Connolly, W. E., 'Tocqueville, Territory and Violence', unpublished manuscript, Johns Hopkins University, Winter 1993, p. 8.

ism by which the international division of labor (with its categories of legal and illegal immigrants, guestworkers and resident aliens) is produced.[10]

Daniel Warner's paper is sensitive to the challenges and implications for social attachments and spatial delineations – and the relationship between the two – posed by the dynamics of globalization, integration and fragmentation afoot in the world (though I would argue, contrary to him, that 'the modern crisis of identity' was a response to, rather than cause of, those processes). Nonetheless, somewhat like Liebich's lowest common denominator proposition, Warner is of the view that, even though 'we are not sure what the state is', we should accept that in a discussion of citizenship the state is 'the major actor'. And echoing Liebich's distinction between the facts and symbols of citizenship, Warner's argument operates in terms of the 'objective' (meaning political and civil) aspects of citizenship, and the 'subjective' (or social) aspects of citizenship.

Such distinctions seem to me to downplay – although this is perhaps more obvious in Liebich than in Warner – the centrality of citizenship's political functioning as an important regulative ideal in the inherently contested domains of politics. Regardless of whether the material conditions or legal rights of citizens and non-citizens are converging, the production of political distinctions between the two groups, and the construction of new differences from within each group, under the rubric of 'citizenship' is of increasing salience in communities that perceive themselves to be under siege. And in our postmodern world where there is often a hankering for (mythological) premodern times, that category incorporates a large number of communities. Think, for example, of the conflicts (regardless of whether the people involved are actually citizens or not) surrounding the Palestinians in Kuwait after the Gulf War; Arab-Americans in the United States during the same period or, more recently, after the bombing of the World Trade Center in New York; and the Turks in Germany. Likewise, although the political fault lines of debates concerning membership in a community (such as those understood in terms of 'multiculturalism' in countries such as Australia, Britain, and the U.S.) may not fall exactly on

[10]Sassen, S. *op. cit.* (note 3), p. 36.

the contours of citizenship, those notions are implicitly evoked if not explicitly articulated.

Where Liebich's conclusions and/or prescriptions are positive in their hoped-for pluralism, Warner concludes his reflections on citizenship and identity in the changing global order with a cautionary and negative note, highlighting the exclusionary cast which inheres in any notion of citizenship. Warner argues that 'the separation between citizens and non-citizens in and of itself is not a problem, but rather that the difficulty lies in the understanding of what the separation means'. I take this to mean that it is the so-called subjective distinctions rather than objective differences which are of the most importance; that being the case, I certainly concur. However, I would actually go one step further.

Although – as I indicated in my remarks on André Liebich's aspiration for less state control over people – my immediate normative preference would be for at least an amelioration of the meaning attributed to the difference between citizen and non-citizen, I do not think such a prospect likely. Principally, this is because I hold to the view that meaning and identity are constituted in their relationship to difference. As such, the production of difference is an essential corollary to the containment of identity, and given that to be (literally) requires an identity, no subject, individual or collective, is apt to escape that problematic. However, as Daniel Warner recognizes, the nature of the relationship between identity and difference is open to negotiation, for the logic of identity and difference need not give in to the temptation of otherness.

In the ambit of citizenship, however, the problem is that the temptation of otherness is increased by the state's need to secure its identity. In consequence, the gap between the symmetry and estrangement of the subjective and objective elements (Warner's terms) is not only increased, it is *necessary* for the production, maintenance and containment of a state's identity. This is because states are unavoidably paradoxical entities which do not possess prediscursive, stable identities.[11] As a consequence, all states are marked by an inherent tension between the various domains that need to be aligned for an 'imagined political community' to come into being, such as territoriality, and the many

[11]These comments draw upon my *Writing Security: United States Foreign Policy and the Politics of Identity*, Minneapolis 1992, especially the introduction.

axes of identity, such as citizenship, and the demand that such an alignment is a response to, rather than constitutive of, a prior and stable identity (such as 'the nation'). In other words, states are never finished as entities; the tension between the demands of identity and the practices that constitute it can never be fully resolved, because the performative nature of identity can never be fully revealed. This paradox, inherent in their being, renders states in permanent need of reproduction: with no ontological status apart from the many and varied practices that constitute their reality, states are (and have to be) always in a process of becoming. For a state to end its practices of re-presentation (such as labelling some people 'citizens' and others 'aliens') would be to expose its lack of prediscursive foundations; stasis would be death.[12]

Moreover, the drive to fix the state's identity and contain challenges to the state's representation cannot finally or absolutely succeed. Leaving aside the recognition that there is always an excess of being over appearance that cannot be contained by disciplinary practices implicated in state formation, were it possible to reduce all being to appearance, and were it possible to bring about the absence of movement which in that reduction of being to appearance would characterize pure security, it would be at that moment that the state would wither away. At that point all identities would have congealed, all challenges would have evaporated, and all need for disciplinary authorities and their fields of force would have vanished. Should the state project of security be successful in the terms in which it is articulated, the state would cease to exist.

Such reflections are not an excuse for political fatalism in the face of the disciplinary strategies of the state with respect to its population. We need not accept without question the citizen/non-citizen distinction. Instead, they are a call for the recognition that proposals which advocate quick and easy escapes from the worst of these disciplinary strategies – or the transcendence of them altogether – are bound to be frustrated. Moreover, they are a call for a radically democratic politics which has as its *raison d'etre* the struggle *for* – or *on behalf of* – alterity, rather

[12]In his account of the importance of speed and temporality to politics, Paul Virilio observed, somewhat grandiosely, that '*Stasis is death* really seems to be *the general law of the World*'. Virilio, P., *Speed and Politics*, translated by Mark Polizzotti, New York 1986, p. 67.

than a struggle to efface, erase, or eradicate alterity.[13] One might never escape the aporias of identity and the temptations of otherness to which they give rise, but one can certainly engage in political contestations and negotiations as a response to them.[14]

[13]See Campbell, D./Dillon, M., 'The Political and the Ethical', in Campbell, D./Dillon, M. (eds.) *The Political Subject of Violence*, Manchester 1993.

[14]A recent remark by Derrida is pertinent in this context. Writing of the concern over European cultural identity, he noted that 'if it is necessary to make sure that a centralizing hegemony (the capital) not be reconstituted, it is also necessary, for all that, not to multiply the borders, i.e., the movements [*marches*] and margins [*marges*]. It is necessary not to cultivate for their own sake minority differences, untranslatable idiolects, national antagonisms, or the chauvinisms of idiom. Responsibility seems to consist today in renouncing neither of these two contradictory imperatives. One must therefore try to *invent* new gestures, discourses, politico-institutional practices that inscribe the alliance of these two imperatives, of these two promises or contracts: the capital and the a-capital, the other of the capital'. Derrida, J., *The Other Heading: Reflections on Today's Europe*, translated by Pascale-Anne Brault and Michael B. Naas, Bloomington, IN 1992, p. 44.

COMMENT ON PAPERS BY DANIEL WARNER AND ANDRÉ LIEBICH

Tamas Földesi

Daniel Warner gives a thorough analysis of the national and individual identity crises surrounding the problem of citizenship. In general, I agree with his main statements about the differences between Western and Eastern Europe. One of his main theses is that state identity and national identity coincide in the so-called nation-state. This nation-state is an ideal because in reality, as the consequence of historical development, there are no clear nation-states. I would like to emphasize that if, in reality, there are no nation-states, then the idea is very dangerous, for one of the crucial problems for the Eastern European area is closely connected with the nation-state concept: what should be the main goal of a state and of the ruling political parties in a mixed country where there is a leading nation but, unfortunately, there is at least one minority?

The idea of the nation-state could be fulfilled only if these minorities disappeared. There are many unacceptable methods of realizing such a programme; these were used especially in the former totalitarian states. In Bulgaria in the 1980s, it was denied that there were Bulgarian citizens who were Turkish; it was said that there were only Bulgarians of the Islamic faith. In Romania, many Hungarians and Germans were expelled from their homes, and Romania, in effect, sold its German population. I would like to emphasize that the Turks in Bulgaria, and the Hungarians and Germans and others in Romania, were formally citizens, but in reality they were second- or third-class citizens who did not have the same rights as the citizens of the majority.

We can observe the most dangerous consequences of the nation-state idea in the contemporary Yugoslavian war. The main idea of the attacking Serbs, and of Croatians and Muslims as well, is to construct a nation-state, and everything, including human life and human values, is absolutely subordinated to this goal. '*Fiat justitia at pereas mundus*' is replaced by '*Fiat* nation-state *at pereas mundus*'. But if you ask the reason for these absolutely inhuman attitudes, you will find a very special motivation: one cause of this nation-state-dominated attitude was the very serious neglect of the minority problem in Eastern Europe. The Serbs are not confident that if, in the future, they are a minority in a Croatian or Muslim state, they will enjoy the same rights as the leading nation.

The lesson of the history of the totalitarian state in Eastern Europe is very clear. If there are basic problems of legitimacy concerning unsolved economic, political, moral and other problems, then one of the best solutions is to generate nationalistic feelings, to try to show that at least the members of the leading nation have more rights than the second-class citizens and that they can hope in the near future for the construction of a pure nation-state.

Therefore, I find that one of the main problems, at least in Eastern Europe, is how to diminish or end the possibility of creating first-, second- and third-class citizens and how to counterbalance nationalism and growing xenophobia. To fulfill the desire of most Eastern European states to join the European Community, there needs to be a precondition: the acceptance of the European Convention on Human Rights, which includes the same rights for all citizens of a nation. But the problem is very difficult because nationalism is based on deep and irrational feelings.

The second unsolved problem mentioned in Daniel Warner's paper is the contradiction inherent in obtaining a new citizenship. The relevant regulation of the Human Rights Convention says very clearly that everybody has the right to be a national and to obtain citizenship. But, at the same time, in the Human Rights Convention we cannot find any obligation on a certain state to bestow citizenship on those needing it. Granting citizenship is part of the sovereignty of a state. Sovereignty was strongly limited by the internationalization of human rights. There are certain obligations for a state which is a member of the UN or of the European Community. But there is no obligation to give citizenship to everybody. Analogically, we can observe something similar in the regulations of refugee law, because, according to the International Refugee Convention, everyone is entitled to request asylum if persecuted for certain reasons by one's state, but no state is obliged to grant asylum to all those requesting it.

I agree with André Liebich's main idea that it would be desirable if, in the future, the difference between citizens' rights and human rights diminished and perhaps eventually disappeared. But I am not so sure about the validity of his second thesis, that the importance of citizenship is diminishing inside one's own country and that it remains a great problem only when the citizen leaves his country. It seems to me that the author took into consideration only the experiences of the Western countries. As he mentioned, it is natural for the state to defend and protect a Western citizen, and it is natural that he have the right not to be expelled, to reenter his country and not to be extradited. But the same rights were not so natural for the citizens of the so-called 'socialist' countries. The expulsion of some members of the opposition was practised; leaving the country and not coming back was a serious crime, and, those who committed it were deprived of their right to reenter the country. Also, the socialist governments extradited refugees coming from each other's countries. The most serious case was when Imre Nagy was extradited to Hungary and later executed.

Similarly, the author is right in supposing that voting in Western countries is sometimes not of primary importance because there is a well-functioning democracy. But this is quite different in the new Eastern European countries where voter participation was very high in the first free elections in 1990 and 1991. Voting is now substantial in Hungary; the ruling coalition endeavours to secure for all Hungarian citizens the right to vote, regardless of whether they are at home or abroad. And the real aim could be for every Hungarian, including those who are not citizens, to also have the right to vote.

André Liebich's idea about the average emigrant – if we can speak about an average emigrant at all – is also based on Western experience. Considering the new possibilities presented by the development of EU regulations, he emphasizes that it is perhaps now more important for an emigrant to have the possibility of moving from one country to another, enjoying the possibilities of a free market, than to acquire the citizenship of a particular country.

The way of thinking of the Eastern European emigrants is quite different. First of all, they are dissatisfied with the economic and, sometimes, political situations of their countries. Their real desire is to find a Western European or perhaps an American country where they can reside and be granted citizenship. Therefore, the idea of the author that it would be desirable to render the obtaining of citizenship easier is very sympathetic, but given the current situation in which the Western European countries are flooded by Eastern European emigrants, and the Western European states are trying to stop them at their borders, it seems unrealistic to require such openness from the state. The Hungarian citizenship law requires the fulfillment of stringent conditions before citizenship can be granted to an applicant.

Last, but not least, the ideal of *plurality* of citizenships is again very appealing to me, and perhaps it will be the only solution to the problem of citizenship later on. However, the idea of having not only one homeland, but perhaps two or more is now a very difficult problem in Eastern Europe. In Hungary, for example, one of the dividing lines between the ruling coalition and the opposition concerns the importance accorded to one's identification as, primarily, a Hungarian or a human being. The important question is how to unify citizenship, the fact that one belongs to at least one country, with the fact that one is part of mankind. Historically, this has been a very difficult issue.

DISCUSSION 2

In the discussion of the papers by André Liebich and Daniel Warner and of the commentaries by Tamas Földesi and David Campbell, several issues were raised: the nature of the modern state in America and in Western and East-Central Europe, the relationship between identity and difference, the concept of the 'cost' of citizenship, the attractiveness of certain states as destinations for immigrants, and the idea of citizenship implying the acquisition of civil and political rights, with particular reference to voting participation in post-communist East-Central Europe.

Krzysztof Jasiewicz began the discussion by arguing that the notion of the nation-state in the Eastern European context could be problematic, depending on the definition given in this region to the term 'nation': if it is understood as a 'community of citizens' in the Western European liberal sense, the state becomes an inclusive and even desirable framework; if, however, 'nation' is understood in ethnic terms, the concept of the nation-state is, potentially, very dangerous. Kenneth Minogue agreed with this distinction, adding that it is important to recognize that no modern state is actually a nation-state in the literal sense of the term: both Britain and France, in fact, contain several nationalities, although they have traditionally been considered nation-states. For Kenneth Minogue, however, a certain national pride – a sense of 'Britishness' or 'Frenchness' – overrides their internal ethnic identities, while such a sense of solidarity has always been much more difficult to achieve in East-Central Europe. This national pride is, in essence, exclusive and based on differentiation, Minogue claimed, thus labelling André Liebich's notion of citizenship as 'neo-nomadism' for its alleged neglect of the close interrelation between identity and difference. According to Minogue, one must be realistic in determining the function of citizenship: if citizenship allows the inclusion of all of humanity, then it loses its purpose of identifying people. Finally, Minogue raised the notion of the 'cost' of citizenship: the idea that the requirements which need to be fulfilled in order to acquire citizenship are related to the state's ability to provide for the new influx of immigrants. To illustrate this point, he referred to the more stringent requirements demanded for the acquisition of ancient Athenian citizenship while the state was engaged in the Pelopponesian War, and the increasing difficulty of obtaining United States citizenship once the state was faced with the rising cost of new immigration. In this sense, Minogue felt that André Liebich's conception of citizenship was essentially a consumer's conception, and that it did not take into account the notion of cost.

Martin Palous expressed concern over the tendency to dichotomize Eastern and Western Europe in reference to the two notions of 'nation' (the liberal and the ethnic) and questioned David Campbell's claim that states are constantly in the process of 'becoming'. Palous argued that the state is based on a foundation that is not invented or man-made; this foundation consists of an ethnic group which exists prior to the state. For Palous, the problem in both Eastern and Western Europe is how to create a new, different foundation for the state and, thus, also for the concept of citizenship. David Campbell replied that the idea that 'states are in the process of becoming' does not deny that a certain foundation exists at the outset. The point is, however, that states are constantly recreating their own foundations, both in East and West, and that this is an ongoing process which is never really resolved, forgotten and transcended. Peter Paczolay added that citizenship in the old-fashioned sense is bound to survive as the means of defining the relationship between individuals and the government. He expressed scepticism concerning the possibility of creating new forms of citizenship both in Western and Eastern Europe.

Professor David Sylvan of the Graduate Institute of International Studies questioned the appropriateness of using dichotomies in discussing citizenship. He stressed that a number of possible relations exist between citizens and non-citizens, and that the number and complexity of such possibilities cannot be captured by the simple dichotomy of identity/difference. Sylvan illustrated this point with three examples of multiple statuses. First, he cited the change in the citizenship law of ancient Athens which required that both parents of a prospective citizen be Athenians, concluding that logically this implied that women, as well as their female offspring (and a certain number of male children who would remain outside the political life of the state in the future), were, from a certain standpoint, Athenians, although they did not and would never enter into the full rights of participation in the affairs of the *polis*. Sylvan's second example raised the issue of military service, such as that of recent immigrants in the United States during the Civil War, while his third illustration of multiple statuses concerned police harrassment of darker-skinned individuals in most Western countries, regardless of their citizenship. These examples suggest to Sylvan that simple semiotic dichotomies such as identity/difference or even trichotomies of identity/difference, where difference is in turn divided into something relatively benign and something else that is called 'otherness', are inadequate. Sylvan listed a series of possibilities for the relations between citizens and non-citizens: those who are not identical may nonetheless be similar, or complementary, or oppositional, or external to each other. He concluded that in thinking about less violent and exclusive alternatives for the future, this multiplicity of statuses should be taken into account.

Edmund Wnuk-Lipinski brought up the issue of why citizenship of certain states is infinitely more attractive than that of others. By examining the new phenomenon of immigration to Poland, Wnuk-Lipinski concluded that Poland really represents only a temporary stopover for emigrants from Ukraine, Belarus and the Baltic states whose real destination is Germany. According to him, Germany's attractiveness lies in its economic development, which gives its residents greater opportunity for consumption, financial aid and employment. Immigrants, Wnuk-Lipinski stated, are not losing their identity or ethnic roots, especially if their religion is different from that of their host country. Motivation for migration to a particular country thus derives primarily from economic considerations, he concluded. Kenneth Minogue disagreed with the claim that economic betterment was the only factor rendering certain citizenships more attractive. To him the Western countries' attractiveness is due also to a certain 'moral openness of life' unavailable to these immigrants in their own countries.

Pierre Hassner raised the issue of political rights associated with citizenship. He argued that the Turks in Germany are very anxious to get dual citizenship, not only for economic reasons, but, more importantly, because they believe that if they become voters they will be able to influence the German government's effort to protect their rights. A similar type of reasoning is at hand in the French government's recent attempts to change the citizenship law: making access to French citizenship more difficult will make the extradition of foreigners easier, it believes. In both cases, Hassner stated, the issue is that citizenship implies political influence and the protection of human and civil rights. In this context, Hassner raised the question of voting in East Central Europe. This newly acquired political right in the postcommunist states (voting during the communist period was more of a farce than an actual right) would lead one to assume that voter turnouts would be very high, while it can be argued, as André Liebich did in his paper, that voters in Western liberal democracies are prone to apathy and abstention. Hassner pointed out that in some Eastern European countries this has not been the case and that voter turnout has been comparatively low. He asked his Eastern European colleagues to explain this paradox.

Martin Palous and Olga Gyarfasova provided the statistics for Czecho-Slovakia: participation in elections has generally been very high, between 80% and 90%. In Martin Palous' opinion, politicians throughout the region are able to mobilize the public with claims that the revolution is still going on; the 1992 elections in Czecho-Slovakia serve as a case in point. Palous believed that this tendency was unlikely to disappear for some time.

Krzysztof Jasiewicz argued that it is necessary to consider two factors when undertaking a comparative analysis of voting in the region. First, voter turnout differed from country to country: in Czecho-Slovakia, Bulgaria and Romania, for example, it was very high, while in Hungary and Poland it was considerably lower. Even in the first free elections in Poland in 1989 turnout was only between 60–62%, as in the presidential elections of 1990, while the legislative elections of 1991 had an even lower participation of only 42%. Jasiewicz does not believe that future voter turnout will be any higher. Second, he argued, the process of transition in these countries largely accounted for the differences between them. Jasiewicz referred to the study of transitions in Latin America and Southern Europe by Schmitter and O'Donnell,[1] who developed the concept of 'founding elections' characterized by very high participation. So, why was Poland once again an exception to this rule? Jasiewicz argued that the transition process in Poland lasted almost a decade, and that popular mobilization was highest in 1980–81 when elections did not take place. Maintaining such a high level of mobilization over a long period of time is impossible, Jasiewicz explained, so that by 1989 a degree of apathy had set in. Furthermore, the first elections tend to be a plebiscite against the *ancien régime*, but with the evolution of a pluralistic political spectrum and multiplicity of choice, abstention becomes an easier option. Unlike Martin Palous, he foresaw a decline in turnout for the Czech Republic and Slovakia in the future. Piotr Ogrodzinski also attempted to account for the over 30% abstention rate in the first Polish elections. He argued that it was evidenced primarily in the second round of the elections, which concerned candidates who were mainly non-members of Solidarity, so that not voting in this case became a manifestation of support for Solidarity. Krzysztof Jasiewicz, however, argued that the abstainers in the 1989 election were an amorphic group and that only a minority acted in the way described by Ogrodzinski. The majority of the abstainers, according to Jasiewicz, were simply apathetic, while the cost of not participating had, of course, declined, since these elections were no longer obligatory as were those in the past.

Some controversy surrounded the discussion of voters' participation in Hungary. Gabor Nagy argued that the 70% turnout in the 1990 elections was not really low. The earlier 98–99% turnouts were due mainly to the fact that elections were not free. Tamas Földesi predicted that there would be at least an 90% participation rate in the upcoming May 1994 elections. Pierre Hassner responded, however, that other Hungarian specialists lamented the terrible state of apathy in their country and the lack of public involvement in politics. Gabor Nagy replied that, although turnout may be lower when the political

[1]O'Donnell G., and P. Schmitter, *Transitions from Authoritarian Rule: Tentative Conclusions about Uncertain Democracies*, Baltimore 1986.

spectrum is widened (rendering choice more difficult), this makes the votes cast much more important.

In their concluding remarks, Daniel Warner and André Liebich addressed some of the issues raised in the discussion. After noting that he was surprised at the apparently general agreement on the importance of exclusion for citizenship, Daniel Warner focussed on the issue of universality in terms of the necessity of articulating identity/difference, and the notion of the 'cost' of citizenship. He returned to David Campbell's point about the necessity for the state to articulate identity/difference, and noted that this seems to be a universal drive behind such articulation in both the East and the West. If one accepts the importance of the articulation of identity/difference in citizenship, the point becomes to look at the nature of superiority and the costs involved for the state to make this articulation. In certain countries, he said, there are enormous tensions over citizenship and non-citizenship, while in other countries the commodity value of citizenship seems much less important. In fact, in many countries the acquisition of citizenship is similar to buying a cheap product. It is within the differences in the 'cost' of citizenship that nuances may arise in terms of universality. If the articulation of identity/difference is universal, the costs of that articulation may be very different.

André Liebich raised three issues in reply to his critics. First, he argued that although solidarity was indeed lacking in his notion of citizenship, he believes that too much solidarity is dangerous. For the post-communist states of East-Central Europe, the 'newfound joy' in citizenship and the rediscovery of solidarity contain the danger of exclusion and may have negative consequences for those outside the 'charmed circle'. Second, while Liebich agreed with the idea that citizenship is a constitutive element of identity, he saw no reason why it should be exclusive. He restated his point that individuals can have several identities, and even several identities related to a state, without having one exclude the other. He rejected the accusation of 'neo-nomadism' and the imputation to him of the idea that all of humanity should be able to accede to a particular citizenship. He still saw no aberration in giving citizenship to all those individuals who have lived in a particular country, paying taxes, learning the language, and contributing to its economic, social or cultural life. Third, he emphasized the problematic fact that while citizens are equal, citizenships are not: some are simply more desirable than others, as Edmund Wnuk-Lipinski and Kenneth Minogue pointed out. This gradation of citizenships thus seems to go against the very concept of equality inherent in the notion of citizenship. Finally, he brought up one argument that had not been made in the course of the discussion, namely that today only citizens have the right to constitute a minority. Liebich gave the example of the Turks in Germany, who do not make up a 'Turkish minority' in that country simply because they are not citizens, which appeared to him to be a real constraint on his own argument concerning the equalization of treatment of citizens and non-citizens in normal democratic states.

Tamas Földesi stressed the importance of the notions of equality and security in relation to citizenship, while David Campbell brought the discussion to its end by emphasizing the multiplicity of relationships and statuses, which had been raised by David Sylvan, and by concluding that there is no universality concerning the modalities of exclusion; that they depend upon context, and political contestations and visions.

J.D.

POLAND

CITIZENSHIP IN POST-COMMUNIST POLAND: CIVIL SOCIETY OR *DAS VOLK*?

Krzysztof Jasiewicz

Introduction: Who is a Pole?

A parliamentary committee working on a draft of Poland's new constitution was faced recently with a troubling question: are the ethnic Poles who have been living in the former Soviet Union Polish citizens or not? Or, rather, should they or should they not be given Polish citizenship on request, without undergoing a lengthy and complicated procedure designed for aliens? The answer to this question is relatively easy – and positive – in the case of those who, usually against their will, remained on Soviet territory after the Polish-Soviet border had been shifted westward at the end of World War II. But what about those Polish inhabitants of Belarus and Ukraine who were living in the areas awarded to the Soviet Union in the Riga treaty of 1921? Most of them were later (in the 1920s and 1930s) deported to Kazakhstan. Their offspring still live there, preserving the Polish language and Polish identity. Are those children and grandchildren of deportees, born in Kazakhstan, still entitled to Polish citizenship? What if they come from mixed marriages? What about those whom Soviet authorities forced to erase the notification of Polish nationality from their passports? And further: what about grandchildren and great-grandchildren of Polish patriots exiled by the tsars to Siberia in the 19th century? Many of them do not speak Polish anymore but still consider themselves Polish.

There is, it seems, a consensus among the Polish population

79

and political elites that yes, these people should be granted Polish citizenship if they choose to ask for it. Their ties to Poland, or the ties of their forefathers, were broken against their will. In the former communist Poland their fate was a taboo. The new, free Poland should therefore redeem past misfortunes and neglects.

Yet a positive answer to the above-listed questions opens new ones. A great many Poles have emigrated over the course of the last two centuries to Western Europe and both Americas. The surviving emigrés legally hold Polish citizenship. But how should their offspring be treated? Is there a need to differentiate between children of political and economic emigrés? If yes, who will decide which decisions to emigrate were based on political, and which on economic considerations? Again, the Polish public seems to express here an inclusive point of view: If people of Polish extraction consider themselves Poles, there should not be any legal obstacles to their being granted (or rather having confirmed) Polish citizenship. This consensus would, perhaps, fade away if the person in question were a descendant of Polish Jews. Similarly, claims to German citizenship by descendants of ethnic Germans living today in Poland might be considered by many Poles as a voluntary exclusion from the community of Polish citizens. Inclusiveness has its limits, but where exactly are they?

Nation, State, Citizen

Ethnicity has not been the only potential basis for exclusiveness here. A notion of citizenship as a quality ascribed or offered to practically all inhabitants of a state, regardless of their class, gender, race, religion or ethnicity, is a relatively young phenomenon. Indeed, most polities of the past would limit citizenship or its political dimension to certain categories of people: males, the well-born (nobles); the educated; the wealthy (taxpayers) and individuals of a certain race (whites), ethnic origin (Germans, Spaniards), or religion (Catholics, Protestants, Muslims). Constitutions of modern states, as a rule, abolish such restrictions. If political rights are not extended to some categories of people, like those of a certain age (too young), or recent immigrants, there is a broad consensus to accept these limitations as justified. But the exclusive notion of citizenship is still expressed in many legal regulations and actions of political actors.

In Central and Eastern Europe, unlike the western part of the continent or North America, the exclusive notion of citizenship has historically prevailed over the inclusive one. In contemporary Germany, even a third-generation offspring of immigrants is not granted German citizenship, while a descendant of ethnic Germans from Russia or Romania is. In post-communist Eastern Europe, exclusion from citizenship on the grounds of ethnicity has been a particularly strong and widely raised claim. The war in Yugoslavia or the split of Czecho-Slovakia are only the two most spectacular cases.

An in-depth analysis of the background of these developments exceeds by far the scope of this article. It should suffice here to observe that the concepts of nation, state and citizen have developed in the West and in the East on the basis of different forms of social, cultural, political and economic integration. In the West – France, England and the United States being the leading cases – a nation-state emerged relatively early as a political community based on a common economy and cultural uniformity, with one ethnic group clearly dominant over weak minorities. These processes were reflected in and inspired by liberal ideologies. Thinkers like Locke and Montesquieu unfolded to the public visions of social order based on free will and contractual obligation. This contract could have and should have been entered into by each and every individual living on a given territory; each and every citizen of a state. The nation has been conceived as equalizing all inhabitants of a state. Because they were entering this contract as individuals, they had to be granted individual protection and individual rights and freedoms. Hence, within this philosophy the primacy of individual rights over collective ones had to be granted.

In the East, forces of integration interacted with those of disintegration. Political integration occurred on the level of multi-ethnic empires: the Ottoman, the Hapsburg, the tsarist, and, toward the end of the 19th century, the German. But here the consolidating forces were much weaker than in the West; the imperial control over provinces was often intensively exploitative, but also superficial; local and provincial economies were not integrated into a statewide system; cultural amalgamation was achieved – if at all – only on the level of a narrow, cosmopolitan elite. Taxes and military service were the only, unwanted tributes paid by peoples to the sovereign. In addition, this weak integration was countered by political fragmentation: Germany divided into a hundred principalities; Poland partitioned among its neighbors; Jewish communities scattered across the region. Loyalty to a nation-state was not a viable option: there was no proper nation-state around. What was left was integration within an ethnic and/or religious community. Yet even this came late. The Herderian vision of a nation as *das Volk*, a moral community based on common language and ancestry, was not realized until the late 19th, or even 20th, century. But when realized, it erupted with a destructive force. E. J. Hobsbawm may be right that '[...] the mystical identification of nationality with a sort of platonic idea of the language [...]'[1] was a mere creation of Herder and his followers, nationalist intellectuals, but this creation has become the major force of history in the region (and not only), from the 19th-century insurgents to the late–20th-century secessionists. Common language, in particular when reinforced by common religion, has been a *conditio sine qua non* of access to mystical common values and to the lore and wisdom of forefathers. Within the framework, there has been no place for Western individualism; collective rights always have had priority over the rights of an individual.

Of course, Western-style individualism and liberalism have penetrated Eastern and, in particular, Central Europe, as the forces of ethnocentric collectivism never really disappeared from the West. As mentioned above, the constitutional provisions, at least since World War II, but also in earlier times, have provided for protection of individual rights and accepted inclusive rather than exclusive concepts of citizenship. But the abuses of human and civil rights under totalitarian regimes have taken their toll. The rights and freedoms written into the constitution are often perceived by the public as window-dressing: something that perhaps ought to be printed, but not necessarily implemented. And even such assumptions are being questioned. After the fall of old regimes the new ones want to rethink and redo their

---

[1] Hobsbawm, E. J., *Nations and Nationalism since 1780. Programme, Myth, Reality,* Cambridge 1990, p. 57.

laws and customs, and in this process nothing should be taken for granted.

Poland Today

Due to the processes generated by World War II, Poland is now an almost homogeneous state, ethnically and religiously. Nonetheless, the issues of inclusive versus exclusive concepts of citizenship underlie many political debates in Poland today. Certainly, nobody (nobody sane, I should perhaps say) wants to use ethnicity or religion as a basis to strip a person legally of currently held Polish citizenship. But the questions concerning the Polish diaspora, discussed above, are real ones, and they remain highly loaded emotionally. Even more emotions are raised by a different set of issues, concerning the formal and substantive equality of citizens. The question is not whether to include or to exclude somebody from the community of citizens, but whether somebody's values and preferences may be given special treatment, or whether somebody's past deeds may justify limitation of his civil rights. Exclusiveness is expressed here in the form of acceptance of various categories of citizens: those whose values are specially protected and promoted, and those whose values are not; those who morally deserve the right to full civil participation, and those who do not; those who are equal, and those who are less equal than others. In political reality these general questions are being translated into very specific ones which appear to be clustered in three major dimensions:

1. Ethnicity: What should be our attitude toward the Polish diaspora, in particular in the neighboring countries? How should the Polish state treat its own ethnic minorities? Also, should the Poles accept Western standards in politics, culture, and economy, or rather cultivate their 'Polishness', whatever that is?

2. Religion: Should Catholicism and the Roman Catholic Church receive special treatment in a country where the overwhelming majority of citizens is Catholic?

3. Decommunization: Should the former members and

functionaries of the Communist party be held morally and/or legally responsible for damages done to Poland's economy and environment, and be punished by, for instance, a formal exclusion from public office for a certain period of time?

The actual answers given to these questions on the level of political elites are many – hardly surprising in a country where more than twenty parties are represented in the parliament. In this paper, however, I would like to focus on public opinion: the beliefs and attitudes of Polish citizens. As among political elites, among the public as well the two concepts of nation and citizenship compete with one another: one of the nation conceived as contractual relationship (civil society), with an inclusive interpretation of citizenship, and the other of the nation visualized as a moral community, with exclusion of those who do not conform to its moral standards.

The empirical basis for this analysis comes from a major study of voting behaviour and political attitudes, conducted by the Division of Electoral Studies of the Polish Academy of Science's Institute of Political Studies.[2] The two parts of the study were carried out in October and November 1991, before and after the parliamentary elections of 27 October 1991. Altogether, 2,078 complete questionnaires were collected, and the sample was representative of the population of eligible voters. For the purposes of this paper sixteen variables indicative of views on citizenship were selected from the pool of almost 500. An additional eleven variables describing the social status of respondents and their voting preferences were used in cross-sectional analysis. The presentation of data begins with a report on the distribution of views on the issues of citizenship, and continues with an analysis of the internal structure of these views, their social, occupational and demographic correlates, and the relationships between the views on citizenship and voting behaviour.

The variables selected for analysis correspond with the three above-mentioned dimensions. They do not always address the issue of citizenship directly, but they are indicative of general-

[2]Banaszkiewicz, J. Dohnalik, S. Gebethner, K. Jasiewicz, R. Markowski, E. Zebrowska, T. Zukowski, authors, with the collaboration of N. Frentzel-Zagorska and K. Zagorski.

ized exclusive-versus-inclusive attitudes. The presentation begins with the questions concerning ethnicity. The first group of three questions measures opinions about the relationship between Poland and the West. The distribution of opinions is presented in tables 1, 2, and 3.

Table 1 Which of the two contradictory views presented below is closer to your personal position (%)?

Poland should become a country just like the countries of Western Europe	26.7
Poland should be above all Polish: neither like the East, nor like the West	73.3

Table 2 Do you agree or disagree that Poland should not imitate patterns from the West, but should rely on her own traditions and experiences (%)?

Strongly agree	31.9
Agree	33.5
Disagree	19.5
Strongly disagree	4.1
Don't know	10.8

Table 3 Do you agree or disagree that our schools should teach primarily the history of Poland, and not focus on the history of the world (%)?

Strongly agree	19.2
Agree	26.4
Disagree	28.9
Strongly disagree	9.8
Don't know	15.6

These opinions may strike one as decisively anti-Western. Will the Poles, after several decades of involuntary isolation from the West, balk at a chance to (re)join Western Europe? Are those opinions indicative of a strong ethnocentrism? Not necessarily. One ought to remember that the national pride of Poles was severely assaulted during a sequence of foreign occupations and pseudo-patriotic totalitarian regimes. Perhaps these opinions reflect such national pride, which does not include ethnocentrism and hostility against aliens. The data presented in tables 4 through 9 may be helpful in addressing this issue.

Table 4 Do you agree that national minorities should be represented in the Sejm and the Senate (%)?

Yes	45.1
No	19.3
Some yes, others no	5.2
Don't know	30.5

There is evidently some confusion; nonetheless, a plurality has no reservations against parliamentary representation of national minorities. Those few who answered 'some yes, others no' were asked to name the minorities that deserve – or not – seats in the parliament. The list did not bring any revelations: all major ethnic minorities in Poland were indicated positively by some and negatively by others: the Germans (21 indications 'yes', 42 'no'), the Byelorussians (17 and 4), the Ukrainians (15 and 19), the Lithuanians (28 and 4), the Jews (5 and 8).

The last group on this list, the Jews, have shared with the Poles a very complex history, and the mutual relationship of these two nationalities even today, when there are almost no Jews remaining in Poland, is highly charged emotionally and often controversial. Table 5 shows the distribution of opinions on one aspect of this relationship.

Table 5 One often hears the opinion that people of Jewish origin play too big a role in our country. Do you agree with this view (%)?

Strongly agree	12.0
Agree	20.0
Disagree	23.4
Strongly disagree	16.5
Don't know	31.6

This question still is apparently very sensitive (a large percentage of respondents avoid a direct answer), but an affirmative opinion on an overly important role and influence of Jews is more often rejected than accepted.

The view of the Jews as an influential and powerful minority has usually been connected to a broader xenophobia and a conspiratorial view of history. The distribution of opinions on this subject is presented below.

Table 6 Do you agree or disagree that those who claim that there are in the world powerful, hidden forces conspiring against Poland are basically right (%)?

Strongly agree	6.0
Agree	17.1
Disagree	28.5
Strongly disagree	14.6
Don't know	33.9

Again many respondents avoided an answer to this question, but one should note that there are twice as many opponents of this conspiratorial view as supporters. Related to this issue is a more general attitude toward aliens and foreigners:

Table 7 Do you agree or disagree that intensifying the flow of aliens to Poland poses a serious threat to our national culture (%)?

Strongly agree	20.0
Agree	19.2
Disagree	28.3
Strongly disagree	13.1
Don't know	19.3

Here public opinion remains divided, and one can wonder who those threatening aliens are: beggars? street vendors? foreign investors?

Table 8 Do you agree or disagree that foreign capitalists should be prevented from buying our Polish property (land, factories, houses) (%)?

Strongly agree	41.7
Agree	27.7
Disagree	15.9
Strongly disagree	7.5
Don't know	7.1

In this case one can see an almost unanimous objection to foreign capital, which could have been caused to a certain extent by the highly emotional wording of this question (intended by the authors), but also, to a certain extent, by a vision of a growing dependence of Poland's crippled economy on powerful and aggressive foreign partners. This issue has been widely debated in the Polish media, as was the one concerning a possible flow of political and economic migrants from the other countries of the region.

Table 9 Do you agree or disagree that people migrating from the countries of the former communist bloc should be prevented from settling in Poland (%)?

Strongly agree	20.3
Agree	27.5
Disagree	25.4
Strongly disagree	7.3
Don't know	19.4

Compared with the question of foreign capital (table 8), there is here a surprisingly large acceptance of immigrants; still, a sizable plurality would refuse them the right to settle in Poland. Inclusiveness has its obvious limits. There are very few (if any) countries in the contemporary world that would allow in an unrestricted flow of immigrants and foreign capital. The European Community is no exception here (freedom of personal movement and capital transfer is limited to the member nations), nor are the other countries of Western Europe and North America. Polish public opinion does not deviate here from American, German or French. The views on exclusiveness and inclusiveness in the ethnic dimension seem balanced and moderate.

Poles and Catholics

Not so moderate are the views on the role of the Church and Catholicism in the Polish state, at least the views expressed publicly. The Polish Parliament and media have been the fora of endless debates on numerous specific topics related to this question, from the right to abortion to the instruction of religion in public schools to the issue of Christian values in radio and television. Of the seven drafts of the new constitution recently submitted to the parliament, five open with an equivalent of the 'We, the People' phrase, while the remaining two open with the phrase 'In the name of God Almighty'. The whole problem comes down to the question of whether Poland should become a secular or a confessional state. In other words, whether the state should remain secular and promote freedom of worship, or whether it should recognize and accept the fact that the overwhelming majority of its citizens are Catholics, and thus reflect Catholic norms and values in its legislation. The answer given to this question will have profound consequences for the actual meaning of citizenship: were the Catholics granted a preferential position within the state, non-Catholics, non-Christians and non-believers, even if formally equal to Catholics, might feel like (and be treated as) second-class citizens. Legally Polish citizens, they would exist apart from the nation: a moral community of Catholic-Poles. The views of the political elites on the issue are highly polarized. What are the views of the public? Tables 10, 11, and 12 present selected views on the role of the Church and religion.

Table 10 Which of the two contradictory views presented below is closer to your personal position (%)?

Laws and regulations in Poland should be in concord with the spirit of the Catholic religion, even if the majority of citizens do not want it.	20.1
Laws and regulations in Poland should be in concord with the will of majority, even if they are not in accord with the teaching of the Catholic Church.	79.9

Table 11 Which of the following statements about the role of the Catholic Church and clergy best reflects your own opinion (%)?

The role of the Church should increase, and the Church and priests should guide our everyday affairs to make us honest and virtuous.	9.7
The role of the Church and priests should remain as it is now: neither increase, nor decrease.	41.8
The role of the Church should be limited, because currently the Church and priests interfere too much in our everyday personal affairs.	53.9
Don't know	4.7

Table 12 Which method of instruction of religion in public schools would you prefer (%)?

Religion in schools as a compulsory subject	15.7
Religion in schools as an optional subject	31.7
Religion taught outside of schools (in churches)	48.9
Don't know	4.7

The pro-Church, confessional point of view dominates among political elites: here one could hardly find better evidence than the recent legislation on abortion (highly restrictive) or on radio and television (promotion of 'Christian values'). But among the public, an overwhelming majority represents the opposite position. It should also be pointed out that people have opinions on this subject and do not avoid expressing their views (there are very few 'don't know' answers, in particular compared with various questions on the subject of ethnicity). Some actions of Polish parliamentarians may create an impression of a triumphant march of Catholic fundamentalism, while in fact Polish society is secularized and very far from accepting the equation between Catholicism and 'Polishness' as a standard of exclusion or inclusion in citizenship. The Poles, by and large, do not accept elevation of Roman Catholics to the status of first-class citizens at the expense of other denominations and non-believers.

Poles and Communists

Would they accept demotion of some individuals to a second-class-citizen status because of their communist past? This has also been a very hot issue, and the politics of decommunization brought down at least one cabinet (Jan Olszewski's cabinet, in June 1992). Among political elites there is a wide spectrum of views on this subject. At one extreme are those who believe that Poland should undergo a process of decommunization similar to the denazification of Germany after World War II: all members of specific organizations (e.g. secret police) and governing bodies in the Communist Party should be barred from public life for a certain time, and communist leaders should be tried for their political and economic decisions. Others believe that an automatic ban on former communists may not be necessary, but that all officials in all three branches of the present government should be subjected to 'lustration': evaluation of their actions under the communist regime, and, in particular, of possible links to the secret police. Another point of view is that the former officials and beneficiaries of the communist regime should be held accountable only for their individual deeds, and only if they had committed crimes punishable under the law in force at that time. Finally, there are also those who say that all affairs of the communist past should be forgotten, preferably under a general amnesty. The views of the public are presented in tables 14 and 15.

Table 13 There has been a debate about the old communist *nomenklatura*, political and economic. How should those who still occupy important positions be treated (%)?

They should be barred from such positions, because they are responsible for the present condition of our country.	33.8
These positions should be open to competition and such people should be allowed to apply under the same conditions as other competitors.	42.1
They should remain in these positions, because most of them are competent.	7.2
Don't know	16.6

Table 14 If in the near future there were a referendum in Poland, would you vote for or against banning the former functionaries of the Polish United Workers' Party (PUWP, the communist party) from positions in public administration, economic administration, foreign service, etcetera (%)?

For	38.3
Against	36.6
Don't know	24.5

The public remains divided on the issue of decommunization.[3] A plurality seems to represent a liberal point of view: there should not be any collective responsibility; anyone should be accountable only for his personal deeds. Nonetheless, some temporary limitations of civil rights for the former communist *apparatchiks* are acceptable to many Polish citizens.

[3]This observation has been confirmed by more recent public opinion polls, see, for instance, those of Warsaw's Public Opinion Research Center CBOS, published in 4 *Opinia Publiczna* (1993).

Citizenship: Inclusive or Exclusive?

Finally, I would like to discuss opinions about two other issues: one specifically addressing views on citizenship, the other a general question of the relationship between the individual and collective rights.

Table 15 Would you be pleased if your children, living abroad, changed their citizenship (%)?

Strongly yes	2.0
Yes	4.0
No	23.9
Strongly no	52.8
Don't know	17.2

The strong attachment to Polish citizenship expressed above may be viewed in the context of the 'national pride' discussed earlier in this paper. The right of an individual to withdraw from a community of citizens ought to be – in the opinion of an overwhelming majority of Poles – restricted (although in a moral, rather than legal, sense). It is this community that should decide who belongs to it; who is a Pole and who is not. Incidentally in a different panel study of political attitudes and voting behaviour, 48% of respondents accepted legislation allowing dual citizenship, while 39% rejected it.[4]

Does the above observation indicate belief in the supremacy of the rights of the collective over the rights of the individual? When asked about this topic directly, the respondents delivered the following answers:

Table 16 What, in your opinion, should be the more important duty of a state (%)?

To guarantee each citizen maximum liberty and freedom of action within the limits of the law?	54.5
To guarantee maximum compliance of the actions of all citizens with the will of the majority?	26.0
Don't know	19.5

The traditional Polish individualism (traceable back to the

[4]Gebethner, S. and Jasiewicz, K., 'The 1990 Presidential Election', a panel study conducted in November/December 1990.

times of the noblemen's Commonwealth and *liberum veto*) seems triumphant here. The major question is to what extent this attitude, as well as other attitudes analyzed above, constitutes a basis for the development of a modern liberal-democratic state and civic culture. There is no unanimity, and one should not expect it. A majority opts against exclusions from or limitations on citizenship on the grounds of religious beliefs. A majority, or at least sizeable pluralities, speaks in favour of a liberal, pluralist democracy, with equal rights for ethnic and other minorities. But many still would accept limitations on someone else's civil rights, and/or express xenophobic resentments. Public opinion, as always, tends to be inconsistent: even on an individual level, views often contradict one another. How consistent are the views of citizenship? Are those who represent an inclusive point of view on one issue likely to express similar inclusiveness on another? Are there any specific dimensions of this exclusiveness-versus-inclusiveness relationship? These questions have been approached using factor analysis, a statistical technique that reveals the latent structure of a broader scope of views and beliefs by relating particular opinions to hidden, hypothetical dimensions or factors. The study exercised factor analysis on fourteen variables: opinions on the change of citizenship (table 15) were excluded because of skewness of this variable (only a few positive answers), while opinions on collective versus individual rights (table 16) were eliminated after preliminary analyses determined that they are not related to other variables. The final results of factor analysis are presented in table 17.[5]

The assumption that the question of inclusiveness versus exclusiveness in perceptions of citizenship should be analyzed in three separate dimensions is fully confirmed by this analysis. The views on decommunization are not related to the views on the role of religion; the latter, as the former, may be separated from the views on ethnicity. There is no single measure of exclusiveness or inclusiveness of someone's views. One can be for preferential treatment of Catholicism and against a ban on former communists, or vice versa. In addition, factor analysis revealed another very important phenomenon: the views on ethnicity separate into two dimensions. The first is composed

[5]Factor analysis, principal components method, with Varimax rotation.

Table 17 Factor analysis of views on citizenship.

Variable	Factor 1	Factor 2	Factor 3	Factor 4
1. Poland and the West			−.76726	
2. Polish tradition			.78286	
3. Teaching of history			.51610	
4. Minorities in the Sejm		−.47891		
5. Influence of Jews		.48021		
6. Alien conspiracy		.46966		
7. Aliens as a threat		.59743		
8. Western capital		.50156		
9. Emigrants		.60005		
10. Religion and law	−.77590			
11. Role of the Church	.81091			
12. Religion in schools	.76541			
13. Jobs for *nomenklatura*				.82873
14. Former communists				.82520

The numbers of variables correspond to the numbers of relevant tables in the text. Factors scores lower than .35 [indicative of a lack of relationship between a given variable and a given factor] are omitted for the sake of clarity of the table.

of items (1 to 3 in table 17) indicative of 'national pride': views not necessarily directed against other ethnic groups. The second consists of views (items 4 to 9 in table 17) clearly loaded with elements of ethnic xenophobia. This observation is important because it shows that Polish nationalism, while still, in the minds of some individuals, associated with resentments against 'aliens', may also develop its non-aggressive, more inclusive forms. For many Poles, national pride and a reluctance to follow the West in a non-reflective manner may come from considerations similar to those weighed by the nations of Western Europe when they debate, for instance, whether or not to join the European Community. Modern nation-states know nationalism without chauvinism; such nationalism apparently has developed, or is developing, in Poland.

Correlates of Citizenship

With a broad scope of views and opinions represented, one may wonder whether there are any groups, classes or strata that give a social basis to these beliefs. A three-step statistical procedure was used to determine social and demographic correlates of views on citizenship. Step no. 1 selects:

- five variables describing demographical features of respondents and their social status: sex, age, place of residence, education, and professional position (managerial versus non-managerial);

- four behavioural variables describing the individual's political and ideological 'history': religiosity (measured by frequency of attendance of church services), trade union membership in 1981 (on the eve of martial law) and in 1991 (at the date of the interview), and membership in the Communist party (was he/she ever a member of the PUWP?);

- five variables reflecting views on citizenship: one most representative for each of the four dimensions revealed in the factor analysis (view on laws and religion, opinion on whether aliens pose a threat to Polish culture, view on relationship between Poland and the West, vote in a simulated referendum on decommunization), and the fifth reflecting the views on collective versus individual rights.

In the second step, analysis of multiple regression has been performed for each of the five variables describing opinions (defined as dependent), with the remaining nine variables (defined as independent).[6] This revealed the net influence of each of the social-demographic and behavioural variables on particular views on citizenship, and selected those with the most significant influence (the best predictors).

Finally, in step no. 3 an analysis of variance was performed to determine the exact direction and intensity of influence those predictors have on the dependent variables (opinions). The specific outcomes of statistical operations (steps 2 and 3) are available from the author.

Analyses of regression and variance revealed several very interesting, and sometimes surprising, relationships. In the case

[6]Each of the two variables reflecting trade union membership was transformed into two dichotomous variables: membership in Solidarity and membership in pro-communist trade unions.

of views on the church and the state, religiosity – to nobody's surprise – turned out to be the best predictor (the more often people attend services, the less likely are they accept separation of church and state), followed by age, education, membership in Solidarity and in branch trade unions in 1981, and gender. The elderly, women and the less educated are more likely to accept preferential treatment of the Roman Catholic Church than the young, men and the better educated. Surprisingly, one can see a secular position taken by the former (1981) members of Solidarity along with the members of the pro-communist branch trade unions, as opposed to those who were unaffiliated. One should bear in mind, though, that Solidarity was largely an urban phenomenon, with a strong liberal-democratic component, while the category of 'unaffiliated' overlaps with such groups as women, the less educated, the elderly, and those living in rural areas. Still, the net influence (controlling for other variables) of 1981 membership in Solidarity in views on the role of the church in secular life is statistically significant.

The ethnocentric (and at times xenophobic) vision of citizenship finds its best predictors in education, age, place of residence, religiosity and membership in Solidarity in 1991. The more educated and younger people are the more likely they are to reject ethnocentric views. Also, city dwellers, those seldom attending church services, and members of Solidarity tend to be less xenophobic than the others.

Education, sex, age and managerial position prove to be the best predictors of the 'national pride' or 'modern nationalism' dimension. The more educated and younger people are the more pro-Western and less nationalistic they tend to be. On the other hand, women and managers (the leftovers of Communist *nomenklatura*?) express pro-Western views less frequently.

Surprisingly, in the case of decommunization the best predictor is not former membership in the PUWP (this, when controlled for other variables, is statistically not significant), but former and present membership in the pro-communist trade unions, followed by religiosity, education and place of residence. The former and present members of pro-communist trade unions oppose decommunization more vigorously than the others, of course. The discriminating power of the trade union variable takes precedence, however, over membership in the Communist party. In the early and mid–1980s 'membership in the trade union movement constituted a variable which, relatively, was most strongly connected with political views.'[7] This paradox may be explained by the fact that the decision to join the party was, in the 1960s and 1970s, basically a career decision, while the choice of trade union affiliation in the 1980s was almost identical with a political option for or against the regime. We should also add that people who go more often to church, are less educated, and live in either rural areas or big cities tend to support slogans of decomunization more strongly than others.

The views on the supremacy of collective or individual rights are most influenced by education, place of residence, and sex: the more educated, city-dwellers and men more often see the rights of the individual as superior to the rights of the collective. Interestingly, the behavioural (political and ideological) variables don't have statistically significant influence here.

Citizens and Voters

To sum up: the exclusive and inclusive visions of citizenship coexist in Poland, with the latter being somewhat better articulated than the former. They tend to overlap, and to an extent which depends on a particular dimension of beliefs. Both visions are anchored, though not particularly deeply, in elements of social structure and stratification, with the inclusive version being more often expressed in younger, urban, well-educated and more secularized milieus. Past and present political affiliations are also related to these two visions, with supporters of the *ancien régime* generally leaning towards more exclusiveness, and supporters of Solidarity towards more inclusiveness. This observation leads to the question of whether and how the two visions of citizenship were related to voting behaviour. This issue can be addressed by looking at the data collected in the panel study and comparing how constituencies of the candidates in the presidential race of 1990 and of major parties participating in the parliamentary elections of 1991 differ from one another in their views on each of the analytical dimensions distinguished above.

Those who in the first round of the presidential election in November 1990 supported Lech Walesa significantly more often

---

[7]Adamski, W., Bialecki, I., Jasiewicz, K., Kolarska-Bobinska, L., Rychard, A., 'Poles 1980–84: Dynamics of Social Conflict and Consensus', 5 *Sisyphus: Sociological Studies* (1985), pp. 252–3.

than the average favoured decommunization and the primacy of Catholic values. Their views on the other issues were very close to the average. The followers of Stanislaw Tyminski were more often against decommunization and against a confessional state. They also expressed more hostility toward aliens, and more often endorsed a collectivistic point of view. The constituency of Tadeusz Mazowiecki (at that point the prime minister) was, compared to the average, more secular, less xenophobic and more individualistically oriented; it also more often opposed decommunization. This group had the highest ideological profile, differing from the average more often than any other. The supporters of Wlodzimierz Cimoszewicz (a post-communist candidate) opposed decommunization (understandably), as well as Westernization. They, more often than any other group, spoke in favour of the separation of church and state.

One year after the presidential election, in October 1991, came a parliamentary vote. Over the course of this year Poland saw an intense process of political realignment, both on the elite and the public levels. The complexity of this process and the peculiarities of electoral law brought about a competition of 111 parties in the election, and eventually a fragmented parliament (originally 29 parties were represented in the Sejm). I will present here the views of the constituencies of only the eight most important parties. They are: five organizations that sprang from the Solidarity movement [the Democratic Union (the party of former Prime Minister Tadeusz Mazowiecki), Christian-National Union (Catholic fundamentalists), Liberal-Democratic Congress (the party of another former prime minister, Jan Krzysztof Bielecki), Center Alliance (in 1990 closely associated with Lech Walesa, since 1991 vocally opposed to him), and Solidarity – the trade union itself]; the post-communist Alliance of the Democratic Left; the Polish Peasant Party (the successor to a communist ally, United Peasant Party); and the Confederation for an Independent Poland (and old anti-communist organization).

On the issue of church-state relations, the secular point of view was more often supported by the constituencies of the Alliance of the Democratic Left, the Liberal-Democratic Congress and the Democratic Union. The confessional position was very strongly endorsed by the constituency of the Christian-

National Union, giving full justification to depiction of this party as one of Catholic fundamentalists. The pro-Western point of view was expressed more often than average by the supporters of the Liberal-Democratic Congress and Democratic Union. The same constituencies, joined by the supporters of Alliance of the Democratic Left, scored relatively low on the index of xenophobia, while the most xenophobic were the followers of the Christian-National Union and the Polish Peasant Party. The latter also articulated, more forcefully than anyone else, a collectivistic point of view, while the most individualistic was the constituency of the Liberal-Democratic Congress. Finally, decommunization was rejected (again understandably) by the supporters of the Alliance of the Democratic Left, and embraced by the constituencies of the Christian-National Union, Confederation for an Independent Poland, Center Alliance and Solidarity.

By and large, the inclusive vision of citizenship was more forcefully articulated by the supporters of the Liberal-Democratic Congress and Democratic Union, while exclusiveness was promoted by the partisans of the Christian-National Union and Polish Peasant Party. The views of parties' constituencies usually did not, however, differ much from the views dominating in the entire sample, with one notable exception being militant Catholicism endorsed by the voters of the Christian-National Union. The issues of church-state relations, and, to a certain extent, decommunization, were the only ones along which relatively clear cleavages began to form in 1990–91 on the elite level and among the public. Since then, however, after a series of sometimes bizarre turns of political fortunes and misfortunes, a coalition was formed in July 1992 with the parties occupying the extreme positions on the inclusiveness-exclusiveness continuum as major partners: the Democratic Union and Liberal-Democratic Congress on the one hand, and the Christian-National Union on the other. They overcame their ideological differences on the grounds of a common Solidarity heritage and common recognition of the priority of economic reforms above any other issues and considerations. This coalition was also challenged on the grounds of economic policies. And it is likely that things will stay this way. In future elections, Polish political elites may hear from the public the slogan so familiar to the Americans after the 1992 presidential race: 'It's the economy, stupid!' This domination of economic issues cannot be avoided:

the reforms are necessary, but costly (in both a material and a moral sense), and cannot bring considerable improvement overnight. The parties most consistently supporting market reforms are also the most committed to the inclusive vision of citizenship. If they lost in an election, the impact would be felt not only on the economy, but also on the process of legislation in other areas. Poland needs a new constitution, and many other new legislative acts. Each of them should be drafted thoughtfully, to last beyond political disputes of the day. Too often we see acts drafted and approved without this consideration, and with only partisan interests in mind. Some such acts include clauses promoting one or another version of civic exclusiveness. The recent legislation on electronic media, requiring that the content of their messages should conform to 'Christian values', provides a handy illustration here. 'It's the economy, stupid!', perhaps, but the choice between the two understandings of citizenship is, in fact, I insist, one of the most fundamental decisions that Poland's young democracy faces.

COMMENT ON KRZYSZTOF JASIEWICZ'S PAPER

Peter Paczolay

I would like to return to the dichotomy between West and East raised by Krzysztof Jasiewicz. We use the notions of West and East for the sake of methodological simplification; nevertheless, I would emphasize that both Poland and Hungary are in Central Europe, and that this is not a question of etymology, but that it explains some of the outcomes of the surveys undertaken by Krzysztof Jaziewicz. It is very difficult to define where the borders of Western Europe lie, although East and West do show two different patterns of the rise of the nation-state. In France, for example, the unified political power of the state absorbed ethnicity. In the East, the Herderian vision mentioned by Jasiewicz followed the cultural nation-state pattern in which language and culture made up the common heritage and values while, politically, the region remained divided. That is one of the reasons why the Eastern European understanding of the nation-state is still different from the Western one. The later history of this region also contributed to this difference and did not help to resolve it or to make it disappear. This ended with a conflict between citizenship as loyalty to the state and citizenship as national identity. The biggest problem in the entire region has been this conflict between national identity and loyalty to an administrative, political state, and all the turmoils after World War I, World War II, between the two Wars − even today after the collapse of communism − can be traced back to this problem of double identity.

One of the survey questions in connection with this problem shows that Poles emphasize their Polishness and, consequently, they reject both the Western and the Eastern models. Therefore, I believe in the appropriateness of the concept of Central Europe;

a concept which has a long history in Hungary as well. In all these Central European countries there is a conflict between 'Westerners' and 'Easterners', for whom adopting Western values means turning one's back on their Eastern heritage. What is seen in most countries, most importantly in Hungary, is that there is always a temptation for a 'third way'. People do not reject the Western and the Eastern types of development, but are trying to refuse the shortcomings of both capitalism and socialism. The myth of the 'third way' is a very strong ideological force in these countries. It was so already between the two World Wars, and now it has returned again. One may ask whether in Poland the Catholic Church does not contribute to this 'third way' idea, because the Polish pope, John Paul II, always condemns both the sins of capitalism and the sins of socialism. I do not know whether the Polish people are reading *Sollicitudo Rei Socialis*; in Hungary it does not have any direct influence on 'third way' ideologies.

Regarding the inclusion-exclusion problem, I agree to some extent with this approach: seeing a relationship of society versus moral community, and trying to insert the questions into this framework. Even more interesting is to see how the Catholic 'moral majority' compares to the voters' majority, because this reveals the role of the elections. How can somebody specify or identify the 'moral majority' compared to the voters' majority, which, after all, is the greatest source of legitimacy in the constitutional state? I think that there is always a conflict, at least a verbal one, between the constitution and voters' legitimate decisions and the positions of the 'moral majority' that might be different from that of the decisions of the parliament. Some developments indicate that Poland may be moving towards becoming a confessional state, which, unfortunately, would cause problems. While neutrality of the state is problematic, in certain aspects the state must remain neutral, above all with respect to religion and education. This was a much-debated issue in Hungary. Now it seems that Hungary will remain a strongly secular state. There are obviously certain pressures to move toward a more Christian community and politics, especially in educational matters, but still, neutrality has been defended. The Constitutional Court recently published a very long decision on this issue in which it decreed that the state must remain neutral on religious matters. This means that the state can make possible the work of the different denominations, but it cannot give special help to any of them or identify the state ideologically with one of them. So, the state must help all denominations without any discrimination. Hungary is not homogeneous in a religious sense; it is a primarily Catholic country although Protestant denominations are well-established and there is a large Jewish community – the third in Europe. These and the self-restraints of the Catholic Church counterbalance certain pressures throughout the state.

Jasiewicz suggests that citizens in Poland have confused views on Christianity, on the market economy, on Westernization, and on decommunization. The problem is that the societies are more in transition than usual, and people do not have models of thought and beliefs that would let them orientate themselves during the transition. They, therefore, continuously create amalgams of choices in specific cases without fitting them into an integrated *Weltanschauung*, which is one of the reasons why it is so difficult to say why certain social classes answer to this and that question so differently. We don't have the same detailed data on Hungary, but I think the same thing is happening there.

However regrettable from a Western perspective, these confused views on national questions and nationalities also express a reaction to the past or a search for identity. Western nation-states developed organically during the last centuries while Poland and Hungary were suffering from foreign invasions and occupations. One hears of nationalism in our part of the world, but not much mention of patriotism, which is the basic element of the republican tradition of Western political thought. The patriot originated in Greece, and moved through the Italian city-states to modern republican thought, such as that in America, so patriotism as such cannot be confused with nationalism. We have to draw the lines, and not confuse this under the catchword of citizenship. I think we should be more careful with these notions.

Let me mention in connection with this a new type of exclusion in certain ideologies in Hungary and some other Eastern or Central European countries. Actually, this new type of exclusion, which can be called, rightly, nationalist, does not want to exclude certain citizens from citizenship in the legal sense; it does not want to exclude them from voting, but from influential, powerful positions. This is also the case in Poland. So, this is the new type of exclusion that we are seeing and that we can use in the kind of model that was described here: the new nationalists in this region want to exclude certain groups of citizens from certain aspects of civic participation, namely from powerful economic and political positions. This has already happened in history, and it may only be the first act of exclusion from life; but, nevertheless, these groups, at least for the time being, do not question the legal equality of these other groups (there nationalism ends); they just want to limit their influence.

As the paper points out, in certain aspects ethnic prejudices and the 'third way' idea overrule economic rationalism. The paper quotes the overwhelming objection to foreign capital, though it is obvious that foreign capital is one of the necessary means of revitalizing the Polish economy. Yugoslavia experienced an economic upturn, but nobody cared about the economy. Slovak propaganda was that the split would be advantageous for economic reasons, but this turned out to be untrue. So, the history of the region shows that ethnic sentiments are more important in certain questions than rational economic thinking.

People are more sensitive to social rights than to civil liberties. Classical civil liberties are free speech, freedom of association, even freedom of voting, and I doubt that the public in Poland and Hungary are focussing on these. The Constitutional Court has had 2,000 claims and 600 decisions a year, and it is very difficult to find any that refer to classical liberties. In three-and-one-half years, the court has only had one important free speech case whereas there are hundreds of social rights cases: people claming social equality, even in the sense of equal distribution of burdens and advantages and the socialist welfare services. Maybe after the first two or three years of democratic euphoria, the real issue for these new democracies will become how to solve the problem of social rights, and not that of the principal civil liberties, which are more or less guaranteed. Social demagogy from different political parties on the left and the right is quite similar and will have a great impact on the next elections both in Poland and Hungary.

Let us turn to the legal aspects of this problem, and to some Hungarian experiences. In terms of Hungarian minorities living outside the country, Hungarian citizenship regulations are very inclusive. Hungary is in favour of dual and multiple citizenship, but the citizenship law passed last year justifies the continued prohibition of dual citizenship in terms of Hungarian historical traditions. In fact, this prohibition had been forced upon the socialist countries. Hungary is trying to return to dual citizenship for obvious reasons. This would constitute one exception to the principle of exclusion.

The other question that was raised is that the representation of ethnic minorities in parliament is extremely difficult in homogeneous countries, although one would think that it would be easier to solve this problem in homogeneous countries than in those with a great number of minorities. Nevertheless, it seems that both Poland and Hungary are unable to solve this problem; certainly, Hungary has been unable to pass a law on ethnic minorities.[1] And, yes, it is easy to refer to the Finnish example, where there is one minority and everything is written in two languages. But in Hungary, we have six or seven minorities, and the tremendous task of writing everything in seven languages, would benefit only approximately the 1% of the population that comprises them. It would be very difficult to change the electoral system for the sake of their representation, or to create a second agenda, or whatever, because none of the political parties wants to give votes to groups that are politically unidentified and are just minorities. In Hungary it is very difficult to persuade people that it is important to solve this question.

[1]The minority law was passed in Hungary in early July 1993. See Edith Oltay, 'Hungary Passes Law on Minority Rights', *RFE/RL Research Report*, 20 August 1993. [editorial note]

DISCUSSION 3

The discussion of Krzysztof Jasiewicz's paper and Peter Paczolay's commentary centered primarily around the issues of 'lustration', the 'third way', and the debate on Central Europe/ Eastern Europe. The participants from Hungary, the Czech Republic and Slovakia presented the experiences of their own countries, providing a comparative perspective for the discussion on Poland.

Kenneth Minogue opened the debate by lauding the ambition of the project undertaken by Jasiewicz. He noted that for most people, answering a question like 'Should Poland become more like the West?' is bound to be very difficult, and that they would have to balance the advantages of such an evolution with the maintenance of the country's distinctiveness and identity. Piotr Ogrodzinski added that the data based on such limited possibilities for response ('yes'/'no') can be criticized, but that it is very important to take into account that such a survey is much more difficult to realize today than a few years ago. Before 1989 Polish society was relatively homogeneous, making straightforward conclusions possible, Ogrodzinski argued, but since then it has become extremely differentiated. He recounted his surprise at discovering that he had become a citizen and a taxpayer, rather than a mere subject, and that he could have an opinion about the way the state used the taxpayers' money: to him this discovery symbolized the tremendous changes that his country and his own thinking had undergone in the last few years. For Ogrodzinski, the crucial factor in these circumstances of rapid change is an individual's capability to adapt to new situations, and while some people manage to do so, others do not. Today it is these different groups of people that participate in elections; some vote for parties that favour reforms and believe that recovery will follow while others vote for parties consisting of 'angry populists' denouncing the new differentiation of society. Ogrodzinski affirmed that most people would still agree that reforms are necessary, but that opinions diverge regarding the extent of these reforms and the manner in which they are being carried out.

Martin Palous briefly commented on Jasiewicz's interpretation of Locke, disagreeing with the idea that Locke proposes a type of universal citizenship for all inhabitants of a state. Palous argued that according to Locke all human beings – formerly free in the state of nature – see their freedom curtailed by a government, but not all *actively* consent to be governed. Palous' second comment opened the debate on lustration. He noted that the issue of lustration is still alive in the new Czech Republic, and presented the three arguments generally given to explain its continuing importance. The first argument is a 'moral' one, based on the belief that one cannot draw a line through the past and simply forget the crimes that were committed. The second, or 'pragmatic', argument resides in the claim that the country is still in a 'state of emergency', necessitating prudence and a continuing struggle against all those who could be used by the 'forces of the past'. For Palous, the third, 'political', argument is the true explanation, although it is not openly articulated: lustration is a part of the political discourse, used very effectively against a certain section of the political spectrum. Now that the issue of lustration has served its purpose and those who used it have won the elections, they no longer appear very interested in it, preferring to shun all responsibility and blame others for its consequences and the country's legal problems.

André Liebich noted that 'lustration' provides an interesting case study for citizenship because, unlike the previous discussion which centered around the acquisition of citizenship, it raises the question of having it revoked. He stated that 'lustration' in Eastern Europe has precedents: the deprivation of citizenship by socialist states which expelled some of their citizens, or by postwar France when it recalled the 'right to national identity' of such individuals as collaborationist police commissioner René Bosquet, or by the Vichy government when it 'de-naturalized' several thousand French Jews. Responding to an enquiry about 'lustration', Martin Palous pointed to the Latin origin of the word, derived from 'lux' and meaning 'the shedding of light' or 'illumination'. Both he and Olga Gyarfasova referred to the fact that it was used long before the present debates by the communist state police to designate the process of investigating the personal records of individuals. Edmund Wnuk-Lipinski stated that the term 'lustration' essentially meant 'monitoring'. Piotr Ogrodzinski provided the origins of the term in Poland, explaining that *lustracja dobr krolewskich* defined the process undertaken by the gentry (*szlachta*) of looking through documents regarding the rental of the crown's property to ascertain whether there was a legal basis for the aristocracy's ownership of land. This process was a part of the gentry's attempts to keep the country united under the sovereign and to curtail the tendency towards disintegration that resulted from the aristocracy's increase of power.

The debate on 'lustration' taking place in Hungary and its legal implications were illustrated by Peter Paczolay. He stated that the debate centers around two issues: first, what to do with former secret police agents and second, how to deal with political crimes committed in the past. The first issue is still being hotly debated in Parliament and is part of the political discourse used by some politicians to discredit others. The second question is legally much more complex. Noting that the political situation was different in Hungary than Czecho-Slovakia in the past, Paczolay affirmed that what is really at stake in his country is punishing the crimes committed after the 1956 Revolution. The Parliament has decided to lift the statute of limitations for political crimes and allow prosecution, while the Constitutional Court turned down the parliamentary act as unconstitutional. The Court's argument is that the transition has to take place within a legal framework, and that it is counter-productive to use double standards such as lifting the statute of limitations for certain groups in society, thus applying *ex post facto* legislation in their case. This issue, Paczolay concluded, remains highly controversial in Hungary and no solution is yet in sight.

Olga Gyarfasova provided information regarding 'lustration' in Slovakia, stating that the law on 'lustration' was a federal law, and that it became defunct with the demise of the federation. So far, no provisions have been made regarding this issue in Slovakia. Gyarfasova believes that the silence on 'lustration' is perhaps due to the presence of many former members of the

Communist Party in the ranks of the new Slovak government, but she added that the general climate in the country is not favourable to dealing with the past. Pierre Hassner concluded the discussion on 'lustration' by stressing that those who demanded retribution most vehemently in the countries of East-Central Europe were not, for the most part, former dissidents. He accounted for Czech Prime Minister Vaclav Klaus' popularity in the Czech Republic by noting that Klaus, like most people, had been neither a communist nor a dissident in the past, and recalled that many former dissidents started out as communists, which estranged them from the majority of the population.

Tamas Földesi brought up the notion of Central Europe and the issue of the 'third way'. He stressed that although the countries of the former Soviet block have some things in common, the differences between them remain great. He pointed to the fear of 'Balkanization' in Hungary, and the desire not to belong to the 'Eastern' part of Eastern Europe – Bulgaria, Romania and some former Soviet states. He stated that Hungary is now in a paradoxical situation: for the West it is East, and for the East it is West. Földesi related this Central European identity to the debate on the 'third way', stating that, in fact, this idea is rather unpopular in his country. For most people the choices between capitalism and the old socialist economic system, or between democracy and totalitarianism, have been made. The 'third way' is seen as a desire to return to the old socialist market. The nationalist populist movement led by Csurka presents another interpretation of the 'third way' as a 'Hungarian way' and refuses foreign capital. Földesi warned that although some of those who are dissatisfied with their economic situation may support the Csurka movement or look to other models of a 'third way', such as Sweden, none are actually rejecting capitalism; they are only claiming that capitalism is variable and that they do not like the way the government is handling the transition. In politics, Földesi concluded, the 'third way' would be represented by neutrality; yet, in this domain too, very few people desire neutrality, most favour joining NATO and the European Community.

Martin Palous agreed that the 'third way' is unpopular in East-Central Europe, as is illustrated by the fact that in the Czech Republic today nobody uses this term except for its critics. Once again, Palous attributed the utilization of this notion to political discourse aiming to discredit opponents: Vaclav Klaus' slogan in the election campaign was 'the "third way" is the shortest road to the Third World'. Piotr Ogrodzinski compared the comments on the Czech Republic and Hungary to the situation in Poland. He cited the Polish economist, Wlodzimierz Brus, who stated that while the 'third way' does not exist, it is nevertheless being pursued in the countries of East-Central Europe, due to the fact that the transition from a state-run economy to a capitalist one takes a long time. He noted Tamas Földesi's use of the same term to define Hungary that the Polish playwright Slawomir Mrozek employed to define his own country – situated east of the West and west of the East. Nevertheless, Ogrodzinski argued that Poland is different from Hungary or Czecho-Slovakia: while in the latter two countries the concept of Mitteleuropa has some appeal, in Poland it is perceived as a threat. He attributed this difference to Poland's historical experience of being partitioned, which gave rise to a traditional perception of Germany as the threat from the West, and to an uncertainty regarding its own frontiers, while expansion of the Polish state tended to take place eastwards. Ogrodzinski's final remark concerned the role of the Church in Poland, and, in particular, the discrepancy that came out in Krzysztof Jasiewicz's paper between public opinion and the policy-makers on this issue. He explained the political strength of the Catholic Church by noting that after the disintegration of Solidarity, only small cadre parties and trade unions came into existence, while the Church as a large and historically important institution with its roots firmly implanted in society naturally remained a key political factor, much more so than its support at the grassroots level would indicate.

Pierre Hassner provided further information concerning the role of the Church in Poland and rounded off the discussion on Eastern Europe/Central Europe and the 'third way'. He referred to the remarks of many of his Polish acquaintances that the Church is vastly unpopular when it comes to issues such as abortion or contraception, and that attempts to create a Christian Party in Poland failed miserably. Hassner also cited the polls ranking the popularity of institutions in Poland, where the Church has progressively declined in rank, and noted his surprise that the top-ranked institution was the army. Second, Hassner wondered whether the 'third way' should rather be called a 'third phase': after the collapse of communism people naturally want its exact opposite (capitalism, the West, and so on), but inevitably a 'third phase' of disappointment and disillusion will set in. The great question for Hassner is what the 'third phase' will culminate in: a return to the past, a revival of nationalism, or perhaps some form of social democracy? Perhaps, Hassner mused, it is at this stage that the 'third way' may come back into fashion. Hassner's final remarks concerned the Central Europe/Eastern Europe debate. He cited the Hungarian historian Jenö Szücs, who argues that three regions have historically existed in Europe, and that Central Europe, which had its development distorted by foreign domination, possesses structures neither like Western Europe nor like Russia, rendering its nationalism and conception of the nation-state different. Hassner concluded that whether one calls this region Eastern Europe or Central Europe, the issue is whether its specific historical conditions and social development have produced fundamentally different conceptions of politics and the nation.

In his closing comments, Krzysztof Jasiewicz addressed the issues raised in the discussion. He began with a short comment on Martin Palous' remark on Locke. He said that Locke never clearly expressed a notion of citizenship in his works, and he preferred to refer to Locke's notion of free will. One can derive from Locke, Jasiewicz maintained, that civil society is a concept in which individuals living on a certain territory accept certain contractual obligations, resulting in the creation of the nation-state. The basis of citizenship is thus the *ius soli*, which Jasiewicz contrasted with the Herderian notion of citizenship based on the *ius sanguinis*. Regarding the Western Europe/Eastern Europe/Central Europe debate and Piotr Ogrodzinski's remark, he felt that a well-known joke best captures the paradox of Poland between East and West: Two planes are flying over Poland, one from Moscow to Paris and one from Paris to Moscow. A thunderstorm breaks just when both are over Warsaw and they are forced to land. The pilot has no time to tell the passengers where they are landing. A Frenchman gets off his plane, looks around, and says 'Moscow, what an ugly city'. A Russian gets off his plane, also looks around, sighs, and exclaims, 'Ah, Paris, what a beautiful place!'

Jasiewicz added that in his paper he included Germany in the East, due to the German notion of citizenship. He stated that the inclusion of countries under the heading 'Eastern

Europe' is necessarily issue-specific, but affirmed his belief in the utility of the East/West distinction. In Yugoslavia, Jasiewicz said, the conflict runs along the ancient line that separated the eastern and western parts of the Roman Empire, which was enforced by the introduction respectively of Eastern Orthodoxy and Roman Catholicism in the 11th century. If one takes the economy into consideration, Jasiewicz continued, the division between areas of predominantly industrial and mainly agricultural structural development since the 15th century runs along the Elbe river in Germany, the Czech lands thus belonging in the West and former Prussia and East Germany in the East.

Jasiewicz then addressed the issue of the Catholic Church in Poland in more detail. He expressed his admiration for the role the Church played in the defeat of communism, affirming that without the Pope's visit in 1979 Solidarity would not have been possible. Nevertheless, he said, when one examines the role of the Church today and the ideas of Catholic intellectuals, one sees that they are essentially attempting to create a 'third way', but in a different sense than that usually given to the term. The Church has traditionally perceived the threat as coming from two directions: it has successfully dealt with that from the East – communism – but it still needs to fight against the threat of Western materialism and liberalism. A Catholic intellectual recently said that, while he knows many social democrats who are good Catholics, he knows no liberal who could be a good Catholic. The Church believes that Poland needs to establish a firm legal and moral framework for society in which economic changes are to take place; its main fear is that Poland will become like another Catholic European country, France. Jasiewicz reaffirmed his belief that the influence of the Church is diminishing in Poland, and that voting practices do not necessarily reflect the opinions of the public: a woman living in the Polish countryside may cast her vote for an ultra-Catholic party, like the Christian National Union, because she was told to do so by her local priest during Sunday service, yet the same woman, if she learned that her unmarried daughter was pregnant, would have few qualms about forcing her to have an illegal abortion. He said that people do not yet connect their voting behaviour with its consequences for their everyday life. Jasiewicz further commented on the Church's double standard on social issues: when the issue of religious minorities comes up, the Church campaigns on the basis that Poland is over 90% Catholic and that minorities must conform, but when abortion is discussed, the Church refuses to let a referendum majority decide on 'moral' issues. In this context, Jasiewicz made a brief remark on the role of the army in Poland, so as to shed some light on its popularity as an institution: while Poland was deprived of statehood for over 120 years, there was often a Polish army in existence somewhere. In this sense, the army has traditionally been a symbol of 'Polishness' and Polish statehood, and its popularity has little to do with its real political role.

In regard to the 'third way' and the economic transition, Jasiewicz expressed his agreement with Vaclav Klaus' argument that the 'third way' was the shortest road to the Third World, and with Martin Palous' statement that only the critics of this notion use it in political discourse to discredit their opponents. Referring to Pierre Hassner's comment on the 'third phase', Jasiewicz affirmed that he did not believe a revival of communism was possible in Poland, whatever the outcome. His final remark concerned the role of the economy in future electoral campaigns in Poland. Although the economy is not the only important issue for voters, it is the one which bears most directly on their everyday existence, and is thus easily manipulated by politicians. For Jasiewicz, the most striking example of the way that the economy played into the hands of politicians is Yugoslavia: had the country's economy been successful, the Croats and the Slovenes would have had little incentive to leave the federation.

HUNGARY

CITIZENSHIP IN HUNGARY, FROM A LEGISLATIVE VIEWPOINT

Gabor Nagy

The Definition of Citizenship

According to one of the most common definitions, citizens are members of a political community. This assumes a treaty between people to establish a political state to serve their common benefit and to protect their individual and collective rights.

Inhabitants are an essential element of the notion of the state. But, the conditions of modern citizenship did not exist until the concept of subject had been replaced by that of citizen, the concept of monarchical sovereignty by that of popular sovereignty, and the concepts of constitutionalism, equality, and national states had appeared. The growing involvement of citizens in the affairs of the state forced the definition of exactly who enjoyed constitutional rights and the protection of the state, and who should pay taxes and serve in the military. Based on this notion, a distinction could be made between 'us' and 'them', between citizens of a state who participate in the political decision process and foreigners, or aliens.

According to T. H. Marshall there are three elements of citizenship: the civil, the political and the social. 'The civil element is composed of the rights necessary for individual freedom, the political element is the right to participate in the exercise of political power, and the social element the whole range from the right to a modicum of economic welfare and security to the right to share to the full in social heritage and to live as a

117

civilised being.'[1] These three elements were differentiated in three steps as a 'gradual addition of new rights to a status that already existed and was held to appertain to all adult members of the community'.[2] Marshall pointed out the 'divorce of social rights from the status of citizenship'.[3]

J. Habermas summarized two concepts of citizenship.[4] In fact, these are based on different meanings of democracy, and they have also appeared in legal philosophy. One is the 'liberal tradition based on natural law, derived from Locke: an individualistic-instrumentalist type of citizen's role. The other is the republican tradition of state theory, which goes back to Aristotle and Rousseau, a communitarian-ethical concept'.[5] Habermas offers a third alternative, the so-called deliberative politics or discourse theory. This is based on conditions and procedures of communication, the institutionalized expression of opinion, and the formation of the will, which bestows legitimacy on the decision.[6]

The liberal model focused on individual human rights, equal treatment and those governmental policies which consider the preferences of citizens. In contrast to this, the communitarian model views participation as self-governing, and as the essential part of the citizen's freedom which must be guaranteed. According to the liberal tradition, the citizen is a member of the state but at the same time an outsider: supporting the state through voting and paying taxes, while being a private individual whose interests are fulfilled in opposition to those of the state.

In the republican tradition, citizenship belongs to an ethnic/cultural community which is so integrated that it can develop a personal and social identity based on common traditions and accepted political institutions. This can only be achieved through the practice of collective self-definition. This model emphasizes that the constitutional institutions have as much value as the

[1]Marshall, T. H., *Citizenship and Social Class*, Cambridge 1950, pp. 10, 11.
[2]*Ibidem*, p. 18.
[3]*Ibidem*, p. 24.
[4]Habermas, J.: 'Allampolgarsag es nemzeti identitas – Töprengések az europai jovorol' ('Citizenship and National Identity – Thought on European Future'), *Beszelo [Speaker]*, (1993)
[5]*Ibidem*. p. 5. The liberal/republican distinction is based on the characterization of C. Taylor. Taylor, C., 'The Liberal-Communitarian Debate', in Rosenblum, N. (ed) *Liberalism and the Moral Life*, Cambridge, MA 1989, p. 178.
[6]Habermas, J., 'Az allampolgarsag harom fogalma' ('The Three Concepts of Citizenship') 8 *Kritika, [Critic]* (1992), pp. 6–9.

population, accustomed to political freedom, can draw from them. 'The legally guaranteed rights of citizens must be embedded in the context of a free political culture'.[7]

Nation-States and Western Integration

The traditional concept of citizenship is based on the nation-state. This was actually one of the conditions for the development of citizenship theory. But what is a nation? What is nationalism? Most objective definitions of nationality rely on the commonality of some particular trait among members of a group. Shared language, religion, ethnicity ('common descent'), and culture have all been used as criteria for defining nations. In much of Western Europe the geographical boundaries of the nation-state preceded the building of the nation itself. Now this concept of nation-states has been challenged on several counts.

First, multicultural societies (like the United States of America, Switzerland, Canada) show that a common democratic and tolerant political culture is not necessarily based on ethnic, linguistic or cultural roots. These societies 'can create a constitutional patriotism, which at one and the same time strengthens sensitivity and respect towards the integration of the different co-existing ways of life'.[8]

The second challenge is the existence of supranational integration.[9] The European Community is tending towards such an integration by establishing a new European identity with a limited form of citizenship. To some extent this is an inclusive process in opposition to the first trend. There are two forces working simultaneously in opposite directions:

a)   the democratic process and representative participation in EC institutions, (i.e. the phenomenon called 'democratic deficit');

b)   the elimination of some of the national characteristics of citizenship, replacing them with a new identity and loyalty towards the EC.

---

[7]Habermas, J., *op. cit.* (note 4), p. 5.
[8]*Idem.*
[9]That integration is supranational which takes over more and more competence from member states, constitutes a rival rule of law and wants to change the political attitude of member states' citizens.

The third challenge is the constant demand for real participation in political decision-making and for social security at the national level. But, in nations with limited public resources, this inevitably means the denial of benefits for those who are not members of the specific community. The current economic stagnation (recession) is accompanied by new problems of xenophobia and far-right extremism with its demands to exclude foreigners.

Additional challenges exist from the economic refugees of the Third World and the politically liberated masses of Eastern Europe who flee towards the West in hopes of escaping their poverty-stricken lives. The question is: How can Western countries face this, one of their biggest challenges?

Universal principles of constitutionalism and democratic ideas must be implemented in specific political contexts which differ very much from one another. Only a population which is accustomed to freedom, which has a democratic political culture, can keep the institutions of liberty alive. That is why Walzer thinks that a limitation on immigration is where a community's right to conserve the integrity of its way of life begins.[10] According to Walzer, a citizen's right to self-determination includes the right to maintain his or her own way of life.

The International Legal Aspect of Citizenship

Citizenship as a legal institution embodies the legal relations of persons to a specific state. From this perspective, citizenship is an institution of both domestic law and international law. Every state can define, according to its laws, whom it considers citizens. Other states must accept this as long as it conforms with international treaties or customs and general principles on citizenship.

In modern international law, the right to citizenship is defined as a human right. The Universal Declaration of Human Rights says: 'Everyone has the right to a nationality' and 'no one shall be arbitrarily deprived of his nationality nor deprived of the right to change his nationality'. (Art. 15. I., II.)

Article 25 of The International Covenant on Civil and Political Rights says:

[10]Walzer, M., *Spheres of Justice*, New York 1993, pp. 31–63.

Every citizen shall have the right and the opportunity without (. . .) unreasonable restrictions:

a) To take part in the conduct of public affairs, directly or through freely chosen representatives;
b) To vote and to be elected at genuine periodic elections which shall be held under universal and equal suffrage and shall be held by secret ballot, guaranteeing the free expression of the will of the electors;
c) To have access, on general terms of equality, to public service in his country.

Also important is Article 12:

2. Everyone shall be free to leave any country, including his own.
4. No one shall be arbitrarily deprived of the right to enter his own country.

As a consequence of Western supranational integration, the Maastricht Treaty established the Citizenship of the Union. This is the first symbolic step towards loyalty to the Community. From the legal perspective, it is important to list rights which will be provided by the EC to member-states' citizens, and which are not owed to anyone else.[11] The most fundamental rights of every citizen of the Union consist of:

– the freedom of movement and choice of residence,
– the right to vote and stand as a candidate at municipal elections in the member-state in which he resides, and also at the European Parliament,
– common protection of diplomatic and consular authorities,
– the right to petition the European Parliament,
– the right to apply to the Ombudsman.

EC citizenship is not a substitute for national citizenships. In fact, the relationship is just the opposite. National citizenship is the indispensable condition to get and use citizenship of the Union. In this way, the citizenship of the Union is derived from national citizenship.

---

[11]Lenaerts, K., 'Fundamental Rights to be Included in a Community Catalogue', 16 *European Law Review*, (1991), p. 384.

Political Background of Central and Eastern Europe

As mentioned earlier, in much of Western Europe the geographical boundaries of the nation-state preceded the building of the nation itself. In Central and Eastern Europe the situation was completely reversed. In these areas, 'nations' were born before proto-nation states. Much of Central and Eastern Europe was controlled by four great multi-national empires (German, Russian, Habsburg and Ottoman). Many of the people who inhabited these empires had no historical state 'of their own' with which they might identify. The Slovaks, Slovenes and Ruthenians, for example, never even had an embryonic state as the Croats, Bulgarians, Lithuanians, Romanians and Serbs had. For the people living in Central and Eastern Europe, the liberal aspirations of nationalism were submerged within the goal of building a nation-state.

After the Soviet bloc collapsed and national states renewed their sovereignty, nationalism became stronger, and repressed national identity was aroused (sometimes by manipulation). The current growth of nationalism is a logical consequence of 40 years of Soviet domination. During that time, the interests and national feelings of the satellite countries were repressed and the 'uniformity' of communism, known as internationalism, was emphasized, although some Soviet bloc countries incorporated nationalism into their official ideologies (which gave rise to the horrible mutations of 'national communism' or 'communist nationalism'). In Hungary that was not the case. Generally, the Communist leaders were indifferent to their co-nationals living as minorities in other countries. It was a kind of negative consensus: 'if you don't mess with me, I don't mess with you'. Nowadays the situation is just the opposite.

Today, Central Eastern European nations want to be independent and want to distinguish themselves from each other. During the current disintegration of the Soviet bloc, oppressed 'minority' nations are striving for a majority political role on their own territory even if the struggle results in a smaller territory. The historical experience has been one of no minority protection, no collective rights, and no effective international institutes to guarantee language, culture or a specific way of life. This is one reason why so many attempts (even a war!)

have been made to create ethnically homogeneous countries, for example in the former Yugoslavia.

All of these changes have consequences for citizenship. Several new countries have appeared and some have regained independence. The latest example is the case of Latvian Way, and its leader Anatolij Gorbunovs, who said that after forming a coalition, the government's first task will be to make the citizens' law of the country.[12]

Connected with this nationalism or even chauvinism, in some places ethnicity has become a more important element of citizenship's definition. In the situation of a civil war, ethnic affiliation and personal emotional identification with the 'nation' can be more important than anything else. In this case, national loyalty is overestimated at the expense of political rights or allegiance to a state. Of course we can find several solutions with differing emphases for these tendencies.

In the Baltic states, such nationalism has become a sensitive domestic political question.[13] The Lithuanian Citizenship Act, adopted in December 1991, provoked criticism from ethnic minorities (Poles, Russians) who are 'afraid of the formation of an intolerant, repressive nation-state', because 'in the law, moral, health and legal principles are mixed up, and some of the exclusionary rules are liable to be interpreted according to manipulation or arbitrariness'.[14]

The Situation in Hungary

Recent political changes in Hungary have made a great difference in migration to and from the country. Hungary has become a 'destination–', or 'transit-country', although some years ago citizens were escaping from it. Tens of thousands of Hungarians have arrived from neighbouring countries, as well as several thousand persons from Africa and Asia who want to get into Europe. Most of these people do not want to live in Hungary. Until immigration laws were amended in 1992, there was a

---

[12]*Magyar Hirlap*, 9 June, 1993, p. 2.

[13]Toth, L., 'Baltikum – a visszanyert szuverenitas utan' ('Baltics – After Regaining Sovereignty') *Tarsadalmi Szemle* [*Social Review*] (1992), p. 58.

[14]*Ibidem*, p. 58, mentions examples from the Latvian draft law on citizenship to show the strict conditions for getting Latvian citizenship.

better chance of getting refugee or residential status in Hungary than in Austria, for example.

The dramatic and rapid political turnaround in itself could not change the political culture of people, either of the new political elite or average citizens. The question is whether the new political structure can transform people from political subjects (who were deprived of political rights) to conscious citizens (*citoyens*).

Parallel with the political changes, public security has weakened, new types of crimes have appeared and anti-Gypsy feelings have become stronger among youth who have no future perspectives, no positive values and no communities. These youths also can be characterized as victims of the transition. They are potential skinheads, and some of them have already committed aggression against Gypsies, foreign students, travellers and even diplomats. (One Gypsy citizen was killed.) And there is a new danger associated with 'skinheads'. Some political groups are trying to co-opt and organize skinheads to serve their political goals. They have re-named them 'Hungarian Conservative-Minded Youth' instead of skinheads. However, they wear the same short hair, bomber jackets and heavy boots as their counterparts elsewhere in Europe. Their anti-social attitudes are obviously very much the same: hatred of foreigners, immigrants and refugees; attacking mainly coloured persons in the streets. (These attitudes are accompanied by hatred of Gypsies, Jews, other ethnic minorities and the refusal to accept them as equal Hungarian citizens.)

Today these tendencies are not peculiar to Hungary, or even Central and Eastern Europe, but are present all over Europe; from Le Pen in France to Haider in Austria, from German skinheads attacking refugees in Rostock to Polish skinheads beating German truck drivers. Extreme nationalists are playing on and responding to the same kinds of difficulties: declining economies, growing unemployment and the release of pent-up anger. But the roots are different. In Eastern Europe, societies are struggling with the legacy of forty years of communism during which a civil society and a value-system based on tolerance were lacking.

Current Hungarian Law On Citizenship

On 1 June, 1993, the Hungarian National Assembly (Parliament) adopted a new law on citizenship. The Act on Citizenship is only a framework; some essential points will be or already have been regulated at the lower level.

The real meaning of Hungarian citizenship can be understood from all kinds of legal norms (including the constitution, political institutions, mass media, social welfare, etc.) and the actual practice of citizens' rights. In principle, during the recodification of citizenship not only the direct citizenship law should be reviewed, but also those legal norms which have significance for the meaning of citizenship.[15]

The Hungarian Constitution provides a broad range of theoretical citizens' rights. The problem with the list is that there are few guarantees for people if their rights are violated. Currently there are new possibilities; after regular legal procedures (court of justice, constitutional court etc.) Hungarian citizens can turn to the European Court of Justice in Strasbourg.

It is also interesting to note that the Local Election Act of 1990 provided voting rights in municipal elections to non-citizen permanent residents. This point was mentioned in the Maastricht Treaty. But the question is to what extent these voting rights can be exercised. How many residents of Hungary at the moment are not of Hungarian nationality? Only a few thousand. Therefore, we cannot compare these voting rights with future EC citizenship, even though the legal framework was constructed earlier.

The most important points in the draft law on citizenship were:

a) elimination of the government's right to take away citizenship (deprivation);

b) conditions for acquiring Hungarian citizenship (naturalization) are becoming stricter: eight years of permanent residence status are required, (instead of three years), a person must have no criminal past, s/he must have a minimum of financial security, naturalization must not violate the interest of the Hungarian Republic, and s/he must meet a language and citizenship examination requirement;

[15]Szamel, L., 'Az allampolgarsagi jog reformjarol', ('On the Reform of Citizen's Law') 3 *Magyar Közigazgatas [Hungarian Administration]*, (1991/3), p. 200.

c)   principle of descent (*ius sanguinis*); all descendants of Hungarian citizens shall be Hungarian citizens too;

d)   a special status for people of Hungarian nationality who have lived outside the borders of the country since Hungary lost its former territories, which entitles them to a 'preferential' and simplified procedure (three years of permanent residence status).

It was obvious that the political intentions of the governing conservative coalition during the debate were to:

(1)   offer special treatment for Hungarian minorities from the neighbouring countries in their efforts to acquire Hungarian citizenship if they wanted it (preferential naturalization);

(2)   to hinder non-Hungarian immigrants applying for Hungarian citizenship. This purpose coincides with Western European intentions;[16]

(3)   to activate as many former Hungarian citizens as possible, even dual citizens, who may not have actual connections with their native country.

'Let All Hungarians Vote!' – is how the government's spokeswoman summarized the draft of the Electoral Law which will be proposed by the government.[17] This confirms the opposition's suspicion that the government wants to use former emigrés for their political purposes. According to the draft, all Hungarian citizens can vote. Non-residents could vote for national lists in Hungarian embassies. Those who have no passport, identification, or any paper confirming their Hungarian citizenship would get a citizenship-certificate from Hungarian authorities. This would mean hundreds of thousands of people could vote who have no permanent connections to Hungary, who do not pay taxes, and who are not living under the authority of the Hungarian government. Most of them have another citizenship as well. The most debated points were:

[16]Népszabadsag, 29 May, 1993.

[17]See the statement of the Minister of Interior, Mr. Boross: 'Hungary is full!' Opening speech in the debate on draft law on 'Foreigners' Travel in Hungary. Their Stay There and Their Immigration', on 20 April, 1993 in the Hungarian Parliament, *Parliamentary Record*, (1993), p. 25931 and his deputy, Mr. Jozsa, State Secretary, Interior Ministry: 'a person must be worthy to get Hungarian citizenship', *Magyar Hirlap*, 30 March, 1993.

a) The unlimited application of *ius sanguinis*. This concerns Hungarian emigrants and their descendants who still have citizenship, but who might have no family, cultural or economic connections with Hungary such as knowledge of the Hungarian language. It means that all descendants of former Hungarian citizens (and there is no time limitation in it) still have citizenship, although they might have grown up in another country and have no direct connections with Hungary. The problem here is the very large number of uncertain Hungarian citizens.

Opposition parties wanted to limit the application of *ius sanguinis*. They offer a similar solution to the one applied in the United States. If somebody does not express his/her interest in maintaining a connection with Hungary for a period of time (eight years), he or she will automatically lose citizenship. In addition, children will not automatically get Hungarian citizenship unless their Hungarian ancestors have maintained contact during the last eight years. In these cases, persons could request preferential naturalization. These terms of the opposition proposal did not receive the support of the parliamentary majority.

b) The condition for access to the citizens' political and social rights were also debated. According to the government's proposal, those Hungarian citizens who are also citizens of another state at the time of application of the Hungarian laws should be considered as Hungarian citizens with all material and political demands connected with citizenship rights (i.e., compensation, family support, voting). For example, this would mean an American-Hungarian could use Hungarian social insurance although he or she never paid any contribution to it. The intention of this point was to incorporate emigrés into the political decision-making process, namely elections. According to the opposition, at least two conditions must be met for a person to benefit from Hungarian citizens' rights:

(1) permanent residence in Hungary, and

(2) regular tax payments.

At the opposition's insistence, the government accepted

this argument and eliminated the above-mentioned proposal.

c) The third point was dual citizenship. According to the draft, multiple-citizenship is allowed and accepted, but there was a debate about whether it is an asset or a liability. What can be the message in this for ex-Hungarian citizens who emigrated to Western Europe or America, and for those minorities who lost their citizenship because of the Peace Treaties after the First and Second World Wars? Emigrés to the West are considered Hungarian citizens. But what about the Hungarians who remain in their villages, outside post-Trianon Hungarian borders? Are they Hungarian according to our laws? And what does Hungarian mean? This is a subjective element of national identity. According to the law, people are Hungarians who consider themselves Hungarians. This means that people's passports are in their hearts, which might be too flexible for a legal category. During the debate there were arguments against the unlimited and frequent opportunity for dual citizenship, claiming that this goes against European standards.[18]

As a result of a long debate, the three relevant parliamentary committees wrote a joint report on the draft law in which they recommended a compromise alternative. It means that both the government and the opposition gave up some proposals. The atmosphere and the procedure were democratic, and perhaps because of that, the Parliament finally adopted the new law, almost unanimously.

---

[18]See: Recommendation of Council of Europe on Reducing Cases of Multiple Nationality, 1963.

COMMENT ON GABOR NAGY'S PAPER

Guy Goodwin-Gill

I come to the issue of citizenship with a background in international law, and a specific interest in issues of migration, refugees and the 'responsibilities' of states, especially towards *non*-nationals – those, as Gabor Nagy emphasized, who are excluded from the political community.

My other qualification for being here, perhaps, is that I am also a dual citizen, having recently acquired the citizenship of Canada in addition to my citizenship of origin of the United Kingdom. Canada, like many other countries built on immigration, is concerned to forge a national identity while remaining faithful to the claims of its two so-called founding nations, the English and the French, and to the increasing demands for recognition by those who really were there first, the native North Americans, and by other constituent ethnic groups who contributed so much to opening up the country in the late 19th and early 20th centuries. Like other countries of immigration, however, Canada, with its policy commitment to multiculturalism, shows how ethnic diversity can be maintained within political community.

My comments will, therefore, reflect this background – and may do less than justice to Gabor Nagy's paper, although fortunately he does make several references to international provisions – while offering a number of other thought-provoking insights into the challenges now facing existing, emerging and consolidating democracies as they encounter the demands for recognition and protection by both citizens and non-nationals.

Preliminary Points

Non-nationals are often on the periphery of effective protection. In part, their vulnerability stems from the fact of state sovereignty, from the particular role ascribed to states themselves as guardians or protectors of human rights, and from a tendency to confine certain rights within a context of community or citizenship. Non-nationals, simply because of their lack of citizenship, are perceived as standing outside the community, and on that basis may be denied the substantive and procedural entitlements normally accorded to members.

Most provisions of most human rights instruments, and most states in most of their practices, draw no distinction between nationals and non-nationals – the right to life, for example, or the right to integrity of the person and to human dignity, are guaranteed to everyone without distinction. Recent international trends, however, have called into question the principle of non-discrimination as it applies to certain other human rights and procedural guarantees, and as it affects entry into or membership of the body politic.

Citizenship and the Nation-State

It is interesting how everyone seems to come back to Locke. The 17th-century idea of civil society, particularly his, was founded upon obedience to a common law and judicature deriving from tacit consent.[1] But merely submitting to the laws and enjoying the privileges and protection of another government did not make foreigners into subjects or members of the commonwealth; something more was required, 'actually entering into it by positive engagement and express promise and compact'.[2] Whatever the implications for *naturalization*, however, the foreigner was not to be denied that 'local protection and homage due to and from all' who, not being at war, come within the territory and jurisdiction of the government.[3]

The true end of government – dispensing justice and deciding rights by promulgated laws rather than absolute, arbitrary

---

[1] Locke, *The Two Treatises of Government* (1690); *Of Civil Government*, etc., ss. 87, 106.
[2] *Ibidem*, ss. 119, 122.
[3] *Ibidem*, ss. 122.

power – together with the promotion of the good of the people[4], would seem to suggest the relative *un*importance of the narrow badge of citizenship when it comes to fundamentals, and that in turn may carry implications for the criteria of membership.

A recent commentator argues that only those committed to and dependent on a social collective have rights against that group[5], but this leaves begging essential, perhaps unanswerable, questions about commitment and dependency; moreover, the adversarial approach to rights clumsily obscures the complexity of relations existing between a community and its parts, whatever their degree of 'membership'.

The national/non-national distinction, nonetheless, is alive and well, at least in certain political contexts. In *Cabell* v. *Chabez-Salido*, for example, the United States Supreme Court observed:

> The exclusion of aliens from basic governmental processes is not a deficiency in the democratic system but a necessary consequence of the community's process of self-definition. Self-government, whether direct or through representatives, begins by defining the scope of the community of the governed and thus of the governors as well. Aliens are by definition those outside of this community.[6]

State practice commonly excludes non-nationals from a narrow class of political rights, but by no means is this a necessary consequence of community self-definition. Some countries already accord the right to vote in all or certain elections to resident non-nationals, and others are moving in that direction. On any interpretation, the notion of community is hardly coterminous with the formal category of citizenship, and if definition is to ground the denial of rights, competing interests will also be ignored or overridden.

Countries with settled minority or migrant populations (and settlement is a fact that repeated statements of national exclusiveness will not change) must address the consequences. These include not only the socio-economic and cultural situation, but also minorities' claims, as contributing members of the community, to a say and a share in the conditions of admission.

The issue of participation, or membership, and exclusion is

---

[4]*Ibidem*, ss. 132, 136, 137, 142.
[5]Benditt, T. M., *Rights*, Totowa NJ 1982.
[6]Vol. 454 US Supreme Court (1982) pp. 432, 439–40.

not so hard and fast as lawyers might like to believe. Rather, the relationship is relative, because membership is not merely a legal tag, but also a factual condition. The community's own decisions on membership remain, but are conditioned by facts, linkages and obligations; this in turn raises the diverting question or whether the mere fact of birth within the territory of a state should be considered a sufficient condition for citizenship, as, for example, in the United States, or whether additional evidence of commitment should be required.

Citizenship and International Law

A valuable and surprisingly useful approach to citizenship from the perspective of international law emerges in the jurisprudence of the World Court. From having earlier confirmed the principle that such issues are, in principle, 'within the reserved domain of domestic jurisdiction'[7], the International Court of Justice emphasized in the Nottebohm Case in 1955 that if nationality rules are to be entitled to recognition, they must accord with the individual's genuine connection with the state. 'Nationality', said the Court, 'is a legal bond having as its basis a social fact of attachment, a genuine connection of existence, interests and sentiments, together with the existence of reciprocal rights and duties'.

International law also recognizes that nationality falls within the broad field of human rights, where everyone's right to a nationality is proclaimed even if nothing specific is said about *which* nationality.

Citizenship, or nationality (the terms are frequently used interchangeably in practice), serves a *functional* role in international law, attributing persons to particular territorial units for various legal purposes and identifying certain normative implications for the responsibility of states, both in relation to other states and in relation to people.

New States, New Citizenship

The challenge for new states, as Gabor Nagy explains, is to see whether people can be transformed from *political subjects* to

7*Nationality Decrees Case*, P.C.I.J. (1923), Ser. B., No. 4, p. 23.

conscious citizens. The new Hungarian citizenship law aims to play a part in this process. Voting rights will be granted to non-citizen permanent residents, thus reflecting the realities of factual membership in a way hitherto rejected by the Federal Republic of Germany, with regrettable consequences. The power to deprive a person of citizenship is eliminated, but naturalization is made harder: citizenship will be transmitted by descent, but not necessarily by reason of birth within the territory of the state; and preferential access to citizenship will be accorded to those of Hungarian 'nationality', considered in the ethnic or cultural sense.

The last-mentioned provision has been criticized as providing a too-easy path to the right to vote, but this sort of preferential treatment is common in the practice of many other states. So far as citizenship equates with the enjoyment of political and social rights, however, there may be a case for achieving a better balance between recognizing historic ties and preserving more than just a formal commitment to the body politic; that is, in linking the right to vote, for example, to the 'social fact of attachment' evident in residence and payment of taxes.

For similar reasons, I am sceptical that recent developments with respect to a 'European citizenship' are anything more than sloganeering, notwithstanding the fact that the citizens of member states of the European Community do enjoy certain common legal, economic and other rights. It seems doubtful whether Community citizenship can be created other than as a pure, and therefore sterile, exercise of legal power. On the contrary, the social 'distance' between individuals and the institutions of Europe is likely to enhance citizenship at the local or peripheral level, no matter what the degree of economic or even political integration. This progress will be encouraged in turn by the essentially non-democratic and non-participatory nature of decision-making at the level of European institutions.

The international dimension to each state's decisions on membership is likely to acquire greater importance as nations, territories and boundaries are opened to review. With renewed attention now being given to sovereignty as a functional attribute in the community of states, one of the most intriguing challenges for international law will be to reconcile claims for national identity on the one hand with the conditions of membership and the criteria of responsibility on the other.

DISCUSSION 4

The discussion of Gabor Nagy's paper and Guy Goodwin-Gill's commentary focussed on the international law implications of citizenship, and on the principles of *ius sanguinis* and *ius soli* in Hungary's new citizenship law.

Daniel Warner started the discussion by invoking the Nottebohm case mentioned in Guy Goodwin-Gill's commentary; he asked for clarification of the criteria used by the International Court of Justice in this instance. Guy Goodwin-Gill explained that the case involved a German citizen who had established himself in Guatemala and had lived and worked there for approximately twenty-five years when World War II broke out. Late in the war, Guatemala joined the Allies and declared war on Germany; at this time, it also expropriated Mr Nottebohm's property and expelled him from the country. Mr Nottebohm had, however, taken precautions against such an event, and had previously gone to Liechtenstein to acquire citizenship of that country. The requirements for acquiring Liechtenstein citizenship were fairly simple: he had to go there, swear an oath of allegiance to the prince and pay a sum of money, whereupon he picked up his passport and returned to Guatemala. The case came before the International Court of Justice when Liechtenstein challenged Nottebohm's expulsion and the expropriation of his property on the grounds that, at the time, he was a Liechtenstein and not a German citizen, and could not be considered an enemy alien. The Court ruled that Nottebohm's Liechtenstein citizenship could not be recognized because of the absence of any social factor of attachment to that country. According to Goodwin-Gill, the further implication of the Court's judgement was that Mr. Nottebohm's effective citizenship was of Guatemala, since that was where his life and work had been for a considerable time, rendering his links strongest with the country that was expelling and expropriating him. Unfortunately, Goodwin-Gill concluded, the Court's ruling did not solve the problem, nor did it give Mr. Nottebohm any satisfaction.

André Liebich added that it was his understanding that the Court did not rule that Nottebohm's Liechtenstein citizenship was ineffective or that it did not exist, but that he could not use it against the state to which he really belonged – Guatemala. In this sense, Liebich asked, did this mean that Nottebohm could have used his Liechtenstein citizenship in a case involving a third country to which he had no links? Guy Goodwin-Gill replied that it is not clear whether Nottebohm could have used it *vis-à-vis* other states; the same problem of his links to Liechtenstein would have come up in any case. Kenneth Minogue noted that many authors writing on the case argued that Nottebohm was no longer German since his links were so obviously to Guatemala, and Krzysztof Jasiewicz wondered whether Nottebohm had ever requested Guatemalan citizenship. Guy Goodwin-Gill explained that Nottebohm had never asked for Guatemalan citizenship, but that if he had been a Guatemalan citizen, he would not have been able to plead his case before the International Court of Justice: he would have had to find another state to protect his rights in Guatemala. Nottebohm, Goodwin-Gill added, was like many resident foreigners – they prefer to maintain links with their own states in case anything goes wrong. If the Guatemalans had tried to expropriate his property in times of peace, he could have appealed to Germany. Daniel Warner followed up on this example by asking how one would deal with the question of individuals of Hungarian ancestry living in other countries: is the Hungarian state in any way responsible for these people, and what kind of attachment would follow that kind of reasoning? Guy Goodwin-Gill replied that that kind of reasoning would not apply to Hungarians in the United States, for example, since the United States, like Guatemala in the Nottebohm case, could resist a Hungarian claim on the basis that there is no effective attachment of American citizens of Hungarian descent to Hungary. Goodwin-Gill stated that this did not mean that their newly acquired Hungarian citizenship or their legal links to Hungary were invalid, but that from an international law perspective, Hungary's right *vis-à-vis* its citizens in the United States had a defined limit.

Daniel Warner's third question concerned the issue of protection: he cited the case of the American intervention in Mexico to kidnap a Mexican suspect and bring him to justice in the United States, on the basis that they were acting to protect US citizens on foreign soil. Warner wanted to know how the United States could justify its action. Guy Goodwin-Gill did not see any possible justification for the American intervention: he replied that the United States did not seriously try to justify it either, knowing that the action was illegal under international law. David Campbell interjected that the U.S. Supreme Court had ruled that the action was valid, while Guy Goodwin-Gill pointed out that the Supreme Court was not the proper institution to decide the question. He stated that the case involved the intervention of American agents, or individuals funded by them, on the territory of a foreign sovereign state, which is, *par excellence*, a breach of international law. Martin Palous gave another example of the problems that can be caused between states by unresolved dual citizenship issues. He told of the current debate between the Czech Republic and Liechtenstein concerning the considerable former property of the Liechtenstein princely family, which had once lived in Czecho-Slovakia, registered as Czecho-Slovak citizens. In the 1937 census, Palous said, the Liechtensteins declared themselves to be German, and when Czecho-Slovakia was dismembered in 1938–39 they received German citizenship. After the war, they were thus subject to President Benes' decree expropriating the property of all Germans in Czecho-Slovakia. Liechtenstein argued that these people were not Germans but Liechtensteiners. Palous explained that this is an ongoing problem between the two countries, and apparently Liechtenstein has threatened first Czecho-Slovakia and now the Czech Republic with blocking its membership in the Council of Europe and other European institutions if the Czech authorities do not recognize that they unjustly expropriated the property of the Liechtenstein family.

André Liebich raised the question of *ius sanguinis* and *ius soli* as the principles underlying citizenship laws. He noted that Switzerland uses the principle of *ius sanguinis* indefinitely through the male line: this means that any number of foreigners who rediscover their 'Helvetism' after decades, if not centuries, can come back to the 'homeland' and claim Swiss citizenship. Gabor Nagy stated that *ius soli* is a secondary principle in Hungarian law, used only for persons who are stateless. While stateless persons born in Hungary are automatically eligible for Hungarian citizenship, Nagy continued, those whose ancestors belonged to another state were encouraged to get the other country's citizenship rather than Hungarian. Nagy thus illustrated how Hungarian law automatically used the *ius sanguinis* principle, in contrast to, for example, the United States. He accounted for this by stressing the countries' difference in size and population density. The only reason for the Hungarian government to encourage attribution of citizenship to Hungarians living abroad, Nagy argued, is to gain political support. Guy Goodwin-Gill compared the trend in Hungary with the new British citizenship law, which has gone back a step from the principle of *ius soli*. Gabor Nagy pointed out that the unlimited application of *ius sanguinis* represented an interesting problem for the authorities: he referred to the pre–1918 period in which the people of most of the nations under the Austro-Hungarian empire had Hungarian citizenship; this allows many Slovaks, Romanians, Croats and Serbs today to claim Hungarian citizenship on the grounds that their ancestors were Hungarian citizens. On the other hand, there are some ethnic minorities, like the Gypsies, whose mother tongue is Hungarian and who consider themselves Hungarians, but who live in Romania. The exclusionary movements in Hungary are not in favour of granting even their own Hungarian Gypsies citizenship. Nagy concluded by stating that the three-year requirement was in fact a compromise, giving in to these pressures; the original draft had been in favour of automatically 're-naturalizing' all those people who had been Hungarian citizens but somehow lost this citizenship over time.

J.D.

AFTER CZECHO-SLOVAKIA

QUESTIONS OF CZECH CITIZENSHIP

Martin Palous

Introduction

When we think about the concept of citizenship, which is certainly a fundamental political category, we immediately discover the following ambiguity. According to the standard definition, citizenship is a legally codified relationship between individual and state, a relationship that determines the rights and duties of individuals with respect to the state. However, it is obvious at the same time that such a definition is far from sufficient, for it omits what is perhaps the most important aspect of the problem of citizenship, which can be reduced neither to a legal formula nor to the factual description of its implementation under given historical and political circumstances.

Citizenship, as Daniel Warner points out in his paper, has besides its external or 'objective' aspect, also its inner, 'subjective' dimension. It presupposes that there are individuals in human society who are open to the idea that there are persons who comprehend and understand what it means to be a citizen. Citizenship is not a value-free (*wertfrei*) social fact, but a dynamic element of political reality. It is what literally *makes* the difference between the free life of a citizen and other life possibilities of human beings (between *euzen*, to live well, and *zen*, to live in the Aristotelian sense.[1]) As the constitutive element of civic identity, as an awareness of the difference between the various ways in which human life can be lived, citizenship depends above all on certain states of the human mind and presupposes the willingness of people to become citizens. It is not only that

---

[1]Aristotle, *Politics*, 1252b30: 'the state . . . originating in the bare needs of life, and continuing in existence for the sake of a good life'.

which formally guarantees citizens their status, nor is it part and parcel of 'objective' political reality. In addition, citizenship is what motivates free human beings, what makes their lives 'good', and what inspires them to act in the way in which the founding fathers of the American Republic acted, giving the constitution to the people of the United States in order to promote not only 'the general welfare', but also to 'secure the blessings of liberty to ourselves and our posterity'.

The Legal Implications of the Split of Czecho-Slovakia

There were two major political events which had a decisive impact on the present state of Czech citizenship: the Velvet Revolution (November 1989), which swept away the communist regime, and the split of the common Czecho-Slovak state at the end of 1992. The relation between these two events – the (at least at first sight) strange and paradoxical fact that, due to the collapse of communism, Czecho-Slovakia disappeared from the political map of Europe on 1 January 1993, after more than seventy-four years of existence – will be dealt with in the second part of this paper. This part will concentrate on the legal dimensions of this unexpected development and some of its legal implications.

On 25 November 1992, the Czecho-Slovak legislators who were elected in free and fair elections in June 1992 passed the Act on the Dissolution of the Czech and Slovak Federal Republic. The Federal Assembly of Czecho-Slovakia resolved:

– that on 1 January 1993, the Czech and Slovak Federal Republic would cease to exist and two successor states, the Czech Republic and the Slovak Republic, would replace it;
– that federal legislation would be invalid as of this date and the institutions of the Czech and Slovak Republics would become the sovereign sources of law on their territories;
– that on 1 January 1993 all federal organs, authorities and other institutions financed from the federal budget (such as army, police, etc.) would be dissolved, and all federal powers explicitly stated by the law or implied in the framework of the existing constitutional order would be transferred to the newly founded republics;

– that in order to have all the necessary legal instruments for cooperation between the Czech Republic and the Slovak Republic ready immediately after the split, the Czech and the Slovak governments would be immediately authorized to prepare and ratify mutual international treaties, which would come into force after 1 January 1993.[2]

When the Federal Assembly finally took the decision to terminate the existence of the state they represented there appeared to be no other solution to the Czecho-Slovak problem. Things simply had gone too far and the process of the country's disintegration seemed irreversible.

The referendum, which was originally seen as the only legal mechanism for deciding between the continuation or dissolution of the common state, could not take place because of the absence of the necessary legislation and because of the lack of political will of the parties controlling parliament to enact a constitutional amendment to make the referendum possible.

An independent Slovak constitution which declared its superiority over the federal legal order had already been passed by the Slovak National Council on 1 September 1992. The Czech National Council was working intensively on a similar document for the Czech Republic.[3]

The two major political parties in the Czech and Slovak Republics, the Civic Democratic Party (ODS) and the Movement for a Democratic Slovakia (HZDS), which won the June elections, immediately concluded a mutual agreement to cooperate decisively in dismembering the 'dysfunctional' federation, and implemented their plan step by step. When Václav Klaus and Vladimír Meciar, the new prime ministers, signed the 'Bratislava Declaration' on 23 July 1992[4] in their capacities as party leaders, one could have doubted whether the Czecho-Slovak Federation

---

[2]The Constitutional Act of the Federal Assembly of CSFR 542/92 of 25 November 1992.

[3]The Czech Constitution was passed on 16 December 1992 after tough and difficult discussions.

[4]According to the agreement signed by Václav Klaus and Vladimir Meciar, ODS (the Civic Democratic Party) and HZDS (the Movement for a Democratic Slovakia) – the winners in the parliamentary elections in June 1992 – would propose that the Federal Assembly should enact 'A law on the possible ways of CSFR's termination and on the settlement of questions of property and other relationships.'

was really in such a bad 'dysfunctional' condition; by the end of November 1992 there could be no doubt.

Strangely, the legal solution to the problem of Czecho-Slovak relations appeared to be the most dynamic issue on the political agenda of post-communist Czecho-Slovakia. This had two aspects which could not be separated, but which must be very clearly and precisely distinguished from one another. The split of Czecho-Slovakia and the creation of two independent states means a transformation of the existing constitutional order and, at the same time, a transformation in the relationship of the parties under international law.

From the point of view of international law, Czecho-Slovakia was divided when both partners agreed to dissolve the federation. Both the Czech Republic and the Slovak Republic were created as new states. Succession, however, meaning disconti-nuity of a state as a subject of international law, implies at the same time continuity in its international obligations. Both the Czech and Slovak Republics declared on the first day of their existence (1 January 1993) that they assumed all the obligations of the Czecho-Slovak Republic. This declaration is seen by the international community as an important condition for the inter-national recognition of successor states and their integration into the system of international relations. The fact that both the Czech and the Slovak Republics were quickly and easily recog-nized internationally, and that they entered into practically all the important relationships which had been created and culti-vated by the Czechoslovak state, is one of the key arguments in favour of those who organized the split of the common state. The positive importance of this fact is inestimable.

Nevertheless, for the heirs of Czecho-Slovakia the question of the continuity or discontinuity of the state and the international implications of the dismembering of the Czecho-Slovak Feder-ation represent very sensitive issues. In the present political context, any attempt to problematize the already accepted legal interpretation of the history of Czecho-Slovakia could have far-reaching consequences for the successor states, seriously damag-ing their specific national interests and complicating their mutual relations. This problem can be illustrated by the polemics around the ratification of the Czecho-Slovak-German Treaty in spring 1992. The tendency of the Slovak leaders at that time to cast doubt on the fundamental dogma of Czecho-Slovak statehood – that is, the uninterrupted continuity of Czecho-Slovakia during World War II and the alleged nullity *ab initio* of the Munich Agreement – by raising the question of whether the Slovak state came into existence in 1939 as a subject of international law was rejected vigorously by the Czech side because it touched upon the highly sensitive issue of Czech-German relations.

The question of the continuity or discontinuity of the state also played a very important role in the transformation of the constitutional order.[5] Here it might be useful to recapitulate the legal interpretation of the origin of the independent Czecho-Slovak state in 1918, keeping in mind the fact that uninterrupted existence was seen as the cornerstone of modern Czecho-Slovak statehood. The proclamation of the independence of Czecho-Slovakia on 28 October 1918 was interpreted by leading Czecho-Slovak legal experts as a 'legal revolution' against the Austro-Hungarian monarchy. Legal revolution meant legal discontinuity, the end of the existing legal order and the emergence of a new one. It had a very important consequence: the principle *lex posterior derogat priori*, the new law abrogates the old one, does not apply in this situation and there are no old laws in force after a new legal order has been born. The preservation of legal continuity (which is a necessary condition for stability during an interim period) requires the enactment of the reception norm explicitly enumerating the laws, legal provisions and regulations of the former regime which are valid henceforth. In the case of Czecho-Slovakia, the reception norm was Act 11/ 1918 (the constitution was enacted only in 1920); and this act was, from the legal point of view, the proper centre and origin of the new legal order.

The reception norm also created Czecho-Slovak citizenship: the existing legislation (par. 2 of the Austrian Law of December 1863 and par. 5 of Hungarian Law number XXII of 1886) was declared as remaining valid. All individuals 'who had by the 28th of October, 1918, the right of residence in a municipality in the territory where the Czecho-Slovak state exerts its sovereign power' were considered Czecho-Slovak citizens. The emergence of this new legal order was confirmed and internationally legali-

---

[5]A detailed analysis of the problem can be found in a paper by Václav Pavlícek, 'O kontinuite a diskontinuite' ('On Continuity and Discontinuity'), *Pravni praxe* (1993).

zed at the Paris Peace Conference (1919–1920) as part of a whole package of treaties that said that 'state citizens of Germany, Austria and Hungary should be incorporated within the seceding states'. Taking into consideration that international treaties can only bind contracting parties, i.e., sovereign states in mutual relations, and cannot be regarded as a legal source of individual rights of their citizens, the agreed principles and regulations of these international treaties were later incorporated into the Czecho-Slovak legal order by a special Constitutional Act (236 of 9 April 1920) which then served as the basis for the general regulations of Czecho-Slovak citizenship, defining who was a Czecho-Slovak citizen and how someone could gain or lose citizenship.

The central dogma of Czecho-Slovak domestic and international policy became the assumption of legal continuity, the demand that all subsequent legal acts which together would create the whole corpus of Czecho-Slovak law must be tied to the basic source of law and that they would have to be connected with what is considered to be the real beginning of modern Czecho-Slovak statehood, and that any discontinuity was to be prevented at any price. And it was this dogma, rather than chauvinism of any kind, or Czech imperialism, or Pragocentrism, that caused the idea of the Czecho-Slovak state to fail in the end.

Nothing can better demonstrate how powerful was the conviction that state continuity had to be kept at any price than the peculiar fact that even the communists interpreted their seizure of power after World War II (in which they really succeeded in turning the order of human affairs upside down, and for which they had their revolutionary ideological explanation) as if it complied with the existing legal order. When the government crisis was being resolved in February 1948, it proceeded, according to the official communist interpretation, 'in compliance with valid constitutional provisions . . . combined with distinctively revolutionary means'.[6] Even the proclamations of 'Action Committees', the typical revolutionary organs, were later legalized: what they did was declared to be 'in compliance with the law, and that also in the cases in which they otherwise

---

[6]Quoted from the Commentary on the Constitution of CSFR [Vyklad Ustavy CSFR], Praha 1987.

were at variance with appropriate provisions and regulations'.[7] Constitutional changes during the communist regime – the Constitution of 9 May 1948, the so-called 'Socialist Constitution' of July 1960, and finally the Constitutional Act of October 1968, which transformed the unitarian Czecho-Slovak state into a Federation – never indicated that the otherwise revolutionary communist regime could ever conduct a 'legal revolution' in the sense of the discontinuity of law. The opposite was true: the May Constitution of 1948 explicitly declared its continuity with the first Czecho-Slovak constitution of 1920. In spite of the fact that the communists destroyed the concept of the state which Masaryk and his successor Benes had developed, a state built on the ideals of humanism and on the principles of the rule of law and political democracy, and in spite of the fact that they transformed the whole Czecho-Slovak political system 'in the likeness' of their Marxist-Leninist ideology, the communists stuck to the concept of legal continuity and passed off their revolutionary *opus magnum* as identical to the 'bourgeois', 'pre-Munich' republic.

The unconditional protection of the continuity of the state as it was founded and the rejection of any step which could problematize this foundation was also at the heart of so-called Czechoslovakism. This concept of one Czechoslovak nation composed of two ethnic branches, Czech and Slovak, from the very beginning problematized and burdened Czecho-Slovak relations. Because, in many respects, the Czech side was much stronger than the Slovak side (we will examine this problem in the next section), the relation between them was asymmetrical. From this it followed that the Czechs were always much more committed to the reason of the common state (they considered themselves as both Czechs and Czechoslovaks) than Slovaks (who regarded themselves exclusively as Slovaks and whose political identity had only very loose ties with Czecho-Slovak statehood). This asymmetry continued to characterize the Czecho-Slovak political system until the end of its existence, despite the fact that the Constitutional Act of 1968 transformed the unitarian state into a federation of national republics and gave Czecho-Slovak citizens a new legal identity: having either

----

[7] *Ibidem.*

Czech or Slovak citizenship according to their birthplace, in addition to original Czecho-Slovak citizenship.[8]

No political event was powerful enough to eliminate this asymmetry, except, perhaps, the end of communism. On 1 January 1993, three years after the Velvet Revolution, Czechs and Slovaks finally got rid of the hated totalitarian regime, and seventy-four years after they spontaneously rejoiced over the first 'legal revolution' in this century, which brought them together, the second 'legal revolution' came and this time split them apart. The return from the Babylonian captivity of totalitarianism initiated a political process which discontinued the long-lasting legal continuity. Czechs and Slovaks, whose marriage in 1918 turned out to be rather difficult and not particularly happy, are legally divorced now and both are facing an entirely new, unknown and unpredictable situation.

Czecho-Slovak citizenship ceased to exist, and both republics have had to enact their own necessary legislation. Czech citizenship is automatically given to 'those physical persons, which by December 31, 1992, were state citizens of the Czech Republic and at the same time of the Czech and Slovak Federal Republic'.[9] The Czech residents who are Slovaks by birthplace (i.e. who were state citizens of the Slovak Republic and the Czech and Slovak Federal Republic) must now apply for Czech citizenship if they wish to acquire it. Applicants have to fulfill certain conditions: they have to prove two years registered residency and five years with no criminal record. The implications of this decision for the future of Czech-Slovak relations, and its special impact on certain social groups which could become stateless after 31 December 1993, will be examined at the end of this study.

Problems of Czecho-Slovak Citizenship in a Historical Perspective

The communist regime which seized power in February 1948 succeeded in one important respect: it destroyed the public space in this country in such a way that the sheer concept of 'citizen' seemed to lose meaning for the average member of Czecho-Slovak society. This success, however, was not immedi-

[8]The Constitutional Act on the Czecho-Slovak Federation, n. 143/1968.
[9]The Citizenship Law (Law 40/1992 of the Czech National Council), par. 1.

ate. In the first period, Czecho-Slovak civil society was still relatively resistant and only slowly adapted itself to the enforced principles of socialist life and socialist morality. The real crisis of citizenship emerged only in the second period. It was normalization, i.e., the restoration of order after the unsuccessful 1968 'Prague Spring' attempt to open a closed society, which had a devastating effect on the state of the Czech and Slovak political mind. The 'origins of totalitarianism' in Czecho-Slovakia, the revolutionary Stalinist 1950s, were certainly more cruel and more tragic from the point of view of the victims of that criminal regime, but the 1970s and 1980s seemed to be a period in which the social experiment of Marxism-Lenninism, Central European style, reached its height. To quote Václav Havel:

> The past twenty years in Czechoslovakia can almost serve as a textbook illustration of how an advanced or late totalitarian system works. Revolutionary ethos and terror have been replaced by dull inertia, pretext-ridden caution, bureaucratic anonymity, and mindless, stereotypical behaviour, all of which aim exclusively at becoming more and more what they already are. The songs of zealots and the cries of the tortured are no longer heard; lawlessness had put on kid gloves and moved from the torture chambers into the upholstered offices of faceless bureaucrats.[10]

> The war and the killing assume a different form: they have been shifted from the daylight of observable public events, to the twilight of unobservable inner destruction. It would seem that the absolute, 'classical' death of which one reads in stories (and which for all the terrors it holds is still mysteriously able to impart meaning to human life) has been replaced here by another kind of death: the slow, secretive, bloodless, never-quite-absolute, yet horrifying ever-present death of non-action, non-story, non-life, and non-time; the collective deadening, or more precisely, anaesthetizing, process of social and historical nihilization. This nihilization annuls death as such, and thus annuls life as such: the life of an individual becomes the dull and uniform functioning of a component in a large machine, and

[10]Havel, V., *Open Letters, Selected Prose*, Wilson, P. (ed), London-New York 1991, p. 331.

his death is merely something that puts him out of commission.[11]

Havel points to what is the most characteristic feature of a totalitarian regime, that which makes it different from all other kinds of tyranny. The Marxist-Leninist ideological perception of political reality materialized at the end, in the Central European environment, in a more absurd than openly demoniacal world of 'real socialism', a world not so much described by George Orwell as by Jaroslav Hasek and Franz Kafka. The society got used to reality, learned how to live with the 'false consciousness' of ideology, how to use its distorted language, and how to get along without trouble and complications. The paradigmatic hero of 'stories of totalitarianism' became the not very heroic 'good soldier Svejk' or the alienated and lonely individual, Josef K.

The Velvet Revolution in November 1989 meant a great awakening. Whatever the real cause of the collapse of communism was, and whoever organized the course of events from behind the scenes, the situation as ordinary people experienced it was simple: they went to the streets and took part in a festival of freedom which unexpectedly burst out during an unforgettable week of public rallies, demonstrations, street discussions and strikes; they rediscovered and restored their civic dignity. The good soldier Svejk, Josef K., numerous strange heroes who populated the landscape of late totalitarianism, became citizens again. A society which was kept closed for more than forty years finally opened up again.

The fall of communism has brought long-desired freedom into Eastern and Central Europe. It has enabled all the nations which were forced to live behind the 'Iron Curtain' to start designing and immediately implementing their fundamental goal of 'rejoining Europe'. They want to do away with all the consequences of decades-long totalitarian government, to profoundly transform their political and economic systems, to reintegrate themselves into all the Western structures, and to make themselves part of its freedom and prosperity.

However, liberation from Babylonian captivity has turned out to be more complicated than it seemed at the beginning: the end of the Cold War era has initiated a very dynamic, barely controllable and, in many ways, very risky and dangerous pro-

---

[11]*Ibidem*, pp. 329–30.

cess. It has meant not only the revitalization of the ideals of open civic society in East Central Europe, but also the re-emergence of very complicated ethnic and political relationships which have been developing for centuries. With their program of 'rejoining Europe', the post-communist nations returned to their history. After a long period when they were living enclosed in the strange, ahistoric timelessness of a well-stabilized late totalitarian regime, they have found themselves suddenly in the midst of a fast stream carrying the boats of their political communities into an unknown and hardly predictable future.

The 'return to history' has also characterized the post-communist development of Czecho-Slovakia and has decisively influenced the genesis of Czech and Slovak post-totalitarian civic identity. Despite the importance of future-oriented goals and objectives connected with the 'rejoining of Europe', the most important part of the post-totalitarian political problem in Czecho-Slovakia has become the question of the still-to-be-realized Czech-Slovak settlement, the question of Czecho-Slovak statehood and the question of the constitutional and legal framework of Czecho-Slovak relations.

Let us look briefly at recent Czech and Slovak political history. The Czecho-Slovak Republic came into existence at the end of World War I amidst the ruins of the Austro-Hungarian monarchy. On 28 October 1918 in Prague, and on 30 October 1918 in Martin, Czech and Slovak political leaders declared the independence of the Czech lands and Slovakia from the governments in Vienna and Budapest, and proclaimed the political will of both nations to jointly found a new democratic state: Czecho-Slovakia. The Paris Peace Conference, which started at the beginning of 1919 with the objective of creating a new international order in Europe, confirmed what had happened, recognized that a sovereign, independent Czecho-Slovak state had been created, and demarcated its borders.

The foundation of a common state represented the fulfillment of long-standing political aspirations both for Czechs and Slovaks. This shared desire, however, was motivated and understood in one way on the Czech side and in another way on the Slovak side. The joint political will masked two different, even potentially conflicting, national interests.

While Czechs have for centuries shared a historical space with Germans, and this mutual history has been a dominant theme of Czech history, Slovaks lived in the territory of the Hungarian Empire, and their principal partners and eventual adversaries in the political process throughout history were Hungarians.

While 'The Lands of the Czech Crown' belonged to the most developed industrial regions of Austria-Hungary, Slovakia was rural and industrially much less developed. In its spirit and character, Czech culture reflected the mentality of the 19th-century urban middle class. Slovak cultural identity was formed by the fact that the decisive majority of the Slovak population was peasantry. (The ruling class and the aristocracy in Slovakia were Hungarian and the urban population predominantly German.)

In contrast to Czech secularism, Slovak national culture was religious and deeply devoted to traditional, conservative values. At the same time, the Slovak nation was relatively young in comparison with Czech history. There was nothing in the memory of the emerging Slovak political mind comparable to the 'glorious past' of the Czech kingdom or the 'Hussite Revolution'. The similar phenomenon of Czech national patriotism which preceded, in Bohemia, the language-oriented national revival in the 19th century, was a practically unknown phenomenon in Slovakia. Before the modern, romantic 'Herderian' concept of nation gained ground here as a reaction to the centralizing efforts of enlightened absolutist rulers who had started to 'Hungarize' the Slavonic population, there was no recognizable Slovak political programme opposing the idea of the Hungarian state and formulating specific Slovak demands.

With the 1867 Austro-Hungarian Settlement, which left the political demands of the Slavonic nations of the Empire unsatisfied, the standing of the Czech lands (which were strong in both economic and cultural terms) did not change greatly. In contrast, the situation in Slovakia dramatically deteriorated as a consequence of the political invigoration of Hungary. The Budapest government, acting out of a fear of 'Pan-Slavism', intensified 'Hungarization' to such an extent that, at the beginning of the 20th century, the fundamental political question in Slovakia did not concern the decentralization of the government and political emancipation, as in Bohemia, but the cultural survival and preservation of the Slovak nation.

From the beginning, the national interests of Czechs and Slovaks, rooted in their historical experience and their basic cultural patterns, differed substantively. From these differences it followed that their attitudes towards the Czecho-Slovak Republic were very different. Czechs felt that they finally had their own state, a state which embodied their long-lasting aspirations and gave them a dignified standing among other nations of the 'New Europe'. 'Czechoslovakism,' the concept of the one 'Czechoslovak' nation composed of ethnic branches, Czech and Slovak, was seen by Czechs as 'part and parcel' of their modern political foundation. This had, of course, a pragmatic dimension (it strengthened the position of the Czech and Slovak leaders who negotiated post-war international arrangements in Central Europe with victorious Allies at the end of World War I), but in the conception of the founding father of Czecho-Slovak statehood, T. G. Masaryk,[12] it was much more than an artificial *ad hoc* creation justified only by its practicality.

For the Czechs, 'Czechoslovakism' was the way in which to resolve the political problem of the Slavonic nations of the dismembered Habsburg Empire in the spirit of the emerging 'New World Order'. It was also a way in which to build a high purpose on the foundations of the new state. In Masaryk's vision, the idea of the Czecho-Slovak state meant the birth of a political nation and the creation of a new political identity through a free decision of Czechs and Slovaks to live together. It presupposed a shared will to commit themselves to the same ideals and values and to enter and inhabit the common space of national political culture.

While from the Czech perspective, Czecho-Slovak statehood was perceived as a definitive solution of the 'Czech question', for Slovaks the existing state of affairs had only a transitory character and was aimed at offering shelter to the still very weak and vulnerable shoot of their modern political identity and independent existence in the family of European nations. From the very beginning of the common state, the key elements of the Slovak political programme were the preservation of Slovak cultural identity and autonomy. Permanent appeals to the May 1918 'Pittsburgh Agreement' between Czechs and Slovaks in exile and accusations that Czechs did not want to keep to the negotiated agreement were standard arguments of the Slovaks in ongoing Czecho-Slovak disputes and negotiations.

[12]Masaryk, T. G., *The Making of a State: Memories and Observations, 1914–1918*, trans. by Henry Wickham Steed, London 1927.

The Czechs built their positions on the central dogma of legal continuity, and the Slovaks called repeatedly for constitutional change. Their basic goal and ambition was to 'repair' the original foundation of the state and introduce an element of discontinuity into its constitution. No matter how legitimate and justified their endeavour to see through the process of political maturation, it is a bitter irony of history that their 'Parish Republic', the long-desired 'independent' Slovak state, found its place in Europe at the end of the 1930s as an ally of a political power which neglected all the principles of European civilization, exterminated whole nations and waged a horrible war against the whole of civilized humanity.

The political catastrophe of the Czecho-Slovak state in 1938–39 meant that both nations again confronted a fundamental task: to regain and defend their freedom and independence in the shaky space of Central Europe; and to formulate and carry out policies which would enable them to enforce their fundamental objectives and their 'national interests', whether particular and oriented to specific needs or more general and universal. Historical conditions caused Czechs and Slovaks to wait fifty long years before this new opportunity finally came. Eduard Benes (who was, after Masaryk, the second president of Czecho-Slovakia) failed in his three-year attempt after World War II to restore the independence of the country and renew its links to the political order and traditions of the 'First Republic'. The six dark years of Nazi occupation were replaced in February 1948 by the dark age of communism. For more than forty years (excluding only the few months of sudden liberalization in 1968) Czechs and Slovaks had to live under an oppressive totalitarian regime. A real change – which was also the real chance to start anew in solving the Czech and Slovak questions – came with the collapse of communism in the autumn of 1989.

As I have already remarked, the main question which had to be solved in post-communist Czecho-Slovakia concerned Czech-Slovak relations. There was no other way to rebuild the existing legal order and move towards 'rejoining' Europe than to abandon the asymmetry which characterized all the constitutions of the past (the 1968 federalization did not solve the problem at all: in spite of being federalized, totalitarianism remained what it was by nature – totalitarianism), and to design and approve a new, strictly symmetrical model. In general, two alternatives came into consideration and were discussed between 1990 and 1992. On 31 December 1992, the federation finally fell apart.

On the basic constitutional issue of dividing competence and power between the federation and the two national republics, the original positions of Czechs and Slovaks differed considerably. Czechs subscribed to their traditional conception of Czecho-Slovak statehood based on the legacy of the 'First Republic', and they were unequivocally for the primacy of the federal constitution and the derivative character of the constitutions of the two national republics. They were ready to fully respect the principle of subsidiarity within the new constitutional order, the principle today so fashionable in Europe, stressing chiefly the need for the functionality of any adopted solution. But for reasons of principle, they argued, the new foundations would have to be laid at the federal level. This was because it is only possible to delegate power, be it executive, legislative or judiciary, from the federal level down to the next, by definition derivative or secondary, segments which create the whole of the constitutional system. What was unacceptable was the violation of the fundamental rule of uninterrupted legal continuity, a reform scenario whose implementation would presuppose suspension of the existence of the state, however brief such a suspension might be (in the moment when state sovereignty would pass from the federation to the two national republics).

Slovaks, on the contrary, insisted unequivocally on their right to self-determination and on their view that the only possibility for creating a 'genuine federation' (or a 'more perfect union' between Czechs and Slovaks, to paraphrase the American founding fathers) was to build it anew on two independent pillars, with full state sovereignty for the Czech and Slovak Republics who would then delegate some power, to be negotiated between them, to the federation.

No matter how irreconcilable these two positions appeared, the first proposed solution tried to overcome the gap and to negotiate a compromise. This alternative, which was in the end rejected by the presidium of the Slovak National Council by one vote,[13] consisted of three steps: first, a state treaty to be signed

---

[13]*Budovani Statu* 3 ('The Making of a State', Surveys of Czechoslovak Politics), published by the International Institute for Political Science, Masaryk University, Brno.

by two national councils which would delegate the sovereign power of the two national republics to the Federal Assembly. Second, the Federal Assembly, on the basis of this constitutional initiative (which was fully legitimate according to the existing federal constitution), would draft and approve a new federal constitution. Third, the new constitution would be ratified and accepted by the two national councils and, in addition, possibly confirmed by a referendum organized separately in the Czech Republic and the Slovak Republic. This solution was apparently unsatisfactory from the legal point of view and was criticized by its opponents as a 'cat-and-dog' approach, as an attempt to construe an imaginary creature from incompatible elements. What was unclear – the lack of clarity was not an unintended by-product of incompetent legislative work here, but was intentionally and consciously introduced by the legislators – was the legal interpretation of the proposed procedure: the relation between the international and domestic (or constitutional) dimensions of the problem. Should the state treaty which was to be concluded as the first step have been seen as a treaty between two independent subjects of international law in the sense of the Vienna Convention? Or, rather, should it have been understood as a political declaration of the will of two nations to live together in one state, a declaration having its meaning and interpretation only within an already existing legal order? Where was the ultimate source of state sovereignty, in the National Republics or in the Federation? We can have, after all, either one or two sovereign states. Did not the proposed solution imply a strange state where sovereignty is divided and where a one-state system and a two-state system are to coexist?

The second alternative is the one which was adopted by Klaus and Meciar after the 1992 elections, which was discussed in the previous section. This alternative was posed in the following terms: the first alternative was 'unclear' and therefore should be rejected. The logic of this argument was based on the presupposition that a solution of the Czecho-Slovak puzzle was feasible and could guarantee the necessary stability only if defined through a traditional and transparent scheme. If it was not possible to satisfy the legitimate demands and claims of both national political communities within the legal framework created by one constitution, the only solution was a legal 'divorce' and the transformation of the problem in the sphere of international relations regulated by international law.

We are at the beginning of the new legal history which emerged on 1 January 1993, when the Czecho-Slovak divorce, prepared during the last months of the common state, came into force. So far, things have gone fairly smoothly, but many questions remain to be answered. What impact will the split of Czecho-Slovakia have on the geopolitical situation at the 'heart of Europe'? What course will be taken in Czech-German and Slovak-Hungarian relations? How will Czechs and Slovaks be able to overcome the certain psychological shock of being separated now after decades of being together? What about the Czech minority in Slovakia and the Slovak minority in the Czech Republic, and what about hundreds of thousands of people who live in mixed families and are genuine 'Czechoslovaks'? Is it indeed so certain that the international framework will succeed where the domestic arrangements apparently failed? What about the possibilities of economic and political cooperation in the 'rejoining of Europe'? What will happen if the European situation deteriorates dramatically, if a 'black hole' opens again in the East, leaving Central Europeans trying to escape its influence and provide safeguards for their own nations through a place in the geopolitical space of the West?

We can now see the development of new political and civic identities on both sides of a newly created Central European border. The fact that the split of Czecho-Slovakia has radically dynamized the Czecho-Slovak differentiation is natural and, in essence, positive. What is disturbing, however, is that this process is progressing along ideological lines. The fundamental fact of post-totalitarian development is that the false consciousness which dominated an enslaved totalitarian society has not disappeared with the elimination of communist ideology, but has remained, still ready to be filled with new ideological content. A belief which now surfaces frequently in the Czech political environment and even finds spokepersons on the official Czech political scene is dangerous and should be de-mythologized as soon as possible; it is the belief that the Czech Right, which proved victorious in the June 1992 elections, is correct, and that Czechs, by nature endowed with a Western, i.e., European, mentality should go to the West, while the less European Slovaks, who succumb easily to the trap of state socialism and populist nationalism, are doomed to stay in the East.

Even more problematic and very dangerous flaws appear in the legislation. The most egregious example is the new Czech Citizenship Law. Article 18 of this law states, as I already mentioned, that in order for 'Slovak nationals' to acquire Czech citizenship, it is necessary to prove two years registered residency and five years with no criminal record. The effect of the law is to discriminate against Romany ethnic groups in particular.

In the years following the Nazi Holocaust, many Romanies moved from Slovakia to the Czech lands.[14] According to the 1969 Czecho-Slovak Constitution (which remained in effect as far as citizenship was concerned until the end of 1992), these Romanies continued to have Slovak citizenship and nationality in addition to their Czecho-Slovak citizenship, despite living in the Czech part of what was Czecho-Slovakia. This is also true for their children and grandchildren who were born in the Czech lands, many of whom have never been outside Bohemia and Moravia. This additional 'Slovak citizenship' and 'nationality' was, in practical terms, a meaningless concept before 1993 and therefore it was not anticipated that it could have negative consequences. Because, according to 1991 Czech government figures, 19% of convicted criminals are Romanies and an estimated 50% of adult Romanies have a criminal record (the other question, which is not touched upon here, concerns reasons of Romany criminality and the social significance and implications of this phenomenon), we can estimate that a large part of the Romany population in the Czech Republic simply will not be eligible for citizenship and will become stateless by the end of this year. Very rough estimates indicate that at least 200,000 people will have to go through the lengthy and humiliating bureaucratic process of naturalization in their own homeland, a process in which many of them cannot succeed. In addition, if we take into consideration the rapidly growing climate of hatred against Romanies in Czech society, which seems to be 'ethnically cleansed' more than ever, and the inability of the post-totalitarian society to find and implement an alternative, non-discrimi-

---

[14]The basic information about the situation of Romanies in CSFR can be found in Human Rights Watch, *Struggling for Ethnic Identity: Czechoslovakia's Endangered Gypsies*, New York 1992.

natory and integrationist solution for the Romany problem, we do not need to be overly pessimistic to imagine that we will soon be in an explosive situation with possibly disastrous consequences.

Despite the fact that Czechs and Slovaks (plus national minorities of Hungarians, Romanies, Poles, Germans, Ruthenians and Jews) now live in two different states and that their relations are regulated by international law, they cannot easily separate themselves; their civic societies are perhaps doomed, perhaps blessed, to live next to each other. They simply have to cooperate in all possible ways in the realization of their political goals and, of course, primarily in their economies. But the problems and questions connected with their citizenship and with their new political identities after the disappearance of the common state demonstrate that much more is at stake here. They have no other choice but to struggle together against the paralyzing effects of false consciousness; to cultivate open political cultures through mutual dialogue; to manage mutual conflicts and to settle mutual disputes in order to strengthen the rule of law and recreate civil societies in both states; and to assist each other in all possible ways to fulfill the great task now confronting them: how to dissolve the past and reunite themselves by the end of the millenium, not in a common state (whose era is now finished) but as Europeans, within a European context that will be determined, in part, by them.

COMMENT ON MARTIN PALOUS' PAPER

Piotr Ogrodzinski

Half a year after the dissolution of Czecho-Slovakia and the creation of two independent states, the Czech Republic and Slovakia, there can hardly be a more important issue in the minds of citizens of the East-Central European region. After making a difficult decision with irreversible consequences, the natural attitude of the man of action (i.e. the politician) is to reaffirm on reflection the correctness of his choice. And even those who vigorously opposed the dissolution of the federation probably believe today that it is better to try to understand and to explain the dissolution than to cry over spilled milk. Martin Palous' brilliant contribution leaves one with no doubt that the 'Velvet Divorce' was the only possible and the best feasible outcome. I would like to refer, however, to his last sentence, expressing the expectation that at the end of this millenium Slovaks and Czechs will eventually become co-citizens of the same extra-national political body (together with Poles and Hungarians, I hope). We can, with some legitimacy, question whether this divorce has made the integration of East-Central European countries into the EC easier or more difficult. There is no simple answer, but it is worthwhile to reflect on this issue, and to try to combine it with the broad question of citizenship.

I propose to situate the issue within Daniel Warner's distinction between the 'objective' and the 'subjective' dimensions of citizenship. This implies setting the citizen in an environment of formally defined institutions, and points to the need for the individual to use the freedom and opportunities provided by such an environment. According to this view, citizenship is a quality of life which is a form of wealth in itself. What is more, the state, the citizen, the market, the civic law, etc., are all distinct features of Western civilization.

That the utopian claim of the totalitarian left to make people happy by force proved to be a disaster requires no additional explanation. The gigantic experiment of real socialism largely failed in its attempts to create a new social reality. It did create a coercive apparatus, qualitatively different and extremely efficient, but it failed to initiate a new type of civilization. To the end of its existence, at least as it looked from the perspective of East-Central Europe, real socialism was an abortive attempt to improve on Western civilization. In the early 1960s, a Warsaw satirical play said it simply: 'Pipes and notebooks are neither socialist nor capitalist, they are only good or bad'. The initial success of rapid extensive modernization only increased the civilizational gap later on, and generated the painful disparity between people's aspirations and the bleak reality of everyday life. What dissidents and eventually the democratic opposition voiced was the demand for citizenship, understood as a type of human wealth, a quality of life. The spectacular events of 1989 and beyond in the eastern part of Europe were, to my mind, predominantly a gigantic return to Europe, 'moving forward backwards', in Kolakowski's words, that is, reclaiming Western civilization.

The constant presence of Western civilization as an external threat and as a partly interiorized model (after all, industrialization meant the creation of a mass society) brought with it the continuous presence of Western institutions, though in grievously distorted form. Parliamentary elections, citizenship, law, market and money all shared only the external appearance of their Western equivalents; still, they were there from the beginning to the end. In this sense Havel's 'living in truth' could always have additional meaning – not only overcoming lies that had been interiorized but also demanding what was formally present but in reality was systematically negated. Ethically driven protest against totalitarian authority made sense only because real socialism was a system founded on the appearance of a truth which was necessary for the very existence of the system. Public declarations of the truth, negating the systemic lies, changed subjects into citizens. I can imagine that in Czecho-Slovakia between 1968 and 1989, where moral terror was exceptionally severe, this phenomenon must have been especially important. So was the strength of the joy felt by the liberated people during the 'Velvet Revolution'.

It seems, however, that the semblance of continuity in formal institutions after the communist take-over in Eastern Europe was the rule rather than a Czecho-Slovak exception. There was a legal revolution accompanying the communist take-over in 1918 in the Soviet Union, and in 1945–46 in Yugoslavia; in both cases the take-over was genuinely internal. Certainly, in Poland after World War II there was legal continuity. The Soviet Union had to pretend to treat the Yalta accord seriously: nations within its sphere of influence were to decide freely on their political order. It also needed the pretence that the imposition of real socialism in this region was not enforced by the presence of the Red Army. In this sense, legal continuity after World War II in Czecho-Slovakia was not predominantly a consequence of the inherent legalism of this state.

I find it rather difficult to believe that legal niceties were the real cause of the Republic's disintegration. I am more convinced by Martin Palous' statement concerning the issue of the referendum, that there was no political will to make the necessary amendments in the constitution. Given the political will, difficult constitutional problems surely should have eventually found a solution. Remembering the emotional reaction of the Bratislava crowd to Vaclav Havel on his unsuccessful mission to save the Federation, one can doubt whether only political elites were responsible for the disintegration. Still, one has the impression that the end of Czecho-Slovakia was directly caused by political games and popular emotions, with little regard for the interests of individual citizens. It seems to me, looking from afar, that Vladimir Meciar, who was brought to power in Slovakia on a wave of national feelings, wanted a vastly increased autonomy for his country, not full independence. Vaclav Klaus then calculated that the Czechs could travel into Europe quicker on their own; and so the idea of disintegration initiated by Slovakia was brought into reality mainly by the decisions of the Czech ruling elites. Certainly the historical differences between the two nations jeopardized the existence of the Federation. And perhaps one should not be surprised that little attention was paid to the splendid democratic tradition of the inter-war period. The prewar political experiences seem to have little influence in the newly founded democracies in the region. Keeping this in mind,

I am still convinced that the division of the Federation was a sad event, an event that brings more negative than positive consequences to international relations.

On the international scene the split of the Czecho-Slovak Federation was indeed accepted, but was it generally approved? Was not the EC casually expressing its reservations? After World War I, two multi-national states were created in Europe; both of them have disintegrated more-or-less simultaneously. Comparing this case with the former Yugoslavia we can only most warmly congratulate the Czechs and the Slovaks on the civility of their conduct. Their 'Velvet Divorce' can be understood as part of two more general tendencies. In Eastern Europe we observe a general revival of strong national emotions; it appears easier to create a new nation-state than to secure proper guarantees for the national minorities. In Western Europe we observe a tendency to demand more autonomy for regions within the democratic state (in Italy and Spain, for example). Perhaps this proves the correctness of Pierre Hassner's vision of a new European structure like the medieval one: a multitude of small societies joined by a common civilization. In light of this, we should perhaps treat the 'Velvet Divorce' with some apprehension but, in the end, as a positive event. Like the first Danish referendum, it adds complexity to the situation but it also builds a more democratic community of Europeans, embraces more diversity and reduces domination by rigid state and inter-state structures. Though sometimes I have the feeling that the idea of nationhood is becoming more important to citizenship, perhaps Europe will eventually find a means of reconciling these two tendencies.

But I am far from being too optimistic. A glance at a map shows that within a few years Poland shifted from having three neighbouring countries to having seven, all in some sense new entities. Within this area the inter-state political situation looks unstable virtually everywhere (even in Germany, the obvious dominating power of this region) and extreme nationalist political tendencies are present everywhere. We add to this picture the complete incapacity of international society to do anything in a consistent way to save human life in the former Yugoslavia. This failure amounts to an indirect acceptance of the habit of setting borders by means of slaughter.

It seems obvious to me, then, that one should not overestimate the security situation in Europe. The 'Velvet Divorce' is an element contributing to this feeling of international instability. It largely spells the end of the Visegrad Group. The Slovak Republic will have much bigger problems with its economy than it would have had within the Federation. The same can be said about minority problems, especially with the Hungarian minority (this issue is accurately described by Martin Palous), which has already created strains in Hungarian-Slovak relations. It will also be more difficult for Slovaks alone to meet the requirements for joining the European Community. The Czech political elites seem to be convinced that their nation belongs more to the West than others in the area. This might be true, but in all official utterances of the EC the sequence of new admissions into the Community is considered in groups: first the EFTA states, then the Visegrad Group. It is doubtful that the Community will decide to give priority to one nation in either of these groups, since this would cause serious diplomatic havoc and provoke protests from the states that have been left behind. Considering the difficulty of integrating the former GDR into Germany, it also seems doubtful that the traditionally warm relations between Czechs and Germans will benefit the former in a clear way. Because neither the western nor the eastern part of Europe is politically stable, the closer cooperation of the Visegrad Group would have been useful. A creative attitude towards integration by these countries would have smoothed the process of receiving full EC membership. Collaboration of these four states on security issues (unlike efforts to bring in Ukraine) could hardly be treated by Russians as moves endangering their international safety. It is therefore a pity that cooperation within the Visegrad formula seems to be an idea with little prospect.

SLOVAKIA AFTER THE SPLIT: DILEMMAS OF THE NEW CITIZENSHIP

Olga Gyarfasova

'We, the Slovak nation, . . .'
(Preamble of the Constitution of the Slovak Republic)

Modern European history began in 1789 and exactly two hundred years later another major event of comparable historical importance transpired. Seen from a geopolitical point of view, the Soviet imperium broke down; seen from an ideological point of view, the communist experiment came to an end.

Nearly four years later it is probably too soon to carry out a historical analysis, but some consequences are already clear. The period when Europe was divided by precisely defined borders into two blocs is over. The post-communist world has begun to move. Between 1990 and January 1993, fourteen new states were set up in this part of Europe. The two latest ones are the Czech Republic and Slovakia.

This paper will try to analyse the social background of the breakup of Czecho-Slovakia. It will also take into account the consequences of the split as viewed by Slovak citizens, and the development of their attitudes, their reflections and their priorities with respect to the social and political reality of their country. My approach is based on the results of sociological surveys which were conducted within the last three years by the Centre for Social Analysis in Bratislava.[1]

[1]The Centre for Social Analysis (CSA) is an independent research institution. Beginning in spring, 1990, the research team of the CSA conducted twelve sociological surveys focussing on attitudes of the Slovak population towards the current social, economic and political problems of Slovakia. Two of the surveys covered all of Czecho-Slovakia. The sample, about 1200 respondents for Slovakia, was always representative with regard to sex, age, education, nationality, and size and place of residence.

The Legacy of Real Socialism

The terms which seem to best describe society in the Czecho-Slovakia Socialist Republic are 'totality, inertia and passivity'. The political system was centralized and directed from above, political pluralism did not exist, and neither democratic institutions nor the legal system guaranteed civic freedom and human rights. Socialist citizens could not influence the governing of the state; they had minimal possibilities to assert their individual or group interests. They were forced to be passive.

Nevertheless, the social status of the socialist citizen appeared to have some advantages. The regime, especially in its later phase, did not oblige citizens to identify with the official ideology in any other than a purely formal way. The ideology was replaced by corruption and clientelism. For the overwhelming majority of citizens, there was a gap between themselves and the state which enabled the people to exploit the state and to despise it at the same time.

The communist regime attempted to create an egalitarian society. In relative terms, everybody had the same social status of state employee, a similar standard of living and the security of social insurance. The threat of unemployment was eliminated and everybody was entitled to subsidized education, housing and health care. The security of the passive citizen was guaranteed by the state.

The revolutionary movement came relatively late to Czecho-Slovakia. After forty years of communism, society was full of apathy, passive waiting and learned helplessness. There had been no experience with democracy and pluralism; legal consciousness was lacking. Experience with the spirit of enterprise was limited to the shadow economy. Citizens did not recognize their rights and duties, and they were not accustomed to bearing responsibility for their decisions and facing the consequences of their actions. The optimism of 1989 proceeded from a mistaken presumption: that the monolithic ideology, when deprived of the protective power of the state, would be automatically thrown away. Also, the presumption that citizens were looking forward to establishing clear rules for economic, social and political freedom was not accurate. The ideologically empty socialist society did not provide any concept beyond the assumption that without the communist regime a normal democratic society would develop, and that, for that to occur, it would suffice to set up political parties and to privatize the economy. The illusion that everybody was *against*, was transformed into the illusion that everybody was *for*.

Such simplified expectations also provided a basic framework for the first period of post-communist development in Czecho-Slovakia, from November 1989 to the first free elections in June 1990. All the parties campaigned for democratic pluralism and economic transformation leading to a free market economy. These two basic pillars of the democratic revolution were so self-evident that they did not provide a profound differentiation among the political parties.

At the very beginning, the dismantling of the communist regime proceeded rather smoothly. However, the consequences of economic transformation coupled with the impact of unknown phenomena such as unemployment, the increase in social inequality, competitive work conditions and social insecurity brought about nostalgia for the previous regime. This was evident especially in Slovakia, where the impact of economic reform hit harder. The legacy of real socialism was rooted much more deeply than one would have expected. The fear of economic failure stemming from social insecurity and a pessimistic evaluation of the possible effects of the economic reform were further compounded by the fear of the economic, political and cultural consequences of the pro-Western orientation.[2] People who had been subjected to a forced ideology for decades were now looking for a new ideology which they could share and which would provide a feeling of security and a sense of belonging because, as Dahrendorf says: 'It is evident that political democracy and the market economy are cold projects. They are civilized inventions of enlightened minds and communities, but they do not touch the heart, nor are they intended to do so'.[3]

---

[2] 44% of the Slovak population was afraid of excessive American influence (compared to 30% of the Czech population), 63% felt distrust towards the European Community, 33% of the Slovak population and 26% of Czechs feared a loss of national identity and national self-esteem after the eventual entry into a united Europe. Center for Social Analysis, *Topical Problems of Czecho-Slovakia*, Bratislava, January 1992.

[3] Dahrendorf, R. 'Liberty and Social Bonds. Notes on the Structure of an Argument', Lecture to the Colloquium of the Academic Advisory Board of the Institute for Human Sciences, Vienna. August 1992.

Survey after survey indicated that initial euphoria and exaggerated expectations were gradually replaced by mistrust and dissatisfaction. People started to long for those things with which they were familiar. Let me summarize the most evident tendencies:

1) The majority of people believe that the economic changes will bring injustice and social inequality, and would prefer that egalitarianism, one of the main characteristics of socialist society, be preserved.[4]

2) The majority of people expect the state to provide social guarantees, such as employment security, medical care and education. State-paternalistic attitudes are very deep-rooted.[5]

3) In Slovakia, an intense feeling of being threatened by ongoing changes is widespread; more people long for the 'firm hand of a strong personality', a leader who will guarantee order; and peace and order are preferred to freedom and democracy.[6]

4) It seems that people are missing a unifying, common ideology. Individualism and pluralism have a very weak position in post-totalitarian societies. Authori-

[4]Egalitarianism persists among the Slovak population: 69% of Slovaks would welcome a reduction in income differentials. Only 24% support the idea of increasing differentiation. Center for Social Analysis, *Current Problems of Slovakia after the Split of the CSFR, Survey Highlights*, Bratislava, March 1993. In a 1990 survey, the deepening of social inequality was regarded by 74% of Slovak respondents as a negative consequence of the economic transformation. Research Center of Social Problems, *Topical Problems of Czecho-Slovakia*, Bratislava, October 1990.

[5]73% of the Slovak population believe that the state has an obligation to provide work for everybody in accordance with his or her qualifications. *Current Problems of Slovakia after the Split of the CSFR. Survey Highlights*, 24 *loc. cit* (note 4).

[6]65% of the respondents in Slovakia and 49% of those in Bohemia shared the opinion that our country at present needs a strong leader who will put things in order (*Topical* . . . 1992). However, after the experience with a firm-handed government, the Slovak population is inclined to prefer 'patience and negotiations in politics' (53% favour negotiations, compared with 21% preferring the firm hand of a strong personality. *Ibidem*. According to the latest results, 50% of the Slovak respondents agree that 'the most important thing is peace and order', and only 18% agree that 'the most important thing is freedom and democracy', *Ibidem*.

tarian and populist political parties and leaders use and misuse this fact.[7]

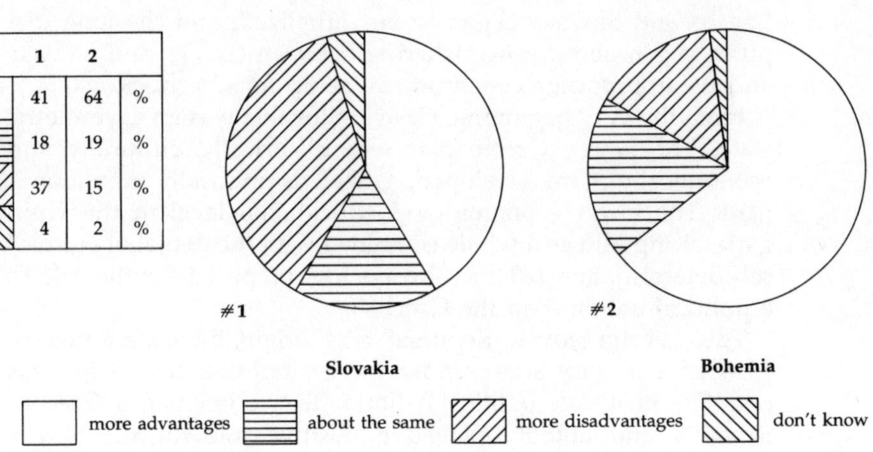

Figure 1   The Present Regime Has in Comparison with the Communist One
(Source: C.S.A. Bratislava, January 1992)

The response of the population of the Slovak Republic to the changes after 1989 is, in many respects, different from that of the population of the Czech Republic. A number of factors account for this: a stronger traditionalism and cultural isolation; less developed democratic traditions; a belated industrialization and urbanization of Slovakia, postponed during the period of socialism; and a less favourably structured and less efficient economy. All these factors formed the heritage with which the Slovak society started its transition.

[7]*Ibidem.* 40% of the respondents agree that the most important thing is unity and togetherness of people; 31% share the view that plurality and democracy are the most important attributes.

Czechs and Slovaks Searching for a New Modus Vivendi

I see as very symptomatic the fact that at the same time the adjective 'socialist' had to be removed from the official name of Czecho-Slovakia (Spring 1990), the national problems between Czechs and Slovaks began to be verbalized, and the long disputes began about power-sharing between Czechs and Slovaks and the appropriate constitutional setup for Czecho-Slovakia.[8]

From the very beginning, Czecho-Slovakia was an asymmetric state. The larger, Czech, part was historically, culturally and economically more developed, as well as politically more dominant. The lower economic and educational level in the Hungarian Kingdom as a whole combined with the denial of cultural self-determination left the Slovaks less prepared for the role of a political nation than the Czechs.

The Czecho-Slovak Republic was originally constituted in 1918 as a unitary state, under the assumption that there was one 'Czechoslovak' political nation with two languages. Czecho-Slovakia undoubtedly played a positive role for the Slovak nation. Within the first Czecho-Slovak Republic (1918–1939) a modern structure of Slovak politics was formed and the educational and cultural levels were raised. The foundation of Czecho-Slovakia made it possible for Slovakia to become a part of modern democratic Europe and, paradoxically, contributed to the national self-determination of the Slovaks.

However, the search for national and political identity of the Slovaks met with a lack of understanding by all regimes in Prague and recurred as a pressing problem:

> With the Slovak ideas of a more equal partnership never being quite fulfilled, the 'Slovak question' had a way of resurfacing whenever there was a crisis or a major political change, be it in 1938, 1946, 1948, 1968 or 1990. It was a cruel paradox for the Slovaks that any improvement in

[8]In March 1990 President Havel proposed modifying the official name of Czecho-Slovakia by omitting the adjective 'socialist'. This evoked a polemic – the so-called 'war over the hyphen', in which 'frozen' tensions and friction between Czechs and Slovaks emerged. Some Slovaks were particularly aggrieved by their lack of 'visibility' to the outside world as an independent and sovereign nation. The discussions resulted in the adoption of a new name, the Czech and Slovak Federative Republic, as an international official name; with Czecho-Slovakia as the Slovak name. The 'hyphen war' provided the most national-oriented political party – the Slovak National Party – with increasing popularity.

their political status was connected with the intervention of a foreign power hostile to the independence of Czecho-Slovakia.[9]

Efforts towards a federative constitutional arrangement lasted many years, and when the federation was finally constituted in 1968, it was implemented half-heartedly and inconsequently because of so-called 'normalization'. 'Federalized Totalitarianism', as Vaclav Havel put it, followed.[10]

Under communism, a simple regulation guided the interpretation of history: i.e., what is good for communism is good for the nation. The collapse of communism initiated in Czecho-Slovakia the sometimes very painful process of the country rediscovering its own history. Jacques Rupnik compared this process metaphorically to defrosting a refrigerator.[11] But the former one-sided approach provoked a new, contrary one. In Slovakia, this was the idealization of the Slovak state established during World War II under Hitler's protection as a period when Slovak state sovereignty was achieved, without regarding its totalitarian character.[12]

While the Czechs take pride in pre-war Czecho-Slovakia and the democratic tradition it represented, the Slovaks are still searching for historical continuity. While for the Czechs the tradition of democratic Czecho-Slovakia is personified in its first president, T. G. Masaryk,[13] in Slovakia there is a lack of a generally shared historical tradition, event or personality.[14]

[9]Butora. M./Butorova, Z., 'Slovakia after the Split', 2 *Journal of Democracy* (1993), p. 74.

[10]Havel, V., *Summer Meditations*, New York/London 1991. After the 'Prague Spring' movement in 1968 was crushed by the invasion of the Warsaw Pact armies, a period of 'consolidation' or 'normalization' of Czecho-Slovak society followed.

[11]Rupnik, J., 'Eisschrank oder Fegefeuer? Das Ende des Kommunismus und das Wiederwachsen der Nationalismen in Osteuropa', 1 *Transit: Europäische Revue* (1990), pp. 132–141.

[12]This idealization is documented by the results of repeated surveys on the historical consciousness of the Slovak population. According to them, only one-third of the respondents assume a negative attitude towards the Slovak state. In the opinion of another one-third, the virtues of the Slovak state prevailed over its vices, and the last third is unable to adopt any evaluating attitude at all. *Topical Problems of Czecho-Slovakia, loc. cit* (note 4) 1990, 1991.

[13]For almost half of the Czech population, T. G. Masaryk is the historical personality of whom they could be proud. *Ibidem.* 1990.

[14]According to the survey conducted in October 1990, 27% of the Czech population, but 47% of Slovaks, do not refer to any historical event or period from the history of their nations of which they should be proud. *Ibidem.*

The winning of more competencies for Slovakia crystallized viewpoints of all the political parties. They espoused programmes varying from a more-or-less loose form of a common state to complete independence. The argumentation differed, ranging from stereotypes such as 'The Slovaks lost to the Czechs' to the longing for national emancipation: 'Let's enforce independence now; let's take advantage of our historical opportunity'. Further arguments related to the various notions about the method and speed of the economic transformation. Most Slovaks were in favour of slowing down the transformation and taking specific Slovak conditions into account. However, the rational argument that the split of Czecho-Slovakia would bring more social burdens upon Slovakia was a brake to open secessionist efforts.

In Slovakia there was only one political party – the Slovak National Party – which, before the parliamentary elections in June 1992, campaigned openly for an independent Slovak republic.

According to repeated public opinion polls, the majority of inhabitants of both republics preferred the preservation of the common state.[15] Although explicitly declared support for an independent Slovakia was very low, a certain divorce mood gradually grew in the relations between Czechs and Slovaks. A mutual labelling in stereotypes, such as: 'Who lost to whom?', 'Prague tries to keep all decision-making in its own hands', and 'Czechs do not consider Slovaks their equal partners', became widespread. The Czechs frequently took the position of an offended benefactor, as expressed in the statement 'Let them go, if they want to'.

In Slovakia, due to the harsher impact of the economic reform (an approximately three times higher rate of unemployment; problems with the conversion of the military industry concentrated largely in Slovakia; loss of the Eastern market; obsolete industries) a substantial part of the Slovak population found a common explanation of the current difficulties: the radical economic transformation was Prague's instrument for exploiting

---

[15]76% of the inhabitants of the Slovak Republic and 92% of those of the Czech Republic held the opinion that both for the Slovaks and for the Czechs, it was advantageous to preserve the common state. *Topical Problems of Czecho-Slovakia, loc. cit.* (note 4) 1992.

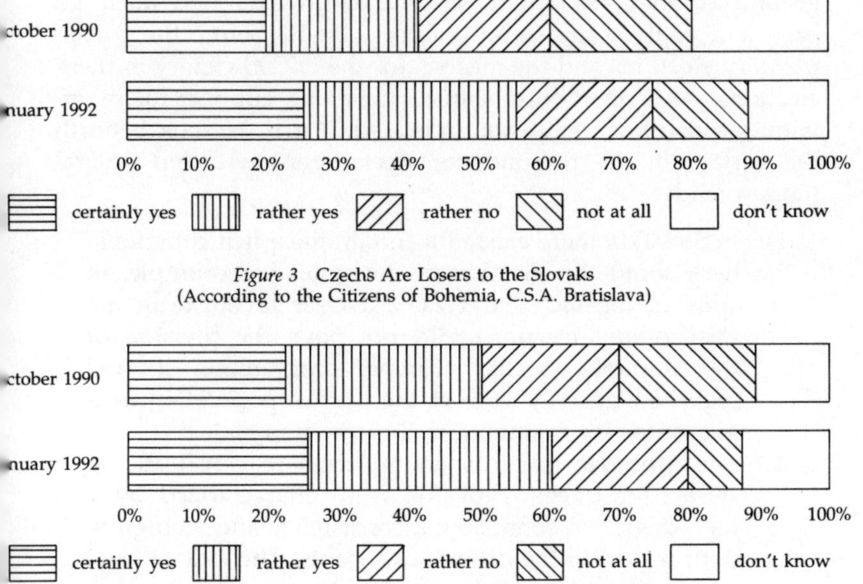

Figure 3 Czechs Are Losers to the Slovaks
(According to the Citizens of Bohemia, C.S.A. Bratislava)

Figure 2 Slovaks Are Losers to the Czechs
(According to the Citizens of Slovakia, C.S.A., January 1992)

and impoverishing Slovakia and for suppressing Slovak national interests.

The linkages between national rhetoric and social demagogy became the obvious argumentation of the opposition parties (before the 1992 elections, the strongest opposition parties were Vladimir Meciar's Movement for a Democratic Slovakia [HZDS], the ex-Communist Party of Democratic Left and the Slovak National Party) and a very effective way to address the electorate and to gain its support.

Splitting the CSFR – Why So Easy?

To cover the current trends in Slovakia and to explain the background of the dissolution of Czecho-Slovakia one must go back and analyze the social-political climate before the parliamentary elections and the reasons for the HZDS victory in these elections. As I mentioned above, prevailing support for maintaining a common state was indicated. But if we look beneath the surface of the respondents' declarations, we find several hidden tendencies:

1) In Slovakia there existed a certain inexplicit consciousness about the division of the state. For example, in spite of the fact that HZDS, a clear favourite in the forthcoming elections, did not have the division of the Republic in its election programme, it was regarded by only 16% of the Slovak population as a guarantee for maintaining the common state.[16]

2) The attitudes towards an appropriate constitutional set-up for Czecho-Slovakia were characterized by a high degree of confusion, inconsistency and ambiguity with regard to the different concepts. The lack of legal and political knowledge opened the door for political manipulation. An analysis based on survey results has found that in Slovakia only 9% of respondents were clear-cut defenders of an independent Slovakia, 17% were clear-cut supporters of the common state, and the rest, that is 74% were people with incoherent notions about the attributes of individual forms of constitutional arrangements.[17]

3) The Movement for a Democratic Slovakia itself largely contributed to this 'fog in people's minds'. The Movement campaigned for a very unclear and ambiguous concept of a confederation that involved preserving a common Czecho-Slovak state while working toward

[16]One-third of those who supported federation, for instance, demanded at the same time the superiority of the Slovak Republic's laws to those of the federation. On the other hand, almost one-quarter of the supports of an independent state did not want an independent Slovak army. There are other examples of such inconsistent thinking. Center for Social Analysis, *Slovakia before the Elections*, Bratislava, April 1992.

[17]Krivy, V., 'Aku krajinu uvidite, ked ustupi hmla?' [What landscape will you see when the fog lifts?] 23 *Kulturny zivot*, (1992).

Slovak national self-determination. On the other hand, Vaclav Klaus, head of the strongest Czech party – the Civic Democratic Party – and the father of Czecho-Slovak economic transformation even before the elections, stressed the fact that he was in favour of a federation with strong competencies and that he would not agree to any other alternative.

4) The future constitutional set-up of Czecho-Slovakia was related very closely to the ongoing economic transformation. On the Slovak political scene, a considerable polarization concerning these two most current topics took place. On the one side, there were parties which supported Klaus' transformation and the common state, while, on the other side, there were parties which demanded a Slovak variant of the economic transformation and a more-or-less unclear concept of independent Slovakia. The vagueness of both concepts as well as the close connection between them found very clear expression in the pre-election programme of HZDS: 'It is necessary to abandon a unified economic transformation and to create within the framework of a joint economic space an independent economic strategy . . . This could be realized only under the presumption that Slovakia would be endowed with state sovereignty'.[18]

The winners of the June parliamentary elections, Vaclav Klaus and Vladimir Meciar, agreed immediately upon the compatibility of their respective viewpoints, and the only subject upon which they could concur was the need to break up the state. This agreement was fulfilled within a very short time, in accordance with the vigorous natures of both leaders. The question of whether the winners, who did not obtain the majority of the popular vote, had or did not have a mandate to negotiate the breakup of Czecho-Slovakia was obscured by the argumentation about the historical necessity of the national emancipation process and its natural evolution into national statehood.

The rhetoric explaining the 'historical necessity' of the split took different forms. The Czechs alleged that it was based on the Slovak longing for independence, on the legitmacy of such

[18]*Volebny program HZDS [Election Programme of the HZDS]*, Bratislava 1992.

a desire and on its unquestionable traits. At the same time, the danger of undemocratic development in Slovakia was accentuated, as were the threat of delaying the economic reform and the advantage of getting rid of the 'uncomfortable Slovak burden' on the road to Europe. Due to the election results, Czech right-wing parties had only a slight majority in the federal bodies, and a coalition of the Slovak and Czech left-oriented parties could hinder the economic transformation or at least slow it down.

In Slovakia, defenders of national emancipation began to doubt the benefits of forming a fully independent Slovak state. 'The balance sheet' was more in favour of a common state, but the political developments could no longer be stopped.

The forthcoming swan song of the 74-year-old state was anticipated with positive feelings by only 27% of the Slovak population, while 36% were clearly negative in their opinions, and the rest shared very ambiguous and mixed emotions. Nevertheless, sporadic meetings and signatures on petitions for the common state could not prevent Czecho-Slovakia's disintegration. Some citizens hoped that they would be given the possibility to express their opinions in the promised referendum. But no referendum was held.

Current Trends in 'Post-Divorce' Society

The inhabitants of Slovakia, citizens of the nonexistent Czecho-Slovakia, became citizens of a newly formed state. In spite of great endeavours on the part of Slovak officials to evoke an atmosphere of joy and jubilation on this occasion, silence and embarrassment prevailed. The pessimistic outlook of the people about the disintegration of Czecho-Slovakia not only lingered but grew in intensity in the presence of everyday reality marked by a deteriorating socio-economic situation. Unexpected complications in Czech-Slovak economic relations arose the very first days of independence: erection of walls and barriers in the areas linking the two republics with natural trade and economic interests, and the numerous improvisations by the Slovak government in its effort to cope with the problems were viewed by the population as proof of Slovakia's lack of readiness for independence. Though most Slovak citizens ascribe an important role in the split of the CSFR to the uncompromising attitude of the Czech side, they do not accept the view that the split

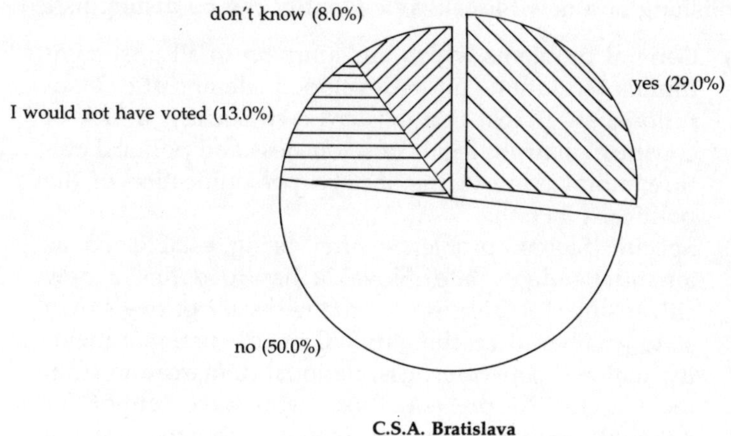

Figure 4 Would You Have Voted for the Dissolution of CSFR?
(Simulation of Unrealized Referendum in Slovakia, March 1993)

was inevitable. The repeatedly invoked official thesis that this is the culmination of the national emancipation process is shared only by 42% of the Slovak population. Much more frequently, independence is seen in the context of the insufficient maturity of Slovakia, the lack of qualified preparation for the process of the division, and the aggravated economic and social situation.[19] The fact that Slovaks now have a state of their own evokes joy for 32% of the population, but almost twice as many are apprehensive toward the future.

If a referendum had been held before the division of the CSFR, only 29% would have voted for the division (see figure 4 above).

Although a certain effect of the 'unbearable attraction of an unrealized possibility' could be found in these answers (maybe the majority of East Germans would not decide now in favour of unification), the widespread embarrassment created an

[19]*Current Problems of Slovakia after the Split of the CSFR, Survey Highlights, loc. cit.* (note 4) 1993.

unfavourable starting point for the identification of the citizen with the new state.

Nowadays, two clusters of determinants which affect the establishing of a new Slovak civic identity can be distinguished:

1) General problems which are common to all post-communist societies: underdeveloped democratic institutions; an almost non-existent civil society; a lack of constitutionalism, legal consciousness and political culture; atomization of the society; personification of the political functions.

2) Specific Slovak problems: after being established as an independent state, Slovakia has to define a new citizenship. Justification for the necessity of one's own state was based on the national issue – national identity, national consciousness, national demarcation from the Czechs. At present, those who have fought for national emancipation and Slovak statehood are not able to provide a concept of citizen identity.

The embarrassment of the citizens presents a very problematic framework for the formation of productive citizen-state relations. Conversely, the fact that Slovakia has to cope with the consequences of its own decisions could provide a positive lesson and help the development process. Adapting to its own independence certainly represents a step forward in the process and inaugurates a period when no excuses can be invoked.

Until now, frustration rooted in a great discrepancy between pre-election promises and current reality has not led to a 'scapegoating' of the national minorities or the Czech nation; rather, it has focussed on the executive power. The Slovak government and the ruling political party have lost approximately half of their supporters. The criticism of government is very reasonable: almost 80% of the respondents were convinced that some government ministers are not competent in their jobs; a substantial part of them shared the opinion that the current set of people in power were not ready to face the complete independence of Slovakia; and only 8% indicated their satisfaction with the way the government handles problems. However, it is necessary to see that the criticism of the government is rooted in disappointment that unrealistic promises about a smooth and painless shift to a prosperous social market economy have not been fulfilled.

But, there has been no sign of a more realistic approach by the Slovak population towards economic reform, no increase of support for privatization, or no effort at active strategies of adaptation to a deteriorated economic situation.[20]

The respondents are mostly concerned about the marked degradation of the contacts with the Czech Republic. This sceptical assessment contrasts with the fact that up to 70% of the respondents gave a very positive evaluation of relations between Czechs and Slovaks from a personal point of view. In spite of the fact that the relations between the Slovak and Czech republics on the political level are not the best the bonds and ties at the interpersonal level have not been adversely affected.

The aggravated socio-economic situation has provoked protests by different groups of the population against decisions of the government and the parliament. These protests received considerable support from the public, especially in the cases where they directly affected the problems of the everyday life of the citizens (health care workers, labour unions, teachers). This could indicate a gradual development of interest groups – a positive indication for building up a civil society.

While federal institutions were viewed with suspicion and distrust in the last years of the federation, nowadays it is clear that power is only in the hands of the Slovak institutions alone, and they are now facing a crisis of confidence. On the other hand, confidence in the European Community has increased, and this provides a supportive basis for Slovakia's integration into European structures.

The most critical issue in the new Slovak state is the social and economic situation. A considerable majority – 70 to 80% – of respondents feel that, since the elections, the situation has grown worse in the public safety, economic and social areas. At present, 87% of the respondents report a decrease in their standard of living since the elections, and 51% of them even speak of a substantial decline. For 74% of the population, this has resulted in the degradation of their personal financial status compared with the year before. Sixty-four percent of the respondents worry about continuing economic decline and poverty. It

[20]Most inhabitants of Slovakia cope with their impaired economic situation using passive means: most frequently they reduce their expenditures by 'tightening the belts' (71%), or using the 'do-it-yourself' strategy (46%). Much less frequently, they use alternatives like setting up their own business (4%). *Ibidem.*

is clear that such a high level of social discontent could affect the further developments of Slovakia, with unpredictable consequences.

Epilogue

Many of those who led the anti-totalitarian democratic revolution in Slovakia have since advocated a common Czecho-Slovak state. However, the idea of Czecho-Slovakia became obsolete surprisingly quickly after the division. Now, all its supporters have to cope with the defeat and adapt to a new reality. Paradoxically, the defeated Slovak 'federalists' may well be those who will formulate a modern and democratic idea of the new Slovak Republic.

COMMENT ON OLGA GYARFASOVA'S PAPER

Edmund Wnuk-Lipinski

One of the crucial phenomena accompanying the collapse of the former system and the gradual emergence of an entirely new social order is a widespread identity crisis of members of the society involved. This identity crisis is being observed in virtually all post-communist societies and, according to certain theories, it is quite a natural outcome of systematic transformation. Under the former regime, as some Polish surveys have shown, social identity was acquired by the definition of an individual's reference to the existing social and political system. As soon as the system collapsed, this peculiar type of social identity vanished.[1] Normative foundations of an old system had been questioned, and later rejected, by a vast majority of the population; consequently, a kind of normative vacuum could be observed.

This vacuum has been quickly filled by various types of axiological systems. For example, in Poland, due to the strong position of the Catholic Church, the vacuum has been at least partially filled by religious values. But we can easily imagine different axiological options entering this 'no man's land': for example, national values, syndicalism, anarchism and many others well-known in 20th-century European history. Looking at the split of Czecho-Slovakia from a distance, I would argue that in this case the national component appeared to be stronger than integrative religious values (especially since Slovakia and Bohemia differ in this respect).

After the communist experience, which did not leave much room for civil society, the latter has to be built up virtually from

[1]Wnuk-Lipinski, E. (ed.), *Nierownosci i uposledzenia w swiadomosci spoleznej [Inequalities and Deprivations in Social Consciousness]*, Warsaw 1987.

181

the beginning. Some Polish studies in the 1980s indicated that deprivations in the status of full citizen were among the strongest felt at that time.[2] The same study revealed the existence of second-rank citizens who were aware of their handicapped position in the system. In the Polish context this phenomenon was a natural backup for widespread contestation of the system and support for the Solidarity movement. It seems to me that in Slovakia, as well as in other then communist countries, this kind of attitude was also present, but at the same time somehow hidden under the surface of a public life controlled by a monocentric power. Once the power collapsed, all these hidden tensions appeared on the surface of public life as the earliest dynamics of an emerging civil society. The question remains as to why in both Slovakia and Bohemia the national issue became a major factor stimulating the dynamics of civil society development.

One may develop a hypothesis that such a quick split must have had solid social, economic and, probably cultural grounds. Otherwise, the split would have been too painful to have been managed by politicians without major resistance from the society. If we accept this assumption then we have to try to formulate as answers to the following questions:

1) Was there an asymmetric economic relationship between Slovakia and Bohemia? In other words, was one nation economically exploited by the other?
2) Was there a cultural and civilizational gap between Slovakia and Bohemia, and, if so, was it big enough to outweigh natural social and economic ties developed in the past?
3) Would the split have been possible if civil society in Slovakia and Bohemia had been better developed? Or, at least, would it have been so easy and peaceful?

Olga Gyarfasova offers partial answers to these crucial questions, and I am tempted to risk adding one explanatory hypothesis.

Both parties involved were, on the level of everyday thinking, victims of a superiority-inferiority complex. Bohemians tended

[2]Koralewicz, J.,/Wnuk-Lipinski, E. 'Vision of Society: Differentiations and Inequalities in the Collective Consciousness', 5 *Sisyphus: Sociological Studies* (1989).

to define the situation in terms of their economic superiority which, because of integration, had to be shared with Slovakia. On the other hand, Slovaks tended to perceive integration in terms of economic and political inferiority, and exploitation by Bohemians. This superiority-inferiority complex was not present much in informal relations between individuals, but it probably appeared as a key issue structuring the emering civil society both in Slovakia and Bohemia. And this had been taken for granted by politicians who have succeeded in making a political issue out of it.

If this line of reasoning is correct, then it is more understandable why the peaceful split was possible in a situation where only a minority (27%) supported the idea of dissolution of the state, whereas half of the population was in favour of remaining together: in both nations the institutions of civil society appeared to be too weak to articulate the majority will. And politicians striving for dissolution did not use such obvious instruments of direct democracy as the referendum.

From an outsider's point of view, independent Slovakia has to face not only serious reconstruction of its economy but also the development of an autonomous civil society. It is an open questions which of the possible patterns will prevail and shape the normative basis of civil society. Here we can enumerate at least some issues which may constitute the dynamics of civil society in the foreseeable future:

1) Universal, European-like institutions of civil society versus domestic, specifically Slovak institutional arrangements referring to local and historical context and tradition;

2) The general orientation of economic policy and politics with respect to integration within the Western hemisphere versus integration within the Eastern hemisphere;

3) Equality versus freedom; in this case the choice is between preservation of economic liberties at the cost of substantial growth in social inequalities, and the preservation of a certain egalitarian policy at the cost of the limitation of economic liberties and economic efficiency. Those whose standard of living deteriorated due to the economic transformation constitute a

natural social basis for egalitarian solutions in macro policy (Olga Gyarfasova's data indicated that this is quite a large segment of Slovak society). On the other hand, those who have rooted their group interests in a market economy constitute the social basis for a liberal macro-social policy.

DISCUSSION 5

The discussion of the papers by Martin Palous and Olga Gyarfasova and the commentaries by Piotr Ogrodzinski and Edmund Wnuk-Lipinski dealt with three broad themes: the relationship between citizenship and nationality, the question of legal and political continuity/discontinuity, and the issue of secession from a federation. The 'Velvet Divorce' between the Czech Republic and Slovakia was the centerpiece of the debate.

David Campbell raised the issue of nationalism, focussing on the relationship between states and nations. He noted that both commentators had apparently worked from the premise that the nation precedes the state. Campbell, on the other hand, had the impression from the two papers that the sense of nationhood often followed the state, especially in Slovakia, where the government's striving for independence went ahead of popular aspirations. Campbell argued that Gyarfasova's paper clearly illustrated the need to work out the sense of nationalism and the broader question of identity, even though the state has already come into being. Campbell thus challenged the traditional notion that national consciousness generally determines a secession and helps produce a state, arguing instead that the state, once formed, looks back to certain distinctions like national identity and consciousness to legitimate itself.

André Liebich followed up on these comments by examining the relation between the notions of nationality and citizenship. He referred to Martin Palous' statement that a type of dual citizenship existed in Czecho-Slovakia (individuals were citizens of the Czecho-Slovak state as well as of their respective republics), and noted the ambiguity in the English language of the terms nationality and citizenship, which are often used as synonyms. Liebich argued that in this case the two terms are not synonymous: one cannot say that Czech citizenship and Slovak citizenship existed within Czecho-Slovak citizenship. Rather, there were Czech and Slovak nationalities within the Czecho-Slovak citizenship – a pattern reproduced in all federal socialist states. Liebich noted that the Russian Empire had also been organized according to this principle: individuals had their *nationalnost'*, which could be Bashkir or Circassian or Polish, but their citizenship – the *grazhdanstvo* – was Soviet. He concluded that a way to distinguish between the two terms might be to use citizenship as a notion of international law, but to emphasize that there can be only one citizenship per state.

Kenneth Minogue agreed that there is confusion regarding the terms nationality and citizenship. Nationalism should be restricted to the project of establishing a state for some ethnic community, and the term nationality should be reserved for a kind of allegiance which is different from citizenship: one that citizens of Britain feel for Britain rather than for Wales and Scotland, or that citizens of France feel for France rather than for Corsica or Brittany or Alsace. Minogue also advanced the hypothesis that it is easier to separate than to unite: most unions have come about by conquest and most established forms of government have been states that were created by armies, while, on the other hand, splitting is easier because it creates whole new governmental structures and job opportunities that are attractive to a large number of people.

Pierre Hassner concluded the discussion of citizenship and nationality by referring to the intellectual origins of this issue: Otto Bauer and the Austro-Marxists believed that it was possible for different allegiances to exist on the same territory (Austria-Hungary). This idea, Hassner said, interests people working on a solution to the Yugoslav problem who are trying to find a mode of coexistence between the warring ethnic communities by distinguishing between citizenship and nationality. The French tradition, on the other hand, has generally been based on the assumption that citizenship and nationality are essentially the same, as expressed by the republican ideal. Hassner's second comment concerned the question of the state preceding or succeeding the nation. He cited the British academic of Montenegrin origin, John Plamenatz, who said that in the West, the state came first and then the nation was created from above, while in Germany and Italy a national linguistic and cultural unity existed before the creation of the state. According to Plamenatz, nationalism in the Slavic and Third World countries arose as a reaction against modernity, and national movements tried to create artificially separate languages and histories. Hassner himself sees the relationship between the state and the nation as a dialectical process: the nation creates the state, which in turn reinforces the national bond. He also emphasized that the civic and ethnic conceptions of nationalism could not be separated. Even in France, where the civic conception originated, the contractual element is combined with a sense of patriotism and of belonging to a particular community.

In reference to Martin Palous' paper, Kenneth Minogue raised the concept of compliance inherent in one notion of citizenship. Palous' paper argues that the only citizenship possible under the communist regime was one based on compliance, while the notion of participation was left by the wayside. Minogue emphasized that the definition of compliance inherent in his theory of citizenship was compliance with an abstract law. Naturally, rule of law did not exist in communist Czecho-Slovakia, and, thus, compliance was reduced to simple obedience to a regime which concretely determined all the circumstances of life – a kind of fake citizenship.

Tamas Földesi noted that one feature of communist dictatorships had been to formally sweep nationalism under the rug, suppressing any manifestations of it. In his opinion, it is hardly surprising that these problems have surfaced with the advent of democracy. In reference to Czecho-Slovakia, Földesi emphasized the difference in the fates of that country and Germany, which has been a problematic neighbour in the past; with the German reunification and the Czecho-Slovak divorce, the distribution of power between the two states has shifted considerably. Although Földesi foresees little likelihood of Germany becoming a political threat to the Czech lands again he believes that the potential for economic meddling exists and may have even influenced the split. Földesi then raised the issue of continuity/discontinuity by emphasizing the totalitarian system's concern with continuity, while being in essence the very expression of discontinuity. He cited the examples of the preservation of the Weimar constitution under the Hitler regime and the maintenance of 'bourgeois law' in socialist Hungary. Daniel Warner followed up on the issue of continuity by stating that today the post-communist states often express their desire to 'return home, back to the European family', without being clear about what they want to return to. He expressed concern with the way federal states broke apart in East-Central Europe, with each faction presenting its own map based on some historical period and claiming some type of continuity, but with different period references and different ideas of which continuity should be preserved.

Peter Paczolay put the issue of legal continuity/discontinuity into a comparative framework. He emphasized that the Czech Republic and Slovakia are very different from Hungary and Poland, since the latter two countries are apparently unable to deal with the problem of legal continuity in a coherent way. Neither country has adopted a new constitution and, thus, their new governments are founded on a sort of legal continuity with the previous socialist regimes. In Hungary, Paczolay explained, the old constitution was merely amended and the old legal system was simply harmonized with the amendments, giving rise to claims that nothing was substantially changed. According to Paczolay, the Czech and Slovak states have been offered an opportunity to create a clear discontinuity with the old regime, thanks to the split. He sees the main problem of the two new states as being their legitimacy: they must prove that they are the only two possible successor states of the old federation. In this context, the questions of Bohemia or the Hungarian minority could resurface on the grounds that they have as much legitimate right to self-determination as the two former republics. Paczolay sees this issue as very similar to the legitimation of the first Czech-Slovak state in 1918. He referred to the writings and speeches of Foreign Minister Benes, which tried to persuade the international community of the need to unite the Czechs and Slovaks because of their historical, cultural and linguistic closeness. From today's perspective, Paczolay said, these arguments appear biased and faulty, but then perhaps so are those given by the new Czech and Slovak governments. What actually legitimizes *these* states, *these* borders and *these* citizenships, and why should they be any more permanent than the former ones? Tamas Földesi expressed concern with the human rights aspect of the new citizenship laws: the only acceptable solution would have been to grant all former citizens of the federal state the opportunity to choose between the citizenship of the two new states. Földesi agreed with Martin Palous' assessment of the Romanies' situation, and, referring to the German concept of the *Untertan* (implying an almost slave-like subjection and subordination), expressed hope that this would not be the fate of people in East-Central Europe again.

Krzysztof Jasiewicz brought up the issue of secession from a federal state. He said that, by definition, no part of a centralized state such as Poland could demand secession with any legal justification. Surprisingly, however, even federal states tend not to have regulations allowing peaceful secession of any of the federal units. Usually the right to secede is guaranteed on a general level, but no procedure for it is set down. From this point of view, Jasiewicz argued, the claims of the Union government of the United States that the Confederacy was responsible for the Civil War because it assaulted federal property (Fort Sumter in South Carolina) are dubious. They were based on the assumption that a part of the territory of the seceding states was the property of the federation. The state in South Carolina in turn argued that once it seceded from the Union, the Union troops were illegally occupying Fort Sumter. Similarly, in the former Soviet Union and Yugoslavia, and also in Canada and present day Russia, no secession mechanism exists. In this ambiguous situation, the Czecho-Slovak divorce may be seen as a sort of 'symmetrical secession' of both federal units based on mutual consent.

The ambiguity concerning the modalities of secession, Jasiewicz continued, also raises the issue of representative versus direct democracy – the question of the referendum. Jasiewicz believes that the lack of a referendum on the split does not automatically make the separation illegal. Martin Palous elaborated the point: there was, in fact, no provision for a referendum in the federal constitution, and the problem was that the constitution could not be revised to provide for a referendum. Jasiewicz explained that if the constitution does not expressly require a referendum, then the representative parties may decide on the issue. Jasiewicz himself would have preferred a referendum in this instance, although he does not believe that referenda are always the best solution (in some countries the political elites seem to want to avoid all controversial issues by simply calling referenda on them). Jasiewicz further expressed his scepticism regarding the outcome of such a referendum, in spite of opinion polls which seemed to indicate strong public opposition to the split. He emphasized that if a referendum had been held, the campaign in favour of the 'divorce' would have articulated its arguments more convincingly. In his opinion, the outcome probably would have been approval of the separation. The issue of the referendum in cases of secession raises other very interesting questions, Jasiewicz added. If, for example, the Slovaks had voted in favour of the split and the Czechs against it, on what level should the decision have been made – on the federal level or that of the republics? In the second case, would it have been enough for *one* of the republics to decide in favour of the separation?

Jasiewicz's final comment concerned the actors involved in the Czecho-Slovak 'divorce'. He felt that both Vladimir Meciar and Vaclav Klaus had overplayed their hands. Meciar, Jasiewicz argued, did not want the split to happen so soon. He presented certain demands representing a Slovak *raison d'état*, expecting that the Czechs would refuse. To his surprise, Klaus called Meciar's bluff, perceiving Slovakia as a burden in the Czech quest to join the EC. The Community position was, however, to give perference to discussions with the Visegard group as a bloc, and the split may in fact have slowed down the admission process for the Czech Republic. Klaus has said openly that he considered the Visegard group an invention of the European Community, but, in Jasiewicz's opinion, this only represented an attempt to justify his policy.

Daniel Warner followed up on the issue of secession. He noted that while Western political theory has been prolific on the question of the social contract, which can be seen as a type of 'marriage', it has not much dealt with the notion of 'divorce'. Did the European Community itself have provisions for 'secession', he wondered, and was that particular 'marriage' perhaps more casual than people thought? Pierre Hassner remarked on the European Community's tendency to promote the integration of others, both as a model and also to prevent them from 'rushing into trouble'. Hassner believes, however, that the effect of these efforts has rather been the contrary – to promote disintegration. Like Vaclav Klaus, the Slovene leadership believed Slovenia would be admitted into the EC more easily without the burden of the poorer Yugoslav republics, and the same concern played a role in the Baltic states' quest for independence. Hassner believes that this represents an interesting dynamic: your own integration, which should promote the integration of others, ends up by causing the disintegration of others by its sheer attractiveness. Regarding secession, Hassner agreed with Jasiewicz's comments, but stated that when unification takes place, the last thing one wants to do is create provisions for secession, since one is trying to establish and strengthen the legitimacy of the new state. In his opinion, most unions do not want to have concrete provisions for secession because they do not want to lay the groundwork for a self-fulfilling prophecy. Daniel Warner remarked that in many American marriages, especially between wealthy people, the divorce settlement is already contained in the marriage contract. Pierre Hassner said that this is due to the tendency of everything to be reduced to a contract, which goes against the more irrational and emotional idea of creating a new kind of attachment, or, in the case of states, a sense of community. Kenneth Minogue backed this statement by citing the example of Stéphane Dion, a Quebécois academic and the son of a well-known Québecois nationalist, who declared his opposition to the right of secession on the grounds that the mere existence of such a right creates a possibility for permanent instability.

Minogue concluded the discussion by commenting more broadly on voting as a political decision-making tool. He stated that voting is in one sense irrational: first of all, the voter is a purely individual interest and has no notion of collective self, and second, voting is a purely instrumental action designed to produce effects. Although this is an abstract model of voting, Minogue affirmed, it does point to the fact that voting as a solution to political problems has very severe limitations. Furthermore, he agreed with Krzysztof Jasiewicz's assessment that a referendum of the Czech-Slovak split might have decided in favour of separation, in view of the effort that would have gone into persuading voters that this was the best solution. Minogue said that voting is an acquired skill. He cited the vote of no confidence that toppled the Polish government in May 1993 as an example of an unintended outcome due to inexperience: a number of people, who for different reasons decided to make a protest vote and voted against the government, suddenly produced a situation which they had neither wished for nor foreseen. Even informed voting has drawbacks, witness the use of tactical voting in first-past-the-post systems, such as that of Great Britain. Committees charged with serious actions and important decisions very rarely use voting, because voting is so crude a way of breaking a deadlock. An acquired sophistication of voting exists, Minogue concluded, citing Winston Churchill's comment that democracy is the worst form of constitution, except for all the rest.

Martin Palous addressed the issues raised in the debate in his closing remarks. First he discussed the distinction between civic society and civil society brought up by Piotr Ogrodzinski. Palous said that Aadm Michnik's and Vaclav Havel's conception of civil society contains the philosophical concept of the European crisis: a discrepancy exists between life as it is experienced by ordinary human beings and life as it is construed by scientists or politicians or ideologues. The basic problem is, therefore, how to go from the latter, alienated description of the world, to the world as experienced by human beings. In this context, Palous explained, he is suspicious of the concept of social rights because it can so easily be 'ideologized'. This 'ideologization' points to the problem of human rights. Palous emphasized that one must not separate human experience from human rights, as the communist world did by perceiving human rights in abstract and very general terms, without content. The ethos, espoused by Havel and Michnik, is based on the idea of 'back to personal experience, back to personal identity' as the foundation on which to rebuild the political world and civil society.

Regarding the question of continuity/discontinuity, Palous emphasized that legal and political discontinuities (revolutions) do not necessarily go together. This issue came up on Czecho-Slovakia in 1989: many people complained that the new regime had not carried out a legal revolution, and that it had only slightly amended the old communist constitution (it excluded the articles on the leading role of the Party). Even the 'Velvet Revolution' itself, Palous explained, was a discontinuity that emerged as the unexpected and unwilled outcome of a process, rather than as the intentional decision of the 'Velvet Revolution-aries' to break with the past.

In reference to this remark, Edmund Wnuk-Lipinski interjected that substantive changes in Czecho-Slovakia, as elsewhere, have generally taken place regardless of their legality, illustrating that the law only follows and confirms changes that have already taken place by the sheer force of history. As an illustration of this idea he told an old Polish joke. After the Polish uprising in 1944, a group of refugees went to Poznan, which had been under Prussian influence for many years, and asked: 'Why didn't you join us? Why didn't you carry out your own uprising?' The Poznanian answered: 'Well, here it was prohibited . . .'

Palous then considered the question of Czech-Slovak relations and the 'Velvet Divorce'. He said that the Czech leadership bears a large responsibility for the disintegration of the federal state. Prior to the 1992 elections, the discussions on reforming the federation resulted in heated debates between Slovak nationalists and Czech federalists, Palous explained. According to him, the Czechs always felt 'Czechoslovak' and responsible for the country as a whole, while the Slovaks only fought for their specific Slovak interests. After the election, however, the situation changed dramatically: Czech separatists were unwilling to listen to any arguments from the Slovak side, while the Slovaks were very moderate and tried to find some common ground with the Czechs. Palous believes that an appropriate metaphor for Czech-Slovak relations is that of the elder and the younger brother. The Czechs had traditionally played the role of the elder brother. In the post-totalitarian political frame of mind, this role became 'ideologized', providing no way out of the trap of the past, no way to create an equal relationship. More generally, Palous argued, it is important for leaders of the post-communist countries of East-Central Europe not to overemphasize the role of history in political debate. As in the case of the former Yugoslavia, the Czech and Slovak negotiators insisted on the role of history, which was, of course, reinterpreted to serve political arguments. Palous believes that certain politicians, and, in particular, Vaclav Klaus, promoted traditional visions of the Czechs being politically more to the right and closer to Europe than the Slovaks, who were accused of being more leftist and more 'Eastern'. The reality is, Palous said, that Klaus has a lot in common with Vladimir Meciar, which explains the facility with which they agreed on the separation of their two republics.

Palous' fourth point concerned the issue of citizenship and nationality. He maintained that the constitutional amendment of 1968 created two distinct sovereignties within the common state and, thus, two separate citizenships within the common citizenship. According to Palous, it was argued at the time that the national amendment did not touch upon the rights and duties of citizens, but that it broadened their national rights. This, of course, was a very ambiguous statement and had no legal meaning. Unfortunately, today it does have meaning, especially regarding the determination of who is eligible for which of the two citizenships. Palous agreed that the Czech citizenship law is discriminatory and needs to be changed. He then turned to the question of the referendum. In his opinion, setting up a referendum would have been desirable, but the problem was what the referendum would have meant in legal terms. He said that unfortunately the Czechs and the Slovaks seemed unable to agree on what would constitute an acceptable union for both. Palous reiterated his hope that the attraction of the European Community would stimulate some form of cooperation between the two new states, and that the virus of disintegration would not turn the Community into another Holy Roman Empire – which was not holy, not Roman, and not an empire.

Olga Gyarfasova agreed with Martin Palous' assessment of the role of 'ideologization' by political leaders in the Czecho-Slovak 'divorce'. She then explained that the public opinion polls used as an *ersatz* referendum did not serve primarily to predict outcomes of a real referendum, had it taken place, but rather to help determine the Slovaks' opinion of their own leadership. As she showed, it is important to note that the relationship between the Slovak people and their state is very ambiguous. She then commented on the question of citizenship and nationality, disagreeing with Martin Palous' argument that two citizenships existed within Czecho-Slovak citizenship after 1968. In her opinion this had only been a formality: in effect, individuals saw themselves as citizens of Czecho-Slovakia, but belonging to either the Czech or the Slovak national group. Gyarfasova then discussed the issue of nationalism and identity in Slovakia. She believes that a certain artificial polarization took place in Slovakia between national and civic values, and that Slovak politicians were considerably more nationalist than the population. She referred to opinion polls conducted in the last three years which asked individuals to rank the problems facing the country. The national question was ranked first only in the autumn of 1990, when the Slovak Parliament was debating the law on language. Otherwise, the national question came in eighth or ninth place, while the most important problems were economic–unemployment, the loss of social benefits, the fear of competition. In her opinion, Meciar's party was so successful in the elections only because it managed to link the national issue with social and economic problems; it would not have carried the election on the national question alone. Gyarfasova believes that this is why the relationship between the Slovak state and its citizens is still, to some extent, an empty concept which needs to be filled. She concluded by expressing her hope that it would be filled by civic rather than nationalist values.

J.D.

PERSPECTIVES

SUMMARY

Pierre Hassner

The subject was 'Citizenship, East and West', and, predictably, we did both more and less. More, because we spoke not only of citizenship, but also of nationality and identity, political life, voting behaviours and specific events of national cultures. We also had an interesting discussion about the unique and peaceful split of Czecho-Slovakia. Less, because although we are all both from the West and the East, the subject of the country studies was East and not West. We did not have papers on France, Germany, the United States and others; rather, we had four papers which correspond to the four Visegard countries, to Central Europe. This does, of course, raise questions, since our discussion has been either very universal, at the level of political philosophy, or particular to these four countries, with occasional comparisons to others, either Yugoslavia or Western countries. The preliminary question, which we could not have discussed but which has to be raised is: to what extent do these countries and the differences between them represent a subject by themselves? Some comparisons have emerged, but, of course, we did not undertake a systematic comparison, except on lustration and on a few aspects of nationality laws. Also, we touched very lightly on the classic subject of what distinguishes Central from Eastern Europe or from the Balkans.

With respect to the question of 'Central Europe', my main references are the two great Hungarian historians, Istvan Bibo and Jeno Szücs.[1] Their argument is that, while Western Europe expanded across the seas, the United States had its own mode of colonization and Russia advanced toward the East territorially,

[1]Bibo, I. *Misère des petits Etats d'Europe de l'Est*, Paris 1993 and Szücs, J., *Les trois Europes*, Paris 1985.

Central Europe, or Eastern Europe, or the 'third Europe' was in a stunted and landlocked situation under the Ottoman, Austrian and Russian empires. It experienced neither Western nor Russian development, with all that this implies in terms of slavery and feudalism. Above all, it saw itself as an object rather than a subject of history. This underlies what Bibo calls the Central European 'hysteria', referring also to Germany's uncertainty about its identity and its borders, which magnifies any quarrel into a challenge to the nation's very existence. The question is whether today a universal 'Central Europeanization' is taking place: whether we feel that we are objects of history rather than it subjects, whether we are sure of our identities, and, precisely, whether problems which used to be specific to Central Europe have become the problems of Europe or of the modern situation more generally. All this puts into question the very identities on which citizenship is based.

Another way of approaching these countries is to say that they are torn between three great influences: they are post-communist countries, facing the problems of post-totalitarianism and the legacy of the past system; they are more receptive than other post-communist countries to the influence of the West and to its economic and cultural penetration; and they are influenced by their own cultural and historical traditions, be they national or regional. In this sense, Piotr Ogrodzinski's remark captures the essence of our subject: the communist system has failed and there is a return to civilization, which begs the question whether there is only one return to universality or whether it is a return to something else. Kryzsztof Jasiewicz has shown very vividly the dilemma of the Church in Poland; it feels that it has defeated the East, but is not sure that it is going to win against the West. Many people, including specialists on China, have remarked that perhaps some elements of the traditional national culture which communist totalitarianism, with its great attention to the 'new man' and 'new society', was not able to efface, will be eradicated much more effectively by capitalism and the consumer society. Aleksandr Solzhenitsyn shares the same fear, and has pointed out that Marxism was a universal creed invented in the West. One may ask: are these countries returning to civilization or, as in the case of Yugoslavia, is this not a return to barbarity? This is the other fear often expressed in the West. Did communism not maintain a universalistic order, even if a stifling one, and is this order now destined to be replaced by tribalism, as some argue, or at least by murderous nationalism?

My main concern is precisely whether the new opening produces universality or whether the removal of barriers will result in reaction. David Campbell has quoted Wendy Brown, who writes that identity politics results from challenges to the postmodern assaults on the integration of community-producing identity. It is these dialectics of opening and of closure which are at the centre of our discussion. We have described the opening, the universalization of these countries. Piotr Ogrodzinski has remarked that in Poland one can now go out without identity papers; I would add that this is no longer the case in France. One has the impression that the West is closing while the East is opening, and some remain in the middle: the refugees, Gypsies, and others expelled from their homes or attracted by prosperity – people who live on the one side without access to the other.

The dialectics of universalization are the essence of our subject. The issue of internationalization and universalization of citizenship and of human rights has been raised by Daniel Warner and is central to André Liebich. Does citizenship remain a vague nostalgia as it becomes universal, synonymous with human rights? Will inclusion or exclusion prevail? These are the prime questions: the spatial one, inclusion-exclusion or globalism-particularism; and the other, perhaps vertical, one, whether under the new conditions citizenship can be reduced to entitlements, whether there is a crisis of participation or, indeed, also of compliance as in Hannah Arendt's argument concering the disappearance of politics.

Kenneth Minogue's analysis is based on these two concepts of citizenship, the basic notions of compliance and participation, and two paradigmatic authors, Hobbes and Rousseau. He pleads for a balance of the two; against an excess of either. The question is whether we can achieve this balance or whether an inherent tension persists. His answer is very much the modern answer: multiplicity of roles. Citizenship is one of our roles and it is expressed as much in compliance as in participation. Particularly in this city of Geneva are we reminded of Rousseau's warning that we cannot be several things at once; we cannot be educated to be both man and citizen; rather, we must choose between these roles.[2] According to Rousseau, we are no longer citizens because we have ceased being Frenchmen, Englishmen, etc. We are all Europeans, we are all bourgeois; this means we are all nothing. Rousseau's advice to the Poles is: if you want to keep your identity against another power, you have to be chauvinistic; you have to distinguish yourself from others, in your dress, customs, and so on.

This is the great challenge, although André Liebich pushes optimism one step further, by defending not only the multiplicity of roles, as Kenneth Minogue, but the multiplicity of citizenships. It is an extremely brilliant contribution – perhaps the most original we have had – but also the most debatable. In my opinion, it shows one side of the question, and, as several contributors have pointed out, multiplicity of citizenships may not apply to the countries discussed here. On the conceptual level, and without going to Rousseau's extreme, one can invoke Spinoza's *omnis determinatio negatio est*, if you are something, it means that you are not something else. Any inclusion means, by definition, exclusion, and, as David Sylvan has noted, one should not see the problem in dualistic terms. Of course there is gradation; the extreme is expounded by Carl Schmitt (deplorably, today in fashion in France), for whom the essence of politics is the opposition 'enemy-friend'. People who are distressed by the end of the Cold War ask: who is our enemy? We cannot have politics if we do not define our enemy. They are looking for a substitute enemy in fundamentalism or something similar. In fact, there are degrees of commitment and of participation. This would also be my reproach to André Liebich: he views citizenship in maximalist or minimalist terms. A voluntary citizen, he claims, does not have to be drafted, but rallies to the flag. The choice is between that and citizenship as various social benefits and a vague nostalgia for participation *à la* Aristotle. For Rousseau and Aristotle, the ideal citizen acts voluntarily at all times, but this requires institutions, celebrations, games and education; behind this socialization of the citizens stands a legislator.

The temptation of stark dualism is everpresent: either Rousseau's *contrat social* and the ideal mythical Greek *polis*, or this very easygoing thing where citizenship represents only the

[2]Rousseau, J. J., *Considérations sur le gouvernement de Pologne*, (1772) Paris-London 1782.

acquisition of certain rights accompanying residence. In fact, there are normally gradations; if not, then we have what Hannah Arendt calls the 'disappearance of politics'. Marx's withering away of the state is already taking place, because politics no longer exists. Regarding social citizenship, the category of the social is extraordinarily ambiguous for Hannah Arendt. The social has triumphed because the division between public and private no longer exists. Hence, there is no more citizenship, but only consumption, communications and the media; there is no interaction or creation. This is also at the core of Daniel Warner's *problématique*. If we were to speak of optimists and pessimists, Kenneth Minogue would be an optimist in the name of moderation and compromise. André Liebich is an optimist in the name of pluralism and individualism, whereas Daniel Warner emphasizes the unresolved tensions and, more specifically the process of exclusion.

The classical theme of the horizontal and vertical contract, the subjective-objective distinction, and T.H. Marshall's differentiation between civic, political, economic and social rights are put into question by the ambiguity of nations. The nation in its social dimension is both the universal *Gesellschaft* – the network of interdependence, exchange and impersonal bureaucratic relationships – and the *Gemeinschaft* – the community, the family or the attempt to recreate them artificially. The issue is: in this prevalence of the social, can one dispense with politics? Is it the politics of Nietzsche's last man: one herd and no shepherd? Or, if not, how can one reconcile pluralism within and among states with political participation and solidarity? This is hotly debated in France today. The former Socialist minister, Jean-Pierre Chevenement and the writer and former editor of *Esprit*, Paul Thibaud, who led the fight against European integration in the name of republicanism, lament that the republican ideal is disappearing, that Europe is undermining French society. They call for the reconstitution of the deep political bond, but in a completely unrealistic way, neglecting both the open character of communities and the fact that our societies do not conform to Greek democracy, Rousseau's ideas or to Hannah Arendt's abstract vision where economics and social division do not exist and everything is politics. The problem is how to rediscover the political in a world in which politics is a secondary activity, regulating and governing relationships which are merely economic or social.

Those who speak of the lack of community or the absence of politics often forget what has been gained by pluralism and openness. Hegel saw this problem, as Kenneth Minogue rightly pointed out. In my opinion, Hegel saw such tensions more than is usually aknowledged, but one basic point is clear: Hegel argues that we must, in some way, bring back citizenship, community, authority. This was the problem for many 19th century thinkers, such as Tocqueville, Comte and Durkheim: how to recreate the social bond which is being dissolved by modern society. One solution was federalism or voluntary association. At the global level one can only have an impersonal relationship: one cannot demand of a complex, moving, open society the qualities of the classical *polis*. On the other hand, one must try to find a context for the dialogue and community which are lacking at the global level. It is here that civil society with its ambiguities intervenes. In the face of totalitarianism, one thought one knew what civil society was. Given the notion of anti-politics and the fact that one now lives in open societies, the meaning of civil society is much less clear, partly because it has become much more complex. Paradoxically, dissidents in the communist states at the time of totalitarianism emphasized the notion of civil society, and we looked to them for inspiration, whereas now the opposite is true: what these countries lack is precisely civil society. Ralf Dahrendorf argues that the transition requires a constitution, a market and civil society.[3] A constitution can be introduced in six months, a market in six years, but the civil society needs at least sixty years. Two generations must accept losing power if the nature of their general relations is to be transformed. This involves the question of attitudes towards the state, the law, and so forth. To conclude these reflections on the moral agenda, let us note the ambiguities of civil versus civic, and two original characteristics of civil society: it is neither military nor religious. Consequently, it is the affirmation of relationships which do not depend on the traditional order of war and religion. Beyond that, can one introduce a moral content of civility, tolerance, responsibility and participation?

In a recent interview, Isaiah Berlin said that we have two

[3]Dahrendorf, R. *Reflections on the Revolution in Europe in a Letter Intended to Have Been Sent to a Gentleman in Warsaw,* London 1990.

kinds of politics: the politics of the soil and the politics of the satellite, global interdependence on the one hand, and the reaffirmation of the small community on the other.[4] What is in question is the intermediate level, the only truly political one: is this the state? Europe? the region? All these institutions which mix elements of *Gemeinschaft* and *Gesellschaft* are in doubt, and the question is that of how to reconcile the opposing elements a little less badly. In short, the central point I want to make is that we are talking about the world, the small community and the uncertain status of what is inbetween.

In an interesting study, Liah Greenfeld crosses two dichotomies, individual-collective and civic-ethnic.[5] She concludes that for the British and the Americans nationality is based on individual rights and individualism, while for the Germans and the Russians it is fundamentally ethnic and collective. Only for the French is it at the same time civic and collective; only they have substituted for the sovereignty of the king the sovereignty of such abstract notions as *volonté générale*, the state and the republican ideal. One can conclude that we do have this reality of society, of individuals, of individual rights on the one hand, and of ethnicity, of the group and of the community on the other. What is in question is republicanism and citizenship; which belong to neither category.

When speaking of political life, we have asked whether it is true, as Gaspar Miklos Tamas and others claim, that there is no citizenship and no sense of the state; that there is complete depoliticization. One may reply that moments of great mobilization can coexist with the apathy of the individual, precluding the danger of unrest. At the other extreme stands mass unanimous mobilization, people looking for scapegoats because they feel presecuted by the rest of the world and have to attack before being attacked. What is in question is a third form of anticipation: citizenship based on people remaining individuals but acting with reciprocity, which then ensures trust.

Regarding the countries discussed, one way of identifying common themes is to apply Krzysztof Jasiewicz's distinction

[4]Gardels, N. 'Two concepts of Nationalism: an Interview with Isaiah Berlin'. *New York Review of Books*, 21 November 1991, p. 22. See also my 'Beyond Nationalism and Internationalism: Ethnicity and World Order'. 34 *Survival*, Summer 1993, pp. 49–65.

[5]Greenfeld, L., *Nationalism: Five Roads to Modernization*, Cambridge 1992.

between inclusion and exclusion at different levels and his differentiation between ethnicity, religion and decommunization. The merit of this approach is that it goes beyond simplistic categorization and shows that attitudes towards these issues do not necessarily go together, that they are different in elites and in the masses, and vary according to social and political position. There is no necessary congruence, so one may express very moderate, guarded optimism that there can be nationalism without chauvinism. Poles (like Hungarians) would not like to have another citizenship because of the influence of religion and the concern with Polishness. There is a fear of foreign penetration and even more of foreign capital, and a rejection of migrants; tensions exist, but they are still in reasonable balance. Ambiguities persist; for instance, borders continue to exist but they are losing meaning, so the issue of changing them becomes less important. We may be witnessing what Gaspar Miklos Tamas called the return to the 'third way', in the sense that we do not have a real distinction between public and private, no real attachment to freedom and choice, a demand for protection by the state even as governments remain unpopular. This seems not all that different from what we have in the West.

Finally, Martin Palous' comments prompt reflection on the international aspect of the question we are discussing. This involves not only the mild, quasi-touristic observation that we go everywhere and that we are pluralistic and tolerant, but that international events – Auschwitz, World War I – intervene in such a way that citizenship and legal institutions can only adapt to them imperfectly. In opposition to this more dramatic view, Palous, himself, emphasized the characteristic peacefulness of the separation of Czecho-Slovakia. Both he and Olga Gyarfasova regretted the split, but were pleased by its non-violent nature. Does this mean that Czechs and Slovaks are Westerners in the sense that they no longer fight for territory? This may be due to cultural features of the Czech tradition, but the Slovaks, who do not have the same cultural tradition, were just as peaceful. The difference with the past was particularly emphasized by Olga Gyarfasova, who also expressed a cautious optimism by noting that there is no hysteria, no search for scapegoats. A very mild tone predominates and hope persists that former federalists may emerge as inspirers of a new faith in the relative convergence between Czechs and Slovaks, between East and West.

The future remains entirely open. I once wrote that we are in a new Middle Ages in the sense of multiple loyalties and different types of actors, but this can be understood in two ways: either it means flexibility and tolerance, or it means anarchy, crusades, pirates, wandering knights, religious wars and the need to reinvent the modern state to bring order and to resurrect citizenship.[6]

[6]Hassner, P., cf. note 4.

DISCUSSION 6

Kenneth Minogue: I am inclined to feel that we went a little too much eyeball to eyeball with this problem: East and West simply meant Eastern and Western Europe. In China, of course, no sentence that we have uttered would have had any significance at all, nor in India, and I was struck by the fact that Islam was never mentioned. Islam is a very interesting and specific case, particularly in France, and also in Britain where there are a lot of Islamic immigrants who have, in fact, set up a thing called the Islamic Parliament of Great Britain. It is of no serious significance at the moment, but it is, in principle, a challenge to the civil coherence of Britain. And Andre Liebich suggested that inclusion was a good thing. I think that this is another of those cases where we need to stand back because we assumed the problem of immigrants and outsiders and aliens was a matter of getting them into the community. And that, indeed, is one problem, but it has a double edge. Salman Rushdie is a superb example of the fact that if you are, as it were, a citizen of Islam, this may be extremely disadvantageous. So, also, is the unfortunate destiny of William Joyce, an Irish-American who applied for a British passport in 1938 and then went off to Germany, where he became a notable broadcaster during the war in the Nazi interest. He was known as Lord Hawhaw, and after the war, of course, he was hanged for treason – another concept which we have not considered – because he had applied for a British passport and therefore had construed himself as a British citizen.

David Campbell: I think the most important motif of the discussion has been the question of inclusion and exclusion because the space or the intersection of inclusion and exclusion is the site of politics. To take Pierre Hassner's point, one would not want to expand politics to cover all relationships, but the point of intersection is a particularly acute moment of politics. If one understands that exclusion can work through a variety of modalities, perhaps just benign differentiation – which is essential for life because if everything were the same things would be intolerably dull, and one would not have the characteristics of life as we know it – then exclusion, to that extent, is essential. I would concur with André Liebich in encouraging multiplicity and pluralism as both an ethical and a realistic stance, because I agree with the historian William McNeill[1] who says polyethnicity has been the norm of civilized life for hundreds of years. The exception to civilized life has been claims or attempts to create homogeneous communities and it is, I suspect, in those attempts or in those aspirations that the greatest degree of violence, exclusion, violent alienation and the problems associated with nationalism and ethnicity will occur. My one doubt – and it's not a doubt about the ethical and realistic position of pluralism and polyethnicity – is that the state will not give up exclusive control, or at least some measure of control, over population because, in order to be a state, the state itself requires territory plus population, which in turn requires some form of definition and exclusion. This is not to say that we just accept that, which would be the pessimistic view. The optimistic view would be that we just try to escape and transcend that. I think that the political option lies between the two: contesting exclusions that we don't like, contesting exclusions which are violent, and negotiating inclusions that we find preferable on whatever grounds. For my final point, I would take Kenneth Minogue's remarks on England slightly differently, in the sense of posing the question not of getting immigrants or outsiders into the community, but perhaps conceiving of a community which tolerates, allows or permits outsiders. The notion of getting them into the community leaves the community as something into which people are brought, whereas perhaps we need a reconsideration of that conception of community that allows for outsiders but obviously has to strike, through negotiation and contestation, a certain balance so that it retains some sense of community.

[1]McNeill, W.H., *Polyethnicity and National Unity in World History*, Toronto-Buffalo-London 1986.

Gabor Nagy: One problem with this very complex discussion of citizenship involving different – philosophical, sociological and legal – points of view is that we considered the Western concept of citizenship but not the Western practice of citizenship, and at the same time we tried to compare the different Central-Eastern European states as Eastern examples on a concrete level; not just on a legal level, but on a political one as well. If we are talking about the Eastern situation, it would be necessary to at least look at current Yugoslavia, Romania, the successor states of the former Soviet Union (at least those states which are actually in Europe, such as the Baltic states and Ukraine), and Bulgaria. That is why I continue to prefer the term East-Central or Central Europe.

Another problem is the model for modernization. What is the model that we would like to follow, and is there any model at all? I mentioned the Maastricht treaty and the whole EC integration process as concrete legal actions towards integration. But is this a real model for East-Central European countries? I think not, because these countries are at a very different stage of modernization. Some of these countries, such as Poland and Hungary, have known statehood for 1,000 years, but Czechs have only 100 years of history, Slovaks fifty years or, if we are very severe, their history has just begun. And we are not even talking about the Yugoslavian case, where the differences between Slovenia and Bosnia and Kosovo are tremendous. Kenneth Minogue mentioned that citizenship as a concept is a global problem, and that it cannot be restricted to Europe.

Edmund Wnuk-Lipinski: If we look at Europe as a whole, we see two contradictory processes. Western European states are undergoing a process of integration into larger entities, while East-Central Europe is on the opposite trajectory of disintegration. This has certain implications for the concept of citizenship. In Western Europe it is becoming larger and larger in geographical and political terms. Some Western Europeans are Europeans first and only then French or British or Italian because they can work and reside in any EC country they wish. This is not the case in East-Central Europe. In some cases, citizenship in this region is even narrowing; this is so in the former Soviet European republics. What kind of regional reintegration can we expect in this area?

Tamas Földesi: If we compare the legal systems of Europe in

1993 with 1953 or 1963, we see that there is a tendency towards convergence. This is due largely to the European Convention of Human Rights, the EC Commission and the European Court of Justice because, beginning with Britain, many countries have voluntarily changed their legal systems. As for citizenship, I cannot see similar tendencies because, unfortunately, the European Convention hardly deals with the subject. It does not provide norms for citizenship and, therefore, differences here are greater. If we combine this problem with that of exclusion, as we should, then we may consider desirable that European legal systems evolve towards convergence on the question of citizenship.

Regarding exclusion, I think that there are two models of democracy, but according to many thinkers only the second one is real. The first model says that democracy is based on the majority principle and that the minority should follow what the majority decides. The second one says that the majority principle is a very limited one because in a democracy the minority opinion should also be taken into consideration. Exclusion does not mean that a citizen has many complex rights and a non-citizen does not have any rights. A crucial challenge to democracy is to bring the legal, social and political position on a non-citizen nearer to that of a citizen.

Piotr Ogrodzinski: When you are immersed in a reality which is changing and diversifying, there is some need for theoretical simplification. I agree with Pierre Hassner that we are returning to Europe but we do not know what sort of Europe it is. This redefinition does not only concern Eastern but also Western Europe. In this context, I would add that there is now a strong need for theoretical practice, a theory which has practical consequences. Krzysztof Jasiewicz has referred to people who do not read the newspaper. But these people have to make decisions, and they have to define their own *Weltanschauung* in a changed reality; they cannot act as they used to. It is very difficult to return to the idea of intellectuals who formulated certain ideas which would then be realized in practice, but the present situation calls for solutions with long-term theoretical implications, and this requires immersion in reality by people who deal with theory.

My last remark is related to the peculiar evolution of European history. If we look back two centuries we have the Vienna

Congress, which defined a certain European order after the Napoleonic wars; then we have the Versailles Treaty after World War I and Potsdam after World War II. Now, we are redefining the European order without wars. This is a novel challenge in European history.

Peter Paczolay: Speaking of dual citizenship and multiple citizenship, one is actually speaking of integration, such as that of the European Community. But, integration must be differentiated from uniformity. Until 1989, Eastern European countries were under very uniform conditions. Therefore, uniformity in itself is not of high value for people in those countries. Consequently, they want to go through a period of diversity and of creating bonds *within* each community and each country. They are looking for community and, after going through this period of diversification, they will seek real integration, not mere reforms. In this sense, it is necessary to have an attractive Western European model in order to promote one's own integration. Sometimes people think of Western European integration as a sort of accidental meeting of countries in the wrong place at the wrong time. That does not really attract East Europeans who are initiating a twofold process of diversification followed by integration.

Olga Gyarfasova: It is good to know that not only countries that have experienced 'divorce' are facing the problem of a new citizenship. The issue of citizenship was discussed in terms of several theoretical polarizations: exclusivity-inclusivity, subjective-objective, East-West, integration-disintegration. What was, or maybe what is, common to both East and West is an identity crisis. The question needs to be raised of the extent to which the concept of citizenship contributes to our countries' general identity crisis in both parts of Europe.

Krzysztof Jasiewicz: I don't see any paradox in the fact that, although our subject is 'Citizenship, East and West', we have been discussing the Central European countries, because these four countries in many ways belong to the West. Certainly, the very concept of Central Europe was invented to emphasize the fact that the people of these countries want to belong to the West, but for political reasons they were in the East bloc. This is the essence of the problem: the concept of West and East ought to overlap somewhere in Central Europe.

Even if we intended to be univeralistic, perhaps we have been excessively particularistic because our discussion focussed on citizenship and the nation-state: a nation-state of a specific kind, where we can presuppose ethnic homogeneity even as we emphasize diversity within the state. We assume Slovakia is the state of Slovaks, Hungary that of Hungarians, France that of the French, and we should remember that the coincidence of the nation-state in the contractual sense with an ethnic group and culture is an exceptional phenomenon. This is so not only in Europe, but also in Eastern Asia, with only two countries, Japan and Korea as homogeneous nation-states. Elsewhere in the world there is either a greater communality, as in Latin America, of the same cultural background and language, among several state entities, or there are multi-ethnic states. So, regarding Kenneth Minogue's point that we have limited ourselves to Europe, one can still raise the question of the universality of the problems with which we are dealing.

Kenneth Minogue: Let me add that in a remarkably large number of cases there are people at the bottom of the heap, which makes the inclusion point highly relevant. The Gypsies are a very interesting hard case for all of our discussions, but in India, there are lower castes, in Japan, there are the Ainu, and nearly everywhere, there does appear to be a kind of hierarchical barrier at the bottom of society which is one of the more acute problems inherent to any discussion of citizenship.

Daniel Warner: One of the subjects that has not been sufficiently discussed is the relationship between citizenship and collective memory. Nowhere is the problem of collective memory more real than when someone sits down to write or amend the citizenship laws of a country. When I was in Moscow two years ago at the Institute of Philosophy, the first question I asked the group was: 'How do you see the last seventy years of your history?', understanding this in terms of the German *Historikerstreit*. They didn't understand the question. Then it occured to me, when did the *Historikerstreit* start? How many years did it take for the debate to take place? In fact, what we may be seeing *à travers* citizenship questions in these specific countries is an unfocussed debate about continuity and discontinuity in their histories.

André Liebich: Allow me to make two self-criticisms. One, on the question of East and West, Gabor Nagy and others have pointed out that we are not really comparing because we don't have people speaking about France, Germany, Switzerland. We have an abstract model somewhere and the East Europeans have been asked, 'how close do you come to this model?' This is a problem, but Providence has intervened in its wisdom and I would join other contributors in saying that we are currently seeing a process of convergence in which we not only have Westernization of the East, but Easternization of the West. Citizenship problems which seemed to have been resolved in France or in Germany are not nearly resolved and are opening up just as much as those in the East. The East-West comparison may be faultily organized because we do not have a balanced comparison, but the comparison still holds because it is not only the East, but also the West which is in flux.

Finally, the concept of citizenship is both an empirical notion and a statement of value. Obviously, when people talk about citizenship laws or opinion polls, they are speaking about citizenship as an empirical given; when they speak about political culture or civic society they mean citizenship as a norm and a value statement. In fact, most of the concepts or problems we deal with have this double nature; they are both normative and empirical. The resulting confusion and even chaos is precisely the stuff of which our daily life is made.

CONCLUSION

The subject of citizenship in the East and West is difficult to define and pinpoint. It involves two variables and their necessarily ambiguous relationship. On the one hand, citizenship itself can be examined from at least the legal, philosophical, sociological or political perspectives. On the other hand, definitions of East and West and the divisions between the two are extremely controversial. While the editors of this volume were aware of these limitations and the eventual confusions that they might engender, they were hopeful that theoretical presentations mixed with specific country analyses of the current situations in Hungary, Poland, the Czech Republic and Slovakia would lead to discussions that were united within central concerns,. The keynote address of Kenneth Minogue and the theme papers by André Liebich and Daniel Warner were meant to present the larger perspective within which the specificites of the Visegrad citizenship problems could be examined. As the lively nature of the discussions recorded and summarized attests, a cross-section of scholars from different disciplines and backgrounds were able to roam through a wide variety of sources and subjects while ostensibly analyzing citizenship in a limited geographic area.

It is the facility with which the participants were able to shift from the general to the specific that marks the various comments and discussions around the papers presented and is encapsulated in Pierre Hassner's summary and the final, general comments. While those who search for order and clear definitions might be somewhat dissatisfied with the breadth of the topics considered, it is more important, we believe, to note the facility with which scholars from different disciplines and different geographic areas were able to converse around a common theme, however vague and undefined that theme may appear. The fact that the discussions and comments were so spontaneous and yet convergent shows the degree to which the question of citizenship in Central Europe touches so many different aspects of political life. Citizenship, in this sense, is a prism through which political life can be studied. And, citizenship in the Visegrad countries at this particular moment in history offers an ideal object to look at through the prism.

What comes out, then, from this volume is how the questions raised by citizenship in the newly democratic countries of Central Europe touch chords of response across a wide spectrum; how all the participants were able to relate to the general and specifics of the questions raised. In his keynote paper, Kenneth Minogue stated that 'the central problem of contemporary politics is that of judging the distinction between those things which should be decided politically in terms of laws, and those which should be decided individually in terms of entering and exiting from loyalties and associations'. The judgement of that distinction knows no geographic or intellectual borders. While Kenneth Minogue and André Liebich warned against overloading citizenship with too many roles and too much importance, it is by questioning citizenship that those very limitations are shown.

Questions raised by the general subject of citizenship become multiplied in importance because of the situation of the Visegrad countries. Following David Campbell's point about countries always becoming, the situation of the Visegrad countries is paradigmatic. Discussions of 'lustration' are configured within the dynamics of normal citizenship debates to show how past, collective memories are part of negotiations within the political process. The notion of continuity or discontinuity in Martin Palous' description of the split in Czecho-Slovakia is one example of the process in which current debates on citizenship are interwoven with historical factors. The ongoing process of state definition is perhaps best captured in the writing of citizenship laws in new countries or countries emerging from totalitarianism. It is here that the debates concerning universalization and particularity are being played out. And it is for this reason that the polling information presented in the country reports is so relevant. As Olga Gyarfasova said, 'it is not only countries after the split that are facing the problem of new citizenship'.

CONCLUSION

In the country papers we see how new citizenship is being confronted in new countries.

It is in this sense also that Pierre Hassner's remarks concerning the dialectics of universalization are so enlightening. Hassner stated: 'The question is whether today a universal "Central Europeanization" is taking place; whether we feel that we are objects of history rather than its subjects, whether we are sure of our identities and, precisely, whether problems which used to be specific to Central Europe have become the problems of Europe or of the modern situation more generally. All this puts into question the very identities on which citizenship is based.' Thus, the Central Europeanization of everyone else or, as André Liebich suggested, 'the Westernization of the East' and the 'Easternization of the West' were sub-themes within the discussions.

In his final comment, Kenneth Minogue mentioned that citizenship in non-European countries had not been considered, raising the question whether the discussion had been too limited in terms of universalization. We leave that decision to others. What is clear, nonetheless, is that the papers, comments and discussions in this volume did go 'eyeball to eyeball', in Minogue's phrase, with the issues surrounding citizenship, whether they be in East or West. Questions of identity, inclusion and exclusion were raised both in general terms and in the specific area of the Visegrad countries. Minogue's comment can thus be understood within the general dialectics of universalization.

Finally, therefore, it is within the context of the dialectics of universalization that this volume should be understood. The free-roaming nature of the discussions bears witness to the universalization of the problems considered. The specificity of the country chapters informs the particularity of a given situation and enriches the general debate on citizenship. But most importantly, the subject of citizenship in East and West gave a cross-section of scholars the opportunity to exchange ideas on the nature of politics and political life in our times. The universalization of that subject cannot be denied and remains the unifying theme throughout this volume.

Daniel Warner

INDEX